THE WORKS OF
SIR JOHN VANBRUGH

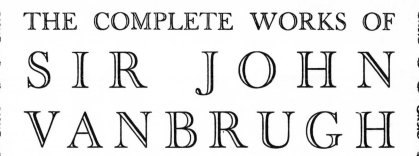

THE COMPLETE WORKS OF
SIR JOHN VANBRUGH

The plays edited by
BONAMY DOBRÉE

The letters edited by
GEOFFREY WEBB

THE SECOND VOLUME *containing*

❡ ÆSOP : PARTS I AND II   ❡ THE PILGRIM

❡ THE FALSE FRIEND   ❡ THE COUNTRY HOUSE

BLOOMSBURY

THE NONESUCH PRESS

16 Great James Street, W.C.

MCMXXVII

AMS PRESS, INC. • NEW YORK • 1967

Reprinted with the permission of
THE BODLEY HEAD LTD.

AMS PRESS, INC.
New York, N.Y. 10003
1967

Manufactured in the United States of America

The Contents

ÆSOP

A

COMEDY

As it is Acted

AT THE

THEATRE-ROYAL

in *DRURY-LANE*

Source

THIS play is from the French of Boursault, *Les Fables d'Ésope*, printed at Paris in 1693, but played under the title of *Ésope à la Ville* on 10 January, 1690, being represented forty-three times. Thus it is possible that Vanbrugh may have seen this play before his imprisonment. Its struggle for recognition is described by Vanbrugh in the Preface in a more detailed manner than Boursault saw fit to do in his *Preface Necessaire :* Le peuple qui s'attendoit à voir une comedie ordinaire . . . fut surpris d'entendre des Fables, à quoy il ne s'attendoit pas, . . . & ne sceut d'abord de qu'elle manière il devoit les recevoir: mais quand il comprit le sens qu'elles renfermoient, & qu'il vit toute l'etenduë de leur application, il se voulut mal de l'injustice qu'il m'avoit renduë; & ses applaudissemens furent, si j'ose me servir de ce terme, comme la reparation de son murmure.

Vanbrugh's treatment is sufficiently explained by his own Preface; but he omits to say that on account of his additions he sacrificed a scene or two of Boursault's. A passage of Boursault's dialogue, and a fable, are given to serve as standards of comparison. This being his first essay in translation, he keeps closer to his original than in later adaptations, as may be seen from the notes. In Part II he resembles Boursault, if only because that author also wrote a sequel, *Ésope à la Cour;* but Æsop II bears the flimsiest relation to this. It is, of course, only a fragment, and was tacked on to the main play.

The addition printed by Stamper, *A Modern Character Introduc'd in the Scenes of Vanbrugh's Æsop,* 1791, is of little interest, except as showing that the play was still read at that date, and perhaps acted. Act II, from the entry of Oronces, may be compared with the corresponding passage in Boursault. *Agenor* has become Oronces and *Euphrosine* Euphronia. The French follows the edition of 1693, which I have not presumed to edit.

> *Agenor.*   Quoy, dans votre entretien avois-je quelque part, Euphrosine?
> *Euphrosine.*   Agenor! que vous arrivez tard!
> *Agenor.*   Il est vray; mais Madame, une tempête étrange . . .
> *Doris.*   Madame est mariée, ou peu s'en faut.
> *Agenor.*   Qu'entens-je Dis-tu vray?
> *Doris.*   Que trop vray.
> *Agenor.*   Quoy, sincérement?
> *Doris.*   Oüy.
> Un Rival venu d'hier, vous en sévre aujourd'huy: Voilà la verité toute pure.
> *Agenor.*   Ah, Madame: Avez-vous pû trahir une si belle flâme? Avez-vous pû. . . .

Euphrosine.   Calmez ces mouvemens jaloux,
Je suis dans ce malheur plus à plaindre que vous.
Lors que de trahison vôtre cœur me soupçonne,
Il ne sçait pas qu'Esope est l'Epoux qu'on me donne.
    Agenor.   Esope! Et le moyen de presumer cela?
L'homme le plus mal fait! le plus laid!
    Doris.   Le voilà
Il s'est rendu fameux par sa méchante mine,
On le connoît par tout.
    Agenor.   Pardon belle Euphrosine,
Vôtre père, sans doute, use icy ses droits:
Vous avez trop bon goût, pour un si mauvais choix.
Esope!
    Euphrosine.   Tel qu'il est, il a charmé mon Pere:
Il est infatué de son esprit austère:
Ses égards vont pour luy par delà le respect.
    Doris.   Choisissez pour gemir un endroit moins suspect.
L'appareil que voilà doit assez vous apprendre,
Que les Cliens d'Esope en ce lieu se vont rendre:
Dans ce Fauteuil douillet, vôtre Epoux prétendu,
Que de tout vôtre cœur vous voudriez voir pendu,
Va donner audiance à qui voudra se plaindre;
Et s'il vous apperçoit vous en devez tout craindre.
Dans vôtre appartement menez Monsieur sans bruit,
Et si vous y parlez, que ce soit avec fruit:
A soûpirer gratis on perd plus qu'on ne gagne;
Il faut aller au fait sans battre la campagne.
    Euphrosine.   Et si mon Pere y vient, quel sera mon dépit?
    Doris.   L'amour que vous avez vous fait perdre l'esprit.
Avant que vôtre Pere ait ouvert vôtre porte,
Monsieur sera sorty, si vous voulez qu'il sorte:
Le petit escalier qui conduit au jardin,
Contre toute surprise offre un secours soudain:
Allez sans hesiter où mon zèle vous pousse—
Hé bien! ne voila pas le Chat-Huant qui tousse?
Passez de ce côté de peur d'être vûs:
L'animal qui paroît rend tous mes sens emus.
Il n'est pas dans le monde un plus hideux visage.
                              End of Scene.

The Chat-Huant is a reference to the previous description of Ésope:

    Que dans sa belle humeur, la Nature en joüant,
    A fait moitié Singe et moitié Chat-huant.
    L'agreable bijou qu'un mary de la sorte.

" a thing that Nature in a merry humour has made half Man half Monkey."

SOURCE

The fable of The Crab-fish and her Daughter may be compared with *L'Ecrivisse et sa Fille*.

> L'écrivisse une fois s'étant mis dans la tête
> Que sa Fille avoit tort d'aller à reculons,
> Elle en eut sur le champ cette réponse honnête:
> Ma Mère, nous nous ressemblons.
> J'ay pris pour façon de vivre
> La façon dont vous vivez:
> Allez droit si vous pouvez,
> Je tâcheray de vous suivre.

It will be seen that Vanbrugh's version (Act III) is longer. This is so in every case.

Text

THE text of the first part is from the first edition of 1697 (Q), which was printed without Part II. This is collated with Q2 of the same year, the 1711 edition, that of 1705 being unobtainable, the collected edition of 1719, and the Dublin edition of 1725. The text has been closely followed, all alterations, except those of obvious misprints, such as *over* for *ever*, being noted. The punctuation has been very charily corrected, and archaistic spelling has been allowed to remain wherever consistent; indeed, where more frequently used than the newer, it has governed alterations: e.g. *Shoe* has been changed to *Shooe* in Acts IV and V, and in the same act *Forty* to *Fourty*. Shooe was Vanbrugh's common spelling, and Fourty seems common sense until usage compels an alteration.

Typographically, occasional italic capitals have been romanised: there seems to be little point in printing *Head*.

The text of Part II is from the 1st edition of 1697 (Q1), collated with the combined edition of that year (Q2), and with the others mentioned above.

Theatrical History

THE first part of *Æsop* was acted at Drury Lane, most probably some time in January, 1697, or perhaps as early as December, 1696. There is no record of the first performance, and one can only guess back from the publication of the printed play, which was late in January, 1697. The expectations Vanbrugh had of it, as well as its success, may be gathered from the Prologue and the Preface; but it was by no means a total failure. Cibber was hugely delighted with his part of Æsop, especially, no doubt, with the fine dress he wore at the end; and he was "equally approved in Æsop" as he had been in Lord Foppington. He acted it, according to Davies, "with that easy gravity which becomes the man who instructs by fable." Doggett acted Learchus, a part which must have well become this fine actor, for though he preferred comic parts, as being nearer to the nature which had come under his observation, he had no tragic fustian to speak here, but a part full of a natural dignity to play. Pinkethman, growing in esteem, and ever popular with the gallery, played Quaint, and was the leading figure in the scene, that of Sir Polidorus Hogstye, which drew the most applause. He had "from Nature a great deal of comic Power about him; but his judgment was by no means equal to it; for he would make frequent Deviations into the Whimsies of an *Harlequin*." He was "rather a droll than a chaste actor." The brilliant Mrs. Verbruggen again appeared, and Roger was played by the madcap Joe Haynes, who, according to Tony Aston, played the character as nobody could play it after him.

The second part was added later in the season, and was acted as a portion of the same play. Ward states that, being a fragment, it was never acted, but the title-page of the first edition clearly says "as acted at Drury Lane"; besides which Gildon, in his additions to Langbaine, in saying that the play was not very successful except in the scenes that were Vanbrugh's own, goes on to associate with them "the three scenes which were since added" as being all of them "received with universal applause, as indeed they justly merited." That puts the question beyond doubt.

It may not have been very successful; Jacob says it was acted "with applause," which is to be distinguished from "with great applause"; but at least it was considered worthy of revival at Drury Lane, for instance on 31 March, 1705, and again in 1709, with Mrs. Oldfield replacing Mrs. Temple in the part of Euphronia, and Cibber and Pinkethman in their original parts. It appeared again on 5 December, 1710, at the same theatre, with most of the actors in their old parts, Euphronia, however, being this time taken by Mrs. Santlow, afterwards Mrs. Booth. She was "a beautiful woman, lovely in her countenance, delicate in her form, a pleasing actress and a most admirable dancer." It was played nearly every year until 1720 inclusive, always at Drury Lane, often with a farce, such as Doggett's *Country Wake* (in 1715), or Gay's *What d'ye Call It* (in 1719). In 1724, 3 November, it was billed as "not acted 4 years," with Cibber in his old part.

On 13th November, 1725, however, Quin seized the part of Æsop at Lincoln's Inn Fields and acted it four times that season, rather putting Cibber's nose out of joint, for until 1734 it appears only to have been acted once at Drury Lane, namely, on 4th February, 1726. In these productions of Quin in 1725 Hippisley played Learchus, and Digges Sir Polidorus, while Mrs. Younger played Euphronia. In these years Spiller, "a master of make-up," took Quaint, and Bullock gained great credit as Roger.

Quin was still playing the part in 1732 to the Hortensia of Mrs. Hallam, and on 26 January, 1734, at Covent Garden; but on 24 September, 1734, it appeared at Drury Lane, "not acted 10 years," at that theatre, it goes without saying, but even then inaccurately. Bridgewater played Æsop; Tony Aston Learchus; and Topham Sir Polidorus. Miss Raftor (Kitty Clive) played Doris, Mrs. Booth being dead, and Mrs. Horton played Hortensia.

Since Quin was then at Drury Lane, when the play was revived there on 5 January, 1738, "not acted 4 years," he took over his old part; Macklin played Quaint, T. Cibber made a hit as Sir Polidorus, and Mrs. Clive, "Fierce Amazonian Dame," took her old part of Doris. It was acted four times. In the next year Yates took over the part of Quaint, one for which he was eminently suited, to judge from Churchill's

> In characters of low and vulgar mould,
> Where nature's coarsest features we behold,
> Where, destitute of ev'ry decent grace,
> Unmanner'd jests are blurted in your face,
> There Yates with justice strict attention draws,
> Acts truly from himself, and gains applause.

Wilkes remarked that " If humour, propriety, and a close adherence to nature render a man valuable in the theatrical world, Mr. Yates claims eminence and distinction." Mrs. Macklin played Mrs. Fruitful at Goodman's Fields early in 1740, and later in the same year Yates repeated his performance at Drury Lane.

Covent Garden, 4 May, 1742. "For the entertainment of the Grand Master and the Brethren of the Ancient and Honourable Society of the Free and Accepted Masons —for the benefit of a brother who has had great misfortunes—not acted 7 years." Bridgewater played Æsop again, and Hippisley Learchus. Woodward, " great master in the science of grimace," took Sir Polidorus, while Mr. and Mrs. Hale took Oronces and Euphronia. It was adorned " with songs in Masonry by Salway and Bencraft." These are mysteries no doubt known to the craft. There was a song composed about 1732 and reprinted 1738 called " To all who Masonry despise," written by some Mason to encourage the craft after certain " secrets " had been disclosed by the *Post Boy* and *Flying Post*, 1723.

In the autumn of the same year it reappeared at Drury Lane as " not acted 5 years," an obvious lie, and Yates went over to Sir Polidorus. Quin, now at Covent Garden, played the name part again there on 9 December ("not acted 7 years "), partnered by Kitty Clive in her old part. Mrs. Clive was, Dr. Johnson said, " a better romp than any I have seen in nature." For him she was " unequalled in the sprightliness of her humour." Davies records that she was " in her comic parts superior to all actresses," and Wilkes describes her as " the Garrick of the ladies." Even Churchill could find nothing to say against " General Clive " except that

> In spite of outward blemishes she shone,
> For humour famed, and humour all her own.

This performance was repeated the same season, and again at the beginning of the next, namely, on 12 December, 1744.

On 21 January and 22 February, 1748, it was again presented at Covent Garden, with Bridgewater back as Æsop, Collins as Learchus, Mrs. Horton as Hortensia, and Dunstall and Mrs. Dunstall as Sir Polidorus and Doris. This year Mrs. Macklin made a great success as Doris in Dublin, for it was a part that perfectly suited her style of acting. She could not rise to the big parts, but in such as were within her compass she excelled, and she is said never to have been surpassed in this one.

At Covent Garden on 22 January, 1753, Arthur played Roger. He was a competent actor, who took many minor parts in Vanbrugh's plays, namely, Sir Francis Wronghead, Galindo in *The False Friend*, Sancho in *The Mistake*, and Alphonso in *The Pilgrim*. His most important character in these plays was Moneytrap.

Some six years later it was revived for seven performances at Drury Lane, beginning on 28 December, billed as "not acted 10 years." The cast included Yates, Holland —"with truly magic stalk He creeps, he flies.—A hero should not walk"; O'Brien, "a very promising comedian, much caressed by the nobility," Palmer, Mrs. Clive and Mrs. and Miss Pritchard. It also included Mossop, who seems to have been a very stiff actor, gesticulating with his right hand only. According to the too acid Churchill:

> With studied impropriety of speech
> He soars beyond the puny critic's reach . . .
> In monosyllables his thunders roll,
> HE, SHE, IT, AND, WE, YE, THEY, fright the soul.

This performance was given "with songs in Masonry," no doubt such things as Lampe's "Hail, Masonry! thou craft divine!" (1723) and Weldon's "Glorious Craft, which fires the mind" (1734).

Twenty years later Thomas Sheridan turned the moral play into a farce, which was acted at Drury Lane on 19 December, 1778, with Henderson in the rôle of Æsop, W. Farren (the elder) in that of Oronces, while Moody played Roger, and Miss Pope —"lively Pope, not without art, but yet to nature true"—played Doris. Yates was in his almost historically old part of Sir Polidorus. Though Henderson gained much applause, "some violent critics insisted upon the piece being withdrawn," and it appears that not only the farce was killed, but the original also, for no further reference is to be found in any place.

PREFACE

TO speak for a Play, if it can't speak for it self, is vain; and if it can, 'tis needless. For one of these Reasons (I can't yet tell which, for 'tis now but the second day of Acting) I resolve to say nothing for *Æsop*, though I know he'd be glad of help; for let the best happen that can, his Journey's up Hill, with a dead English weight at the Tayl of him.

At *Paris* indeed, he scrambled up something faster (for 'twas up Hill there too) than I'm afraid he will do here. The *French* having more *Mercury* in their Heads, and less Beef and Pudding in their Bellies. Our Solidity may set hard, what their Folly makes easy; for Fools I own they are, you know we have found 'em so, in the Conduct of the War: I wish we may do so, in the management of the Peace; but that's neither *Æsop*'s Business, nor mine.

This Play, Gentlemen (or one not much unlike it) was writ in *French* about Six Years since, by one Monsieur *Boursaut*, 'twas play'd at *Paris* by the French Comedians, and this was its Fate.

The first day it appear'd, 'twas routed (People seldom being fond of what they don't understand, their own sweet Persons excepted). The second (by the help of some bold Knight Errants) it rally'd. The third it advanc'd, the fourth it gave a vigorous Attacque, and the fifth put all the Feathers in Town to the scamper; pursuing 'em on to the fourteenth, and then they cry'd out, Quarter.

'Tis not reasonable to expect, *Æsop* should gain so great a Victory here, since 'tis possible by fooling with his Sword, I may have turn'd the edge on't. For I confess in the Translation, I have not at all stuck to the Original; Nay I have gone farther, I have wholly added the Fifth Act, and crowded a Country Gentleman into the Fourth, for which I ask Monsieu *Boursaut*'s Pardon, with all my heart, but doubt I never shall obtain it, for bringing him into such Company. Though after all, had I been so complaisant to have waited on his Play word for word, 'tis possible even that might not have ensur'd the success of it. For though it swam in *France*, it might have sunk in *England*. Their Country abounds in Cork, ours in Lead.

PROLOGUE

GAllants; *We never yet produc'd a Play,*
With greater fears, than this we act to day.
Barren of all the Graces of the Stage,
Barren of all that entertains this Age.
No Hero, no Romance, no Plot, no Show,
No Rape, no Bawdy, no Intrigue, no Beau:
There's nothing in't, with which we use to please ye:
With down right dull Instruction, w'are to tease ye,
The Stage turns Pulpit; and the World's so fickle,
The Play-House in a whim, turns Conventicle.
But Preaching here, must prove a hungry Trade,
The Patentees will find so, I'm afraid.
For though with Heavenly Zeal, you all abound,
As by your Lives and Morals may be found,
Though every Female here o'reflows with Grace,
And Chast Diana's written in her Face;
Though Maids renounce the sweets of Fornication,
And one Lewd Wife's not left in all the Nation;
Though Men grow true, and the foul Fiend defy.
Though Trades-men cheat no more, nor Lawyers lye.
Though not one spot be found on Levi's Tribe,
Nor one soft Courtier, that will touch a Bribe:
Yet in the mid'st of such Religious Days,
Sermons have never borne the Price of Plays.

Dramatis Personæ

MEN.

Æsop.	Mr. *Cibber.*
Learchus, Governour of *Syzicus.*	Mr. *Dogget*
Oronces, in Love with *Euphronia.*	Mr. *Harland.*

WOMEN.

Euphronia, Daughter to *Learchus,* in Love with *Oronces.*	} Mrs. *Temple.*
Doris, her Nurse.	Mrs. *Verbruggen.*
People who come to *Æsop,* upon several occasions, independent one of another.	
Two Country Tradesmen.	} Mr. *Pinkethman,* and Mr. *Smeton.*
Roger, a Country Bumkin.	Mr. *Haynes.*
Quaint, a Herald.	Mr. *Pinkethman.*
Fruitful, an Inn-Keeper.	Mr. *Smeton.*
A Country Gentleman.	Mr. *Pinkethman.*
A Prieſt, Musicians, &c.	
Hortentia, an affeĉted Learned Lady.	Mrs. *Kent.*
Aminta, a Lewd Mother.	Mrs. *Willis.*
Forge-Will, a Scrivener's Widow.	Mrs. *Finch.*
Fruitful, Wife to the Inn-Keeper.	Mrs. *Powell.*

Æ S O P

ACT I.   SCENE I.

Learchus's *HOUSE*.

Enter Learchus, Euphronia *and* Doris.

Lear. AT length I am bleſt with the sight of the Worlds wonder, the delight of Mankind, the incomparable *Æsop*. You had time to observe him laſt Night, Daughter, as he sat at Supper with me.   Tell me how you like him, Child; is he not a charming Person?

Euph. Charming?

Lear. What say'ſt thee to him, *Doris*?   Thou art a good Judge, a Wench of a nice Palate.

Dor. You wou'd not have me flatter, Sir?

Lear. No, speak thy thoughts boldly.

Dor. Boldly you say?

Lear. Boldly I say.

Dor. Why then, Sir, my opinion of the Gentleman is, That he's uglier than an old Beau.

Lear. How, Impudence?

Dor. Nay if you are angry, Sir, second thoughts are beſt; he's as proper as a Pike-man: Holds up his Head like a Dancing-Maſter: Has the shape of a Barb; the Face of an Angel, the Voice of a Cherubin, the smell of a Civet-Cat——

Lear. In short, thou art fool enough not to be pleas'd with him.

Dor. Excuse me for that, Sir, I have Wit enough to make my self merry with him——

Lear. If his Body's deform'd, his Soul is beautiful: Wou'd to kind Heaven as he is, my Daughter cou'd but find the means to please him.

Euph. To what end, Dear Father?

Lear. That he might be your Husband, Dear Daughter.

Euph. My Husband: Shield me, kind Heaven——

Dor. Psha! He has a mind to make us laugh, that's all.

Lear. *Æsop*, then, is not worth her Care, in thy Opinion.

Dor. Why truly, Sir, I'm always for making suitable Matches, and don't much approve of breeding Monſters.   I wou'd have nothing marry a Baboon, but what has been got by a Monkey.

Lear. How dareſt thou liken so incomparable a Man, to so contemptible a Beaſt.

Dor. Ah, the inconſtancy of this World: Out of sight out of mind. Your little Monkey is scarce cold in his Grave, and you have already forgot what you us'd so much to admire: Do but call him to Remembrance, Sir, in his Red Coat, new Gloves, little Hat, and clean Linnen. Then discharge your Conscience, utter the truth from your Heart, and tell us whether he was not the prettier Gentleman of the two——By my Virginity, Sir, (though that's but a slippery Oath, you'll say) had they made Love to me together, *Æsop* should have worn the Willow.

Lear. Since nothing but an Animal will please thee, 'tis pity my Monkey had not that Virginity thou haſt Sworn by. But I, whom Wisdom charms, even in the homelieſt dress, can never think the much deserving *Æsop*, unworthy of my Daughter.

Dor. Now in the Name of Wonder, what is't you so admire in him?

Lear. Hark, and thou shalt know; but you, *Euphronia*,
Be you more especially attentive,
'Tis true he's plain, but that, my Girl's, a Trifle.
All manly beauty's seated in the Soul,
And that of *Æsop*, Envy's self muſt own,
Out shines whate'er the World has yet produc'd.
Cræsus, the prosperous Favourite of Heaven,
Cræsus, the happieſt Potentate on Earth,
Whose Treasure (though immense) is the leaſt part,
Of what he holds from Providence's Care,
Leans on his Shoulder, as his grand support,
Admires his Wisdom, doats upon his truth,
And makes him Pilot to Imperial sway.
But in this elevated Poſt of Power,
What's his Employ? Where does he point his thoughts,
To live in Splendour, Luxury and Ease,
Do endless Mischiefs, by neglecting good,
And build his Family on others ruines?
No:
He serves the Prince, and serves the People too,
Is useful to the Rich, and helps the Poor,
There's nothing ſtands neglected, but himself.
With conſtant Pain, and yet with conſtant Joy,
From place to place, throughout the Realm he goes,
With useful Lessons, form'd to every Rank,
The People learn Obedience from his Tongue,
The Magiſtrate is guided in Command,
The Prince is minded, of a Father's Care:

The Subject's taught, the Duty of a Child:
And as 'tis dangerous, to be bold with truth,
He often call's for Fable to his Aid,
Where under abject Names, of Beasts and Birds,
Virtue shines out, and Vice is cloath'd in shame:
And thus by inoffensive Wisdom's Force
He conquers Folly, wheresoe'er he moves.
This is his Portraite.

Dor. A very good Picture of a very ill Face.

Lear. Well, Daughter; what, not a word? Is it possible any thing that I am Father of, can be untouch'd with so much Merit?

Euph. My Duty may make all things possible: But *Æsop* is so ugly, Sir.

Lear. His Soul has so much beauty in't, your reason ought to blind your Eyes: Besides, my Interest is concern'd: His power alarms me. I know throughout the Kingdom he's the scourge of evil Magistrates: Turns out Governours, when they turn Tyrants: Breaks Officers for false Musters, excludes Judges from giving Sentence, when they have been absent during the Tryal: Hangs Lawyers when they take Fees on both sides: Forbids Physicians to take Money of those they don't Cure: 'Tis true, my Innocence ought to banish my fears. But my Government, Child, is too delicious a Morsel, not to set many a frail Mouth a watering: Who knows what accusations Envy may produce, but all wou'd be secure, if thou cou'dst touch the Heart of *Æsop*. Let me blow up thy Ambition, Girl; the fire of that, will make thy Eyes sparkle at him. [*She sighs.*
——What's that sigh for now; ha?
A young Husband, by my Conscience: Ah, Daughter, had'st thou a young Husband, he'd make thee sigh indeed. I'll tell thee what he's compos'd of. He has a Wigg full of Pulvilio; a Pocket full of Dice: A Heart full of Treason; a Mouth full of Lyes; a Belly full of Drink, a Carkass full of Plaisters, a Tayl full of Pox, and a Head full of——Nothing. There's his Picture; wear it at thy Heart if thou can'st. But here comes one of greater worth.

Enter Æsop.

Lear. Good morning to my Noble Lord; your Excellency——

Æsop. Softly, good Governour: I'm a poor wanderer from place to place; too weak to train the weight of grandeur with me! The Name of Excellency's not for me.

Lear. My Noble Lord, 'tis due to your Employ; Your Predecessors all——

Æsop. My Predecessors all deserv'd it, Sir; They were great Men, in Wisdom, Birth and Service: Whil'st I, a poor unknown decrepit Wretch, mounted aloft for Fortunes Pastime, expect each moment to conclude the Farce, by sinking to the Mud, from whence I sprung.

Lear. Great *Cræsus*'s Gratitude will ſtill support you; His Coffers all are open to your Will, your future Fortune's wholly in your power.

Æsop. But 'tis a power, that I shall ne'er employ.

Lear. Why so, My Lord?

Æsop. I'll tell you, Sir.

> *A Hungry Goat, who had not eat,*
> *Some Nights and Days——(for want of meat)*
> *Was kindly brought at laſt*
> *By Providence's Care*
> *To better Chear,*
> *After a more than Penitential Faſt.*
>
> *He found a Barn, well ſtor'd with Grain,*
> *To enter in requir'd some pain,*
> *But a Delicious Bait*
> *Makes the way easy, though the pass is ſtrait.*
>
> *Our Gueſt observing various Meats,*
> *He puts on a good Modish Face,*
> *He takes his place,*
> *He ne'er says Grace,*
> *But where he likes, he there falls to, and eats.*
>
> *At length with jaded Teeth and Jaws,*
> *He made a pawse,*
> *And finding ſtill some Room,*
> *Fell too as he had done before,*
> *For time to come, lay'd in his ſtore;*
> *And when his Guts cou'd hold no more,*
> *He thought of going home.*
>
> *But here he met the Gluttons Curse,*
> *He found his Belly grown so great,*
> *'Twas vain to think of a Retreat,*
> *'Till he had render'd all h' ad eat,*
> *And well he far'd no worse.*

To the Application, Governour.

Lear. 'Tis easy to be made, My Lord.

Æsop. I'm glad on't.   Truth can never be too clear.

[Seeing Euphron.

Is this Young Damsel your fair Daughter, Sir?

Lear. 'Tis my Daughter, my good Lord: Fair too, if she appears such in the Eyes of the unerring *Æsop.*

Æsop, going up to salute her,] I never saw so beautiful a Creature.

Lear. Aside.] Now's the time; Kiss, soft Girl, and fire him.

Æsop gazing at her.] How partial's Nature, 'twixt her form and mine.

Lear Aside.] Look, Look, Look, how he gazes at her——*Cupid*'s hard at work, I see that already. Slap; there he hits him——If the Wench wou'd but do her part: But see, see, how the perverse Young Baggage ſtands biteing her Thumbs, and won't give him one kind glance——Ah the sullen Jade: Had it been a handsome ſtrong Dog of Five and Twenty, she'd have fallen a Coquetting on't, with every Inch about her. But may be it's I that spoil sport, I'll make a pretence to leave 'em together. Will your Lordship please to drink any Coffee, this Morning?

Æsop. With all my heart, Governour.

Lear. Your Lordship will give me leave to go and order it my self; for unless I am by, 'tis never perfeĉt.

Æsop. Provided you leave me this fair Maid in Hoſtage for your return, I consent.

Lear. My good Lord do's my Daughter too much Honour.

[Aside, going off.

Ah that the Wench wou'd but do her part——

Hark you Hussy—— *[Turning back to* Euphronia, *Aside.*

——You can give your self Aires sometimes, You know you can: Do you remember what work you made with your self at Church t'other day? Play your tricks over again once more for my pleasure, and let me have a good account of this Statesman; or, d'ye hear?——You shall die a Maid, go chew upon that; go. *[Exit* Lear.

Æsop. Here I am left, fair Damsel, too much expos'd to your Charms, not to fall your Viĉtim.

Euph. Your fall will then be due to your own weakness, Sir; for Heaven's my Witness, I neither endeavour, nor wish to wound you.

Æsop. I underſtand you, Lady; your Heart's already dispos'd of, 'tis seldom otherways at your Age.

Euph. My heart dispos'd of?

Dor. Nay, never mince the matter, Madam,

The Gentleman looks like a Civil Gentleman, e'en confess the truth to him: he has a good Intereſt with your Father; and no doubt will employ it to break the Heathenish Match he proposes to you.

To Æsop.] Yes, Sir, My young Lady has been in Love these two years; and that with as pretty a Fellow, as ever enter'd a Virgins Heart. Tall, Straight, Young, Vigorous, Good Cloaths, Long Periwig, Clean Linnen: in brief, He has every thing that's necessary, to set a young Lady a Longing, and to ſtay it when he has done: But her Father, whose Ambition makes him turn Fool in his old Age, comes with a back ſtroak upon us, and spoils all our sport. Wou'd you believe it, Sir? he has propos'd to her to day, the moſt confounded ugly Fellow: Look, if the very thoughts of him don't set the poor thing a crying? And you, Sir, have so much power with the old Gentleman, that one word from you, wou'd set us all right again. If he will have her a Wife; In the Name of *Venus* let him provide her a handsome Husband, and not throw her into the pawes of a thing that Nature in a merry humour, has made half Man half Monkey.

Æsop. Pray what's this Monſter's Name, Lady?

Euph. No matter for his Name, Sir, my Father will know who you mean, at firſt word.

Æsop. But you shou'd not always chuse by the outside alone; believe me, fair Damsel, a fine Periwig keeps many a Fools Head from the weather, have a care of your young Gallant.

Dor. There's no danger; I have examin'd him: His inside's as good as his out: I say he has Wit, and I think I know.

Euph. Nay, she says true; he's even a Miracle of Wit and Beauty: Did you but see him, you'd be your self my Rival.

Æsop. Then you are resolv'd againſt the Monſter.

Dor. Fy, Sir, fy, I wonder you'll put her in mind of that foul frightful thing: We shall have her Dream of nothing all night, but Bats and Owls and Toads and Hedghogs, and then shall we have such a squeeking and squaling with her, the whole House will be in an uproar. Therefore pray, Sir, name him no more, but use your Intereſt with her Father, that she may never hear of him again.

Æsop. But if I shou'd be so generous to save you from the old gallant, what shall I say for your young one?

Euph. O, Sir, you may venture to enlarge upon his Perfeĉtions, you need not fear saying too much in his praise.

Dor. And pray, Sir, be as copious upon the Defeĉts of t'other; you need not fear outrunning the Text there neither, say the worſt you can.

Euph. You may say the firſt is the moſt graceful Man, that *Asia* ever brought forth.

Dor. And you may say the latter is the moſt deform'd Monſter, that Copulation ever produc'd.

Euph. Tell him that *Oronces* (for that's his dear Name) has all the Virtues that compose a perfeĉt Hero.

Dor. And tell him that *Pigmy* has all the Vices, that go to equip an Attorney.

Euph. That to one, I cou'd be true, to the laſt moment of my Life.

Dor. That for t'other; she'd Cuckold him the very day of her Marriage. This, Sir, in few words, is the Theme you are desir'd to preach upon.

Æsop. I never yet had one, that furnisht me more matter.

Enter Servant.

Ser. My Lord, there's a Lady below desires to speak with your Honour.

Æsop. What Lady?

Ser. It's my Lady——my Lady—— [*To* Doris] The Lady there, the Wise Lady, the great Scholar, that no body can understand.

Dor. O ho, is it she? Pray let's withdraw, and oblige her, Madam; she's ready to swoon at the insipid sight of one of her own Sex.

Euph. You'll excuse us, Sir, we leave you to wiser Company.

[*Exeunt* Euph. *and* Dor.

Enter Hortentia.

Hort. The Deess, who from *Atropos*'s Breast preserves the Names of Heroes and their Actions, proclaims your Fame throughout this mighty Orb, and——

Æsop Aside.] Shield me, my Stars, what have you sent me here? For Pity's sake, Good Lady, be more human: my Capacity is too heavy to mount to your stile: if you wou'd have me know what you mean, please to come down to my understanding.

Hort. I've something in my Nature soar's too high
For Vulgar flight, I own:
But *Æsop*'s sphere must needs be within Call;
Æsop and I may sure converse together,
I know he's modest, but I likewise know,
His Intellects are Categorical.

Æsop. Now by my Faith, Lady, I don't know what *Intellect* is; and methinks *Categorical* sounds as if you call'd me Names: Pray speak that you may be understood; Language was design'd for it; indeed it was.

Hort. Of vulgar things, in vulgar phrase we talk,
But when of *Æsop* we must speak,
The Theam's too lofty for an humble stile,
Æsop's is sure no common Character.

Æsop. No truly; I am something particular. Yet if I am not mistaken, what I have extraordinary about me, may be describ'd in very homely Language. Here was a young Gentlewoman but just now pencill'd me out to a hair, I thought; and yet I vow to Gad the learned'st word I heard her make use of, was, Monster.

Hort. That was a Woman, Sir; a very Woman; Her
Cogitations all were on the outward-Man.
But I strike deeper, 'tis the Mind I view.
The Soul's the worthy object of my care;
The Soul, That sample of Divinity, that glorious

Ray of Heavenly Light.   The Soul that awful
Throne of Thought, That sacred Seat of Contemplation.
The Soul, That Noble source of Wisdom,
That Fountain of Comfort,
That Spring of Joy, That happy Token of eternal
Life; The Soul, that——

Æsop. Pray, Lady, are you married?

Hort. Why that Question, Sir?

Æsop. Only that I might wait upon your Husband to wish him Joy.

Hort. When People of my Composition wou'd marry, they first find
something of their own species to join with; I never could resolve to take
a thing of common Fabrick to my Bed, lest when his brutish Inclinations
prompt him, he shou'd make me Mother to a Form like his own.

Æsop. Methinks a Lady so extreamly nice, shou'd be much at a Loss
who to converse with.

Hort. Sir, I keep my Chamber, and converse with my self; 'tis better
being alone, than to mis-ally ones Conversation.
Men are scandalous; and Women are insipid.
Discourse without figure, makes me Sick at my Soul;
O the Charms of a Metaphor.
What Harmony there is in words of Erudition;
The musick of 'em is in-imaginable.

Æsop. Will you hear a Fable, Lady?

Hort. Willingly, Sir, the Apologue pleases me when the Application of
it is just.

Æsop. It is, I'll answer for't.

> *Once on a time, a Nightingale*
> *To Changes prone:*
> *Unconstant, Fickle, Whimsical,*
> *(A Female one:)*
> *Who sung like Others of her kind,*
> *Hearing a Well-taught Linnet's Aires,*
> *Had other matters in her mind,*
> *To imitate him she prepares.*
> *Her Fancy strait was on the Wing:*
> *I fly, quoth she,*
> *As well as he;*
> *I don't know why,*
> *I shou'd not try,*
> *As well as he, to sing.*
> *From that day forth, she chang'd her Note,*
> *She spoil'd her Voice, she strain'd her Throat:*

She did, as Learned Women do,
 Till every thing,
 That heard her sing,
Wou'd run away from her——as I from you.

          [Exit Æsop, running.

    Hortentia *sola.*

How grosly do's this poor World suffer it self to be impos'd upon——
Æsop a Man of sense——Ha, ha, ha, ha, ha. Alas poor Wretch: I shou'd
not have known him but by his Deformity, His Soul's as nauseous to my
Understanding, as his odious Body to my sense of Feeling.
Well;

  'Mongst all the Wits, that are allow'd to shine,
  Methinks there's nothing yet approaches mine:
  Sure I was sent, the Homely Age t' adorn;
  What Star, I know not, rul'd when I was born;
  But every thing, besides my self, 's my scorn.   [Exit.

    The End of the First ACT.

ACT II.

    Enter Euphronia *and* Doris.

Dor. WHat in the Name of *Jove's* the matter with you? Speak for
    Heaven's sake.
 Euph. Oh, What shall I do? *Doris,* I'm undone.
 Dor. What, ravisht?
 Euph. No, ten times worse! ten times worse! Unlace me, or I shall
swoon.
 Dor. Unlace you? Why you are not there abouts, I hope?
 Euph. No, no; worse still; worse than all that.
 Dor. Nay then it's bad indeed.   [Dor. *unlaces her.*
There: How d'ye do now?
 Euph. So; it's going over.
 Dor. Courage; pluck up your Spirits: Well; now what's the matter?
 Euph. The matter? Thou sha't hear. Know that——that Cheat——
Æsop——
 Dor. Like enough; speak, What has he done? That ugly ill-boding
Cyclops.
 Euph. Why instead of keeping his Promise, and speaking for *Oronces;*

      (21)

he has not said one word, but what has been for himself. And by my Father's Order, before to Morrow Noon, he's to marry me.

Dor. He marry you?——

Euph. Am I in the wrong to be in this despair? Tell me, *Doris*, if I am to blame?

Dor. To blame? No by my troth. That ugly, old, treacherous piece of Vermin: That Melancholy mixture of Impotence and Desire; Do's his mouth ſtand to a young Partridge? Ah the old Goat. And your Father? He down right doats at laſt then?

Euph. Ah, *Doris*; What's a Husband do's he give me; and what a Lover do's he rob me of. Thou know'ſt 'em both; Think of *Oronces*, and think of *Æsop*.

Dor. Spitting.] A Foul Monſter. And yet now I think on't, I'm almoſt as angry at t'other too: Methinks he makes but a slow Voyage on't, for a Man in Love. 'Tis now above two Months, since he went to *Lesbos*, to pack up the old Bones of his dead Father: Sure he might have made a little more haſt:

Enter Oronces.

Euph. Oh, my heart; What do I see?

Dor. Talk of the Devil, and he's at your Elbow.

Or. My Dear Soul.   [Euph. *runs and leaps about his Neck.*

Euph. Why wou'd you ſtay so long
From me.

Or. 'Twas not my fault indeed; The Winds——

Dor. The Winds?——Will the Winds blow you your Miſtress again. We have had Winds too, and Waves into the bargain, Storms and Tempeſts, Sea-Monſters, and the Devil an' all. She ſtruggled as long as she cou'd; but a Woman can do no more than she can do; When her breath was gone, down she sunk.

Or. What's the meaning of all this?

Dor. Meaning? There's meaning and mumping too;
Your miſtress is married; that's all.

Or. Death and Furies——

Euph. clinging about him.] Don't you frighten him too much neither, *Doris.* No, my Dear, I'm not yet
Executed, though I am Condemn'd.

Or. Condemn'd? to what? Speak! Quick.

Dor. To be married.

Or. Married? When, how, where, to what, to whom?

Dor. Æsop, Æsop, Æsop, Æsop, Æsop.

Or. Fiends and Speƈtres: What, that piece of Deformity, that Monſter; that Crump?

Dor. The same, Sir, the same. I find he knows him,
You might have come home sooner.

Or. Dear *Euphronia,* ease me from my pain. Swear that
You neither have, nor will consent.
I know this comes from your ambitious Father:
But you're too generous, too true to leave me:
Millions of Kingdoms ne'er wou'd shake my Faith,
And I believe your Constancy as firm.

Euph. You do me Justice, You shall find you do,
For Wracks and Tortures, Crowns and Scepters join'd shall neither fright
me from my truth, nor tempt me to be false. On this you may depend.

Dor. Wou'd to the Lord you wou'd find some other place to make your
fine speeches in. Don't you know that our Dear Friend *Æsop*'s coming
to receive his Visits here.
In this great Downy Chair, your pretty Little Husband Elect, is to sit
and hear all the Complaints in the Town: One of Wisdoms Chief Recom-
pences, being to be constantly troubled with the business of Fools.
Pray, Madam, will you take the Gentleman by the hand, and lead him
into your Chamber; and when you are there, Don't lie Whining and
Crying and Sighing and Wishing——

Aside.] If he had not been more Modest then Wise, he might have set
such a mark upon the Goods before now, that ne'er a Merchant of 'em
all, wou'd have bought 'em out of his hands: But young Fellows are
always in the wrong: Either so impudent they are nauseous, or so modest
they are useless.
Go, pray get you gone together.

Euph. But if my Father catch us, we are ruin'd.

Dor. By my Conscience, this Love will make us all turn Fools. Before
your Father can open the Door, can't he slip down the Back-stairs? I'm
sure he may, if you don't hold him; but that's the old Trade. Ah——
Well, get you gone however——Hark——I hear the old Baboon cough;
Away!   [*Ex.* Or. *and* Euph. *running.*
Here he comes, with his Ugly Beak before him. Ah——a Luscious Bed-
fellow, by my troth.

Enter Learchus *and* Æsop.

Lear. Well, *Doris;* What news from my Daughter? is she prudent?

Dor. Yes, very prudent.

Lear. What says she? What do's she do.

Dor. Do? what shou'd she do? Tears her Cornet; Bites her Thumbs;
Throws her Fan in the fire; Thinks it's dark Night at Noon day; Dreams
of Monsters and Hobgoblins; Raves in her Sleep of forc't Marriage and
Cuckoldom; Cryes: *Avaunt* Deformity, then wakens of a sudden, with

fifty Arguments at her Fingers ends, to prove the Lawfulness of Rebellion in a Child, when a Parent turns Tyrant.

Lear. Very fine, But all this shan't serve her turn.
I have said the Word, and will be obeyed——
My Lord do's her honour.

Dor. Aside.] Yes, and that's all he can do to her.

To Lear.] But I can't blame the Gentleman after all; He loves my mistress, because she's handsome; and she hates him, because he's ugly. I never saw two People more in the right in my Life.

To Æsop.] You'll pardon me, Sir, I'm somewhat free.

Æsop. Why, a Ceremony wou'd but take up time.
But, Governour, methinks I have an admirable Advocate about your Daughter.

Lear. Out of the Room, Impudence: begone, I say.

Dor. So I will: but you'll be as much in the wrong, when I'm gone, as when I'm here. And your Conscience, I hope, will talk as pertly to you, as I can do.

Æsop. If she treats me thus before my Face; I may conclude I'm finely handled behind my Back.

Dor. I say the truth here; and I can say no worse any where.

[*Exit* Doris.

Lear. I hope your Lordship won't be concern'd at what this pratling Wench bleats out; my Daughter will be govern'd, she's bred up to Obedience. There may be some small difficulty, in weaning her from her Young Lover: But 'twon't be the first time she has been wean'd from a Breast, my Lord.

Æsop. Do's she love him fondly, Sir?

Lear. Foolishly, my Lord.

Æsop. And he her?

Lear. The same.

Æsop. Is he Young.

Lear. Yes, and Vigorous.

Æsop. Rich?

Lear. So, so.

Æsop. Well born?

Lear. He has good blood in his Veins.

Æsop. Has he Wit?

Lear. He had, before he was in Love.

Æsop. And handsome with all this?

Lear. Or else we shou'd not have half so much trouble with him.

Æsop. Why do you then make her quit him for me?
All the World knows, I am neither Young, Noble, nor Rich; And as for my Beauty——Look you, Governour. I'm honest: but when Children

cry, they tell 'em, *Æsop*'s a coming: Pray, Sir, what is it makes you so earnest to force your Daughter?

Lear. Am I then to count for nothing, the favour you are in at Court? Father-in-Law to the Great *Æsop*, what may I not aspire to. My Foolish Daughter perhaps may'n't be so well pleas'd with't, but we Wise Parents usually weigh our Childrens happiness in the Scale of our own Inclinations.

Æsop. Well, Governour; let it be your care then to make her consent.

Lear. This moment, my Lord, I reduce her, either to Obedience, or to Dust and Ashes. [*Exit* Lear.

Æsop. Adieu. Now let in the People,
Who come for Audience. [*Æsop sits in his Chair, reading of Papers.*

Enter two Ordinary Tradesmen.

1 *Tra.* There he is, Neighbour: Do but look at him.

2 *Tra.* Ay; One may know him; he's well mark't.
But dos't hear me? What Title must we give him; for if we fail in that point, d'ye see me, we shall never get our business done. Courtiers love Titles, almost as well as they do Money, and that's a bold word now.

1 *Tra.* Why I think we had best call him, His Grandeur.

2 *Tra.* That will do; Thou hast hit on't. Hold still, let me speak. May it please your Grandeur——

Æsop. There I interrupt you, Friend; I have a weak Body that will ne'er be able to bear that Title.

2 *Tra.* D'ye hear that, Neighbour? What shall we call him now?

1 *Tra.* Why, call him, call him, his Excellency: try what that will do.

2 *Tra.* May it please your Excellency——

Æsop. Excellency's a long word, it takes up too much time in business: Tell me what you'd have, in few words.

2 *Tra.* Neighbour: this man will never give
Ten Thousand pounds to be made a Lord.
But what shall I say to him now?
He puts me quite out of my play.

1 *Tra.* Why e'en talk to him as we do to one another.

2 *Tra.* Shall I? Why so I will then. Hem. Neighbour,
We want a new Governour, Neighbour.

Æsop. A new Governour, Friend?

2 *Tra.* Ay, Friend.

Æsop. Why what's the matter with your old one?

2 *Tra.* What's the matter?
Why he grows Rich; that's the matter:
And he that's Rich can't be Innocent, that's all.

Æsop. Do's he use any of you harshly,
Or punish you without a fault?

(25)

2 Tra. No; but he grows as Rich as a Miser;
His Purse is so cram'd, it's ready to burſt again.

Æsop. When 'tis full, 'twill hold no more;
A new Governour will have an empty one.

2 Tra. 'Fore Gad, Neighbour, the little Gentleman's in the right on't.

1 Tra. Why truly I don't know but he may:
For now it comes in my head,
It coſt me more Money to fat my Hog,
Than to keep him fat when he was so.
Prithee tell him we'll e'en keep our old Governour.

2 Tra. I'll do't. Why, look you, Sir, d'ye see me:
Having seriously consider'd of the matter,
My Neighbour *Hobson*, and I here, We are content to jog on a little longer
With him we have: But if you'd
Do us another Courtesy, you might.

Æsop. What's that, Friend?

2 Tra. Why that's this: Our King *Cræsus* is a very good Prince, as a
Man may say: But——a——but——Taxes are high, an't please you;
And——a——poor Men want Money, d'ye see me: It's very hard, as
we think, that the Poor shou'd work to maintain the Rich. If there were
no Taxes, we shou'd do pretty well.

1 Tra. Taxes indeed are very burthensome.

Æsop. I'll tell you a ſtory, Country-men.

> *Once on a time, the Hands and Feet,*
> *As Mutineers, grew mighty great,*
> *They met, caball'd, and talk't of Treason,*
> *They swore by* Jove, *they knew no reason,*
> *The Belly shou'd have all the meat,*
> *It was a damn'd Notorious Cheat,*
> *They did the Work, and——Death and Hell; They'd eat.*

> *The Belly, who ador'd good Chear,*
> *Had like t'have dy'd away for fear:*
> *Quoth he, good folks, you little know,*
> *What 'tis you are about to do;*
> *If I am ſtarv'd, what will become of you?*

> *We neither know nor care, cry'd they,*
> *But this we will be bold to say,*
> *We'll see you damn'd*
> *Before we'll work,*
> *And you receive the Pay.*

With that the Hands, to pocket went,
Full Wrist-band deep,
The Legs and Feet fell fast a sleep:
Their Liberty they had redeem'd,
And all except the Belly seem'd
Extreamly well content.

But mark what follow'd; 'Twas not long
Before the right became the wrong,
The Mutineers were grown so Weak,
They found 'twas more than time to squeak.
They call for Work, but 'twas too late.
The Stomach, (like an Aged Maid,
Shrunk up, for want of human aid)
The Common Debt of Nature paid,
And with it's Destiny, entrain'd their Fate.

Æsop. What think you of this Story; Friends, ha?
Come, you look like wise Men; I'm sure you understand what's for your
good; in giving part of what you have, you secure all the rest; If the
King had no money, there cou'd be no Army; and if there were no Army,
your Enemies wou'd be amongst you: One Day's Pillage wou'd be worse
than Twenty Years Taxes, What say you! is't not so?

2 *Tra.* By my troth I think he's in the Right on't again.
Who'd think that little Hump-back of his
Shou'd have so much brains in't, Neighbour?

Æsop. Well, Honest Men; Is there any thing else that I can serve
you in?

1 *Tra.* D'ye hear that, *Humphrey?*——Why that was civil now.
But Courtiers seldom want good breeding;
Let's give the Devil his due.
Why to tell you the truth, Honest Gentlemen, we had a whole Budget
full of grievances to complain of. But I think——a——Ha Neighbour?
We had e'en as good let 'em alone?

1 *Tra.* Why good feath, I think so too, for by all I can see, we are like
to make no great hond on't. Besides; between thee and me, I begin to
daubt, whether aur Grievances do us such a plaguy deal of Mischief, as
we fancy.

2 *Tra.* Or put Case they did, *Humphrey;* I'se afraid, he that go's to a
Courtier, in hope to get fairly rid of 'em, may be said (in aur Country
Dialect) to take the wrong Saw by the Ear. But here's Neighbour *Roger*,
he's a Wit, let's leave him to him.   [*Exeunt.*

Enter Roger, *a Country Bumkin, looks seriously upon*
Æsop; *then bursts out a Laughing.*

Ro. Ha, ha, ha, ha, ha: Did ever Mon behold the like——Ha, ha, ha, ha, ha.

Æsop. Hast thou any business with me, Friend?

Ro. Yes, by my troth, have I;
But if *Roger* were to be hang'd up for't,
Look you now, he could not hold laughing:
What I have in my Mind, out it comes: but bar that:
I'se an honest Lad as well as another.

Æsop. My time's dearer to me than yours, Friend;
Have you any thing to say to me?

Ro. Gadswookars, do People use to ask for Folks,
When they have nothing to say to 'em?
I'se tell you my business.

Æsop. Let's hear it.

Ro. I have, as you see, a little Wit.

Æsop. True.

Ro. I live in a Village hard by, and I'se the Best Man in it, tho' I say it, that shou'd not say it. I have good Drink in my Cellar, and good Corn in my Barn; I have Cows and Oxen, Hogs and Sheep, Cocks and Hens, and Geese and Turkeys; but the truth will out, and so out let it. I'se e'en tyr'd of being call'd plain *Roger.* I has a Leathern Purse; and in that Purse, there's many a fair half Crown, with the King's Sweet Face upon it, God Bless him: And with this Money I have a mind to bind my self Prentice to a Courtier: It's a good Trade, as I have heard say, there's Money stirring: Let a Lad be but diligent, and do what he's bid, he shall be let into the Secret, and share part of the Profits. I have not liv'd to these Years for nothing: Those that will swim, must go into deep Water: I'se get our Wife *Joan* to be the Queen's Chambermaid; and then——Crack says me I; and forget all my Acquaintance.

But to come to the business. You who are the King's great Favourite, I desire you'll be pleas'd to sell me some of your Friendship, that I may get a Court Place. Come, you shall chuse me one your self; You look like a shrewd Man; by the Mass you do.

Æsop. I chuse Thee a Place?

Ro. Yes: I would willingly have it such a sort of a Pleace, as wou'd cost little, and bring in a great deal; in a word, much Profit, and nothing to do.

Æsop. But you must name what Post you think wou'd suit your humour.

Ro. Why I'se pratty indifferent as to that: Secretary of State, or Butler; Twenty Shillings more, Twenty Shillings less, is not the thing I stand upon. I'se no Hagler, Gadswookars, and he that says I am——'Zbud he lies: There's my humour now.

Æsop. But hark you, Friend, you say you are well as you are, Why then do you desire to change?

Ro. Why what a Question now is there, for a Man of your parts: I'm well, d'ye see me; and what of all that? I desire to be better: There's an Answer for you. (*Aside.*) Let *Roger* alone with him.

Æsop. Very well: this is reasoning; And I love a Man should reason with me: But let us enquire a little whether your Reasons are good or not. You say at home you want for nothing.

Ro. Nothing 'fore *George*.

Æsop. You have good drink?

Ro. 'Zbud the best i' th' Parish. (*Singing*) And dawne it merrily goes, my Lad, and dawne it merrily goes.

Æsop. You eat heartily?

Ro. I have a noble Stomach.

Æsop. You sleep well?

Ro. Just as I drink: till I can sleep no longer.

Æsop. You have some honest Neighbours?

Ro. Honest? 'Zbud we are all so, the Tawne raund, we live like Breether; when one can sarve another, he does it with all his Heart and Guts; when we have any thing that's good, we eat it together, Holydays and Sundays we play at Nine-pins, tumble upon the Grass with wholesome young Maids, laugh 'till we split, Daunce 'till we are weary, eat 'till we burst, drink 'till we are sleepy, then swap into Bed, and snore 'till we rise to Breakfast.

Æsop. And all this thou woud'st leave, to go to Court. I'll tell thee what once happen'd.

A Mouse, who long had liv'd at Court,
(Yet ne'er the better *Christian* for't)
Walking one Day to see some Country Sport,
He met a home-bred Village-Mouse,
Who with an awkard Speech and Bow,
That savour'd much of Cart and Plow,
Made a shift, I know not how,
T'invite him to his House.
Quoth he, my Lord, I doubt you'll find
Our Country Fare of homely kind,
But by my Troth, y'are wellcome to't,
Y'have that, and Bread, and Cheese to boot:
And so they sat and din'd.
    Ro. Very well.

Æsop. The *Courtier* cou'd have eat, at least,
As much as any Houshold Priest,
But thought himself oblig'd in Feeding,
To shew the difference of Town-breeding,
He pick'd and cull'd, and turn'd the Meat,
He champt and chew'd, and cou'd not eat:
No Toothless Woman at Fourscore,
Was ever seen to mumble more.
He made a thousand ugly Faces,
Which (as sometimes in Ladies cases)
Were all design'd for Airs and Graces.

   Ro. Ha, ha.

   Æs. At last, he from the Table rose,
He pickt his Teeth, and blow'd his Nose,
And with an easie Negligence,
As tho' he lately came from *France*,
He made a careless sliding Bow,
'Fore Gad, quoth he, I don't know how
I shall return your Friendly Treat,
But if you'll take a bit of Meat
In Town with me,
You there shall see
How we poor Courtiers eat.

   Ro. Tit for tat; that was Friendly.

   Æs. There needed no more Invitation
To e'er a Country Squire i'th' Nation,
Exactly to the time he came,
Punctual, as Woman, when she meets
A Man between a pair of Sheets,
As good a Stomach, and as little shame.

   Ro. Ho, ho, ho, ho, ho.

   Æs. To say the Truth, he found good Chear,
With Wine, instead of Ale and Beer:
But just as they sat down to Eat,
Comes bouncing in a hungry Cat.

   Ro. O Lord, O Lord, O Lord!

   Æs. The nimble Courtier skipt from Table,
The Squire leapt too, as he was able;
It can't be said that they were beat,
It was no more than a Retreat;
Which when an Army, not to Fight,
By Day-light, runs away by Night,
Was ever judg'd a great and glorious Feat.

Ro. Ever, ever, ever.

Æs. The Cat retir'd, our Guests return,
The Danger past, becomes their scorn,
They fall to Eating, as before,
The Butler rumbles at the Door.

Ro. Good Lord!

Æs. To Boot and Saddle again they sound.

Ro. Ta ra, tan tan ta ra, ra ra tan ta ra.

Æs. They frown, as they wou'd stand their Ground,
But (like some of our Friends) they found.
'Twas safer much to scowre.

Ro. Tantive, Tantive, Tantive, &c.

Æs. At length the Squire, who hated Arms,
Was so perplext with these Alarms,
He rose up in a kind of heat:
Udzwooks quoth he, with all your Meat,
I will maintain a dish of Pease,
A Raddish, and a slice of Cheese,
With a good desert of Ease,
Is much a better Treat.
However;
Since every Man shou'd have his due,
I own, Sir, I'm oblig'd to you,
For your Intentions at your Board.
But Pox upon your Courtly Crew——

Ro. Amen, I pray the Lord. Ha ha ha ha ha. Now the Deel Cuckold me, if this Story be not worth a Sermon. Give me your hond, Sir. ——If it had na' been for your Friendly Advice, I was going to be Fool enough, to be Secretary of State.

Æs. Well, go thy ways home, and be wiser for the Future.

Ro. And so I will: For that same Mause, your Friend, was a witty Person, Gadsbudlikins; and so our Wife *Joan* shall know: For between you and I, 'tis she has put me upon going to Court. Sir, she has been so praud, so saucy, so rampant, ever since I brought her home a Lac'd Pinner, and a Pink-colour pair of Shooe-strings, from *Tickledawne* Fair, the Parson o'th' Parish can't rule her; and that you'll say's much. But so much for that. Naw, I thank you for your good Caunsel, honest little Gentleman; and to shew you, that I'se not ungrateful——Give me your hand once more——If you'll take the pains, but to walk dawne to our Towne,——a Word in your Ear,——Ise send you so drunk whome again, you shall remember friendly *Roger*, as long as you have breath in your Body.   [*Exit Ro.*

Æsop Solus.

Farewell, what I both envy and despise:
Thy Happiness and Ignorance provoke me;
How Noble were the thing call'd Knowledge,
Did it but lead us to a Bliss like thine?
But there's a Secret Curse, in Wisdom's Train,
Which on it's Pleasures ſtamps perpetual Pain,
And makes the wise Man loser by his gain.

                                                     [Exit.

End of the Second Aɛ̃.

ACT III.

Enter Æsop.

Æs. WHo waits there?   *[Enter Servant.*
         If there be any Body that has Business with me, let 'em in.
Serv. Yes, Sir.   *[Exit Serv.*

Enter Quaint, *who ſtands at a diſtance, making a great
many fawning Bows.*

Æs. Well Friend? who are you?

Q. My Name's *Quaint,* Sir, the profoundeſt of all your Honours humble Servants.

Æs. And what may your Business be with me, Sir.

Q. My Business, Sir, with every Man, is firſt of all to do him Service.

Æs. And your next is, I suppose, to be Paid for't twice as much as 'tis worth.

Q. Your Honours moſt Obedient, Humble Servant.

Æs. Well, Sir, but upon what Account am I going to be Obliged to you?

Q. Sir, I'm a Genealogiſt.

Æs. A Genealogiſt?

Q. At your Service, Sir.

Æs. So, Sir.

Q. Sir, I am inform'd from common Fame, as well as from some little private familiar Intelligence, That your Wisdom is entring into Treaty with the *Primum Mobile* of all Good and Evil, a fine Lady.

    I have Travell'd Sir, I have Read Sir, I have Consider'd Sir, and I find

Sir, That the Nature of a fine Lady, is to be——a fine Lady Sir; a fine Lady's a fine Lady, Sir, all the World over; she loves a fine House, fine Furniture, fine Coaches, fine Liveries, fine Petticoats, fine Smocks; and if she ſtops there——she's a fine Lady indeed, Sir. But to come to my Point.

It being the *Lydian* Cuſtom, That the fair Bride should be presented on her Wedding-Day, with something that may signifie the Merit and the Worth of her dread Lord and Maſter, I thought the Noble *Æsop's* Pedigree, might be the wellcom'ſt Gift that he could offer. If his Honour be of the same Opinion,——I'll speak a bold Word; There's ne'er a Herald in all *Asia*, shall put better Blood in his Veins, then——Sir, your humble Servant, *Jacob Quaint*.

Æs. Doſt thou then know my Father Friend? for I proteſt to thee, I am a Stranger to him.

Q. Your Father, Sir, ha, ha; I know every Man's Father, Sir, and every Man's Grand-father, and every Man's Great Grand-father. Why, Sir, I'm a Herald by Nature, my Mother was a *Welch Woman*.

Æs. A *Welch Woman?* prithee of what Country's that?

Q. That, Sir, is a Country in the World's back-side, where every Man is born a Gentleman, and a Genealogiſt. Sir, I cou'd tell my Mothers Pedigree before I cou'd speak plain: which, to shew you the depth of my Art, and the ſtrength of my Memory, I'll trundle you down in an inſtant.

Noah had three Sons, *Shem, Ham* and *Japhet; Shem*——

Æs. Hold, I conjure thee, in the Name of all thy Anceſtors.

Q. Sir, I cou'd take it higher, but I begin at *Noah* for brevity's sake.

Æs. No more on't, I intreat thee.

Q. Your Honour's impatient perhaps, to hear your own Descent. *A Word to the Wise is enough.* Hem, hem: *Solomon*, the wise King of *Judea*——

Æs. Hold once more.

Q. Ha, ha; Your Honour's modeſt, but——*Solomon* the wise King of *Judea*——

Æs. Was my Anceſtor, was he not?

Q. He was, my Lord, which no one sure can doubt, who observes how much of Prince there hangs about you.

Æs. What? Is't in my Mien?

Q. You have something——wondrous Noble in your Air.

Æs. Personable too: view me well.

Q. N—not Tall; but Majeſtick.

Æs. My Shape?

Q. A World of Symmetry in it.

Æs. The Lump upon my Back?

Q. N—not regular; but agreeable.

Æs. Now by my Honesty, thou art a Villain Herald. But Flattery's a Thrust I never fail to Parry. 'Tis a Pass thou shoud'st reserve for young Fencers; with Feints like those, they're to be hit: I do not doubt but thou hast found it so: hast not?

Q. I must confess, Sir, I have sometimes made 'em bleed by't. But I hope your Honour will please to excuse me, since, to speak the Truth, I get my Bread by't, and maintain my Wife and Children: And Industry, you know, Sir, is a commendable thing. Besides, Sir, I have debated the business a little with my Conscience; for I'm like the rest of my Neighbours, I'd willingly get Money, and be Sav'd too, if the thing may be done upon any reasonable Terms. And so Sir, I say, to quiet my Conscience, I have found out at last, that Flattery is a Duty.

Æs. A Duty?

Q. Ay Sir, a Duty: For the Duty of all Men is to make one another pass their time as pleasantly as they can. Now Sir, here's a young Lord, who has a great deal of Land, a great deal of Title, a great deal of Meat, a great deal of Noise, a great many Servants, and a great many Diseases. I find him very dull, very restless, tyr'd with Ease, cloy'd with Plenty, a Burthen to himself, and a Plague to his Family. I begin to flatter: He springs off of the Couch; turns himself round in the Glass; finds all I say true; Cuts a Caper a Yard high, his Blood trickles round in his Veins; his Heart's as light as his Heels; and before I leave him—his Purse is as empty as his Head. So we both are content; for we part much happier then we met.

Æs. Admirable Rogue; what dost thou think of Murder and of Rape, are not they Duties too? Wer't not for such vile fawning Things as thou art, young Nobles wou'd not long be what they are: They'd grow asham'd of Luxury and Ease, and rouse up the old Spirit of their Fathers; leave the pursuit of a poor frightned Hare, and make their Foes to tremble in her stead; Furnish their Heads with Sciences and Arts, and fill their Hearts with Honour, Truth and Friendship; be Generous to some, and Just to all; drive home their Creditors with Bags of Gold, instead of Chasing 'em with Swords and Staves; Be faithful to their King and Country both, and Stab the Offerer of a Bribe from either; blush even at a wandring thought of Vice, and boldly own they durst be Friends to Virtue; tremble at nothing but the frowns of Heaven, and be no more asham'd of him that made 'em.

Q. (*Aside.*) If I stand to hear this Crump Preach a little longer, I shall be Fool enough perhaps to be bubbled out of my Livelihood, and so lose a Bird in the Hand for two in the Bush.

Sir, Since I have not been able to bring you to a good Opinion of your self, 'tis very probable I shall scarce prevail with you to have one of me.

But if you please to do me the favour to forget me, I shall ever acknow-
ledge my self,——Sir, your most obedient, faithful, humble Servant.

[*Going.*

Æs. Hold; If I let thee go, and give thee nothing, thou'lt be apt to
grumble at me; and therefore——who waits there?

Enter Servant.

Q. [*Aside.*] I don't like his Looks, by Gad.

Æs. I'll present thee with a Token of my Love.

Q. A—another time, Sir, will do as well.

Æs. No; I love to be out of Debt, tho' 'tis being out of the fashion.
So, d'ye hear? Give this honest Gentleman half a Score good Stroaks on
the Back with a Cudgel.

Q. By no means in the World, Sir.

Æs. Indeed, Sir, you shall take 'em.

Q. Sir, I don't merit half your Bounty.

Æs. O 'tis but a Trifle.

Q. Your Generosity makes me blush. [*Looking about to*

Æs. That's your Modesty, Sir. *make his escape.*

Q. Sir, you are pleased to Compliment. But a—twenty Pedigrees for
a clear Coast. [*Running off, the*

Æs. Wait upon him down Stairs Fellow, *Servant after him.*
I'd do't my self, were I but nimble enough, but he makes hast to avoid
Ceremony.

Enter Servant.

Serv. Sir, Here's a Lady in great hast, desires to speak with you.

Æs. Let her come in.

Enter Aminta, *Weeping.*

O Sir, If you don't help me, I'm undone.

Æs. Why, what's the Matter, Lady.

Am. My Daughter, Sir, my Daughter's run away with a filthy Fellow.

Æs. A slippery Trick indeed.

Am. For Heaven's sake, Sir, send immediately to pursue 'em, and seize
'em; but 'tis in vain, 'twill be too late, 'twill be too late; I'll warrant at
this very Moment they are got together in a Room with a Couch in't;
all's gone, all's gone; tho' twere made of Gold 'tis lost: Oh! my Honour,
my Honour. A forward Girl she was always; I saw it in her Eyes the
very Day of her birth.

Æs. That indeed was early; but how do you know she's gone with a
Fellow?

(35)

Am. I have e'en her own insolent Hand-writing for't Sir, take but the pains to read what a Letter she has left me.

Æs. Reads.

> *I Love, and am belov'd; and that's the reason I run away.*

Short, but Significant.

—— *I'm sure there's no Body knows better than your Ladyship, what Allowances are to be made to Flesh and Blood; I therefore hope this from your Justice, that what you have done three times your self, you'll pardon once in your Daughter.*

The Dickins.

Am. Now, Sir, what do you think of the business?

Æs. Why truly, Lady, I think it one of the most Natural Businesses I have met with a great while. I'll tell you a Story.

> *A Crab-fish once her Daughter told,*
> *(In terms that savour'd much of Scold)*
> *She cou'd not bear to see her go,*
> *Sidle, sidle, too and fro;*
> *The Devil's in the Wench, quoth she,*
> *When so much Money has been paid,*
> *To polish you like me;*
> *It makes me almost mad to see,*
> *Y'are still so awkward an ungainly Jade.*
>   *Her Daughter smil'd, and look'd askew,*
> *She answer'd, (for to give her her due)*
> *Pertly, as most Folks Daughters do,*
> *Madam, Your Ladyship, quoth she,*
> *Is pleas'd to blame in me,*
> *What, on Enquiry you may find*
> *Admits a passable Excuse,*
> *From a Proverb much in use,*
> That Cat will after kind.

Am. Sir, I took you to be a Man better bred, than to liken a Lady to a Crab-fish.

Æs. What I want in good Breeding, Lady, I have in Truth and Honesty: As what you have wanted in Virtue, you have had in a good Face.

Am. Have had, Sir? What I have had, I have still, and shall have a great while, I hope. I'm no Grand-mother, Sir.

Æs. But in a fair way for't, Madam.

Am. Thanks to my Daughter's forwardness then; not my Years. I'd have you to know, Sir, I have never a wrinkle in my Face. A young pert Slut; who'd think she shou'd know so much at her Age.

Æs. Good Masters make quick Scholars, Lady; she has learn'd her Exercise from you.

Am. But where's the Remedy, Sir?

Æs. In trying if a good Example will reclaim her, as an ill one has debauch't her. Live Private, and avoid Scandal.

Am. Never speak it; I can no more Retire, than I can go to Church twice of a *Sunday*.

Æs. What? your Youthful Blood boils in your Veins, I'll warrant.

Am. I have warmth enough to endure the Air, old Gentleman. I need not shut my self up in a House these twenty Years.

Æs. [*Aside.*] She takes a long Lease of Lewdness; she'll be an admirable Tenant to Lust.

Am. [*walking hastily to and fro.*] People think when a Woman is turn'd Fourty, she's old enough to turn out of the World; but I say, when a Woman is turn'd Fourty, she's old enough to have more Wit. The most can be said is, her Face is the worse for wearing: I'll answer for all the rest of her Fabrick. The Men wou'd be to be pity'd, by my Troth, wou'd they; if we shou'd quit the Stage, and leave 'em nothing but a parcel of young pert Sluts, that neither know how to speak Sense, nor keep themselves clean. But don't let 'em fear, we a'n't going   (*Æsop stares upon her,*
yet.   *and as she turns from*
——How now? what? left alone. An unman-   *him, runs off the*
nerly Piece of deformity. Methinks he might have   *Stage.*)
had Sense enough to have made Love to me. But I have found Men strangely dull, for these last Ten or Twelve Years: Sure they'll mend in time, or the World won't be worth living in.

> *For let Philosophers say all they can,*
> *The Source of Womans Joys is plac'd in Man.*   [*Exit.*

Enter Learchus *and* Euphronia, Doris *following at a distance.*

L. to Eu. I must tell you, Mistress, I'm too mild with you, Parents shou'd never intreat their Children, nor will I hereafter. Therefore, in a word, let *Oronces* be lov'd, let *Æsop* be hated; let one be a Peacock, let t'other be a Bat. I'm Father, you are Daughter. *I* command, and you shall obey.

Eu. *I* never yet did otherwise; nor shall *I* now, Sir; but pray let Reason guide you.

L. So it do's: but 'tis my own, not yours, Hussey.

Do. Ah——Well, I'll say no more; but were I in her place, by the *Mass*, I'd have a tug for't.

L. Dæmon, born to distract me. Whence art thou in the Name of Fire and Brimstone? Have not I satisfy'd thee? have not I paid thee what's thy due? and have not I turn'd thee out of Doors, with Orders never more to ſtride my Threshold, ha? Answer, abominable Spirit; what is't that makes thee haunt me?

Do. A foolish Passion, to do you good in spight of your Teeth. Pox on me for my Zeal, I say.

L. And Pox on thee, and thy Zeal too, I say.

Do. Now if it were not for her sake, more than for yours, I'd leave all to your own management, to be reveng'd of you. But rather than I'll see that sweet thing sacrificed,——I'll play the Devil in your House.

L. Patience; I summon thee to my Aid.

Do. Passion; I defie thee; to the laſt drop of my Blood. I'll maintain my ground. What have you to Charge me with? Speak: I love your Child better than you do, and you can't bear that; ha? Is't not so? Nay, it's well y'are asham'd on't; there's some sign of Grace ſtill.

Look you, Sir, in few Words, you'll make me mad; and 'twere enough to make any Body mad (who has Brains enough to be so) to see so much Virtue ship wreck'd at the very Port. The World never saw a Virgin better qualify'd; so witty, so discreet, so modeſt, so chaſt; in a word; I brought her up my self; and 'twou'd be the death of me, to see so virtuous a Maid, become a lewd Wife; which is the usual effeċt of Parents Pride and Covetousness.

L. How Strumpet; wou'd any thing be able to debauch my Daughter?

Do. Your Daughter? yes, your Daughter, and my self into the Bargain: A Woman's but a Woman: and I'll lay a hundred Pound on Nature's side. Come, Sir, few Words dispatch Business. Let who will be the Wife of *Æsop;* she's a Fool, or he's a Cuckold. But you'll never have a true Notion of this Matter, 'till you suppose your self in your Daughter's place. As thus:

You are a pretty, soft, warm, wishing young Lady. I'm a ſtrait, proper, handsome, vigorous young Fellow.

You have a peevish, positive, covetous old Father, and he forces you to Marry a little, lean, crooked, dry, sapless Husband. This Husband's gone abroad, you are left at home. I make you a Visit; find you all alone; The Servant pulls too the Door; the Devil comes in at the Window. I begin to wheedle, you begin to melt; you like my Person; and therefore believe all I say; so firſt I make you an Atheiſt, and then I make you a Whore. Thus the World goes, Sir.

L. Pernicious Peſtilence: has thy Eternal Tongue run down its Larum yet?

Do. Yes.

L. Then get out of my House, Abomination.

Do. I'll not ſtir a Foot.

L. Who waits there? bring me my great Stick.

Do. Bring you a Stick; bring you a Head-piece, that you'd call for, if you knew your own wants.

L. Death and Furies, the Devil, and so forth: I shall run diſtraćted.

Eu. Pray Sir, don't be so angry at her; I'm sure she means well, tho' she may have an odd way of expressing her self.

L. What, you like her meaning? who doubts it, Offspring of *Venus*. But I'll make you ſtay your Stomach with Meat of my chusing, you liquorish young Baggage you. In a word, *Æsop*'s the Man; and to Morrow he shall be your Lord and Maſter.

But since he can't be satisfy'd unless he has your Heart, as well as all the reſt of your Trumpery, let me see you receive him in such a manner, that he may think himself your Choice, as well as mine, 'twill make him eſteem your Judgment: For we usually guess at other People's Under-ſtandings, by their approving our Aćtions, and liking our Faces: See here the Great Man comes; [*to Do.*] Follow me, Insolence; and leave 'em to express their Passion to each other. [*To Eu.*] Remember my laſt Word to you is, Obey.

[*Do. to Eu. aside.*] And remember my laſt Advice to you is, Rebel.

[*Exit L. Doris following him.*

Eu. Alas, I'm good natur'd; the laſt thing that's said to me, usually leaves the deepeſt Impression.

Enter Æsop. They ſtand sometime without speaking.

Æs. ——They say, That Lovers, for want of Words, have Eyes to speak with. I'm afraid you do not underſtand the Language of mine, since yours, I find, will make no Answer to 'em. But I muſt tell you, Lady, There is a numerous Train of Youthful Virgins, that are endow'd with Wealth and Beauty too, who yet have thought it worth their pains and care, to point their Darts at *Æsop*'s homely Breaſt; whilſt you so much contemn, what they pursue, that a young Senseless Fop's preferr'd be-fore me.

Eu. Did you but know that Fop you dare to term so, his very Looks wou'd fright you into nothing.

Æs. A very Bawble.

Eu. How?

Æs. A Butterfly.

Eu. I can't bear it.

Æs. A Paraquet, can prattle and look gawdy.

Eu. It may be so: but let me paint him and you, in your proper Colours, I'll do it exaćtly, and you shall judge which I ought to chuse.

Æs. No, hold; I'm naturally not over-curious; besides, 'tis Pride makes People have their Pićtures drawn.

Eu. Upon my word, Sir, you may have yours taken a hundred times, before any Body will believe 'tis done upon that account.

Æs. [*Aside.*] How Severe she is upon me.
You are resolv'd then to persiſt, and be fond of your Feather; sigh for a Periwig, and die for a Cravat ſtring?

Eu. Methinks, Sir, you might treat with more respeƈt, what I've thought fit to own I value; your Affronts to him, are doubly such to me; if you continue your provoking Language, you muſt expeƈt my Tongue will Sally too; and if you are as wise, as some would make you, you can't but know, I shou'd have Theme enough.

Æs. But is it possible you can Love so much as you pretend?

Eu. Why, do you queſtion it?

Æs. Because no Body Loves so much as they pretend to: But hark you young Lady; Marriage is to laſt a long, long time; and where one Couple Bless the Sacred Knot, a Train of Wretches Curse the Inſtitution. You are in an Age, where Hearts are young and tender, a pleasing Objeƈt gets Admittance soon. But since to Marriage there's annext this dreadful Word, *For Ever;* the following Example ought to move you.

> *A Peacock once, of splendid show,*
> *Gay, gawdy, foppish, vain——a Beau,*
> *Attackt a fond young Pheasants Heart*
> *With such Success,*
> *He pleas'd her, though he made her smart;*
> *He pierƈt her with so much Address,*
> *She Smil'd the Moment that he fix't his Dart.*

> *A Cuckow in a Neighb'ring Tree,*
> *Rich, honeſt, ugly, old,——like me,*
> *Lov'd her, as he lov'd his Life:*
> *No pamper'd Prieſt, e'er ſtudy'd more,*
> *To make a virtuous Nun a Whore,*
> *Then he to get her for his Wife.*
> *But all his Offers ſtill were vain,*
> *His Limbs were weak, his Face was plain,*
> *Beauty, Youth and Vigour weigh'd,*
> *With the warm desiring Maid,*
> *No Bird she cry'd wou'd serve her turn,*
> *But what cou'd quench as well as burn,*
> *She'd have a young Gallant; so one she had.*
> *But e'er a Month was come and gone,*
> *The Bride began to change her tone,*
> *She found a young Gallant was an Inconſtant one.*

She wander'd to a Neighb'ring Grove,
Where after musing long on Love,
She told her Confident, she found
When for ones Life one must be bound,
(Tho' Youth indeed was a delicious Bait;)
An Aged Husband, Rich, tho' Plain,
Wou'd give a slavish Wife less pain,
And what was more, was sooner slain,
Which was a thing of Weight.

Behold young Lady here; The Cuckow of the Fable. I am deform'd, 'tis true, yet I have found the means to make a Figure amongst Men, that well has recompenc'd the wrongs of Nature; my Rival's Beauty promises you much; perhaps my homely Form might yield you more; at least consider on't, 'tis worth your Thought.

Eu. I must confess, my Fortune wou'd be greater;
But what's a Fortune to a Heart like mine?
'Tis true, I'm but a young Philosopher,
Yet in that little space my Glass has run,
I've spent some time in search of Happiness;
The fond pursuit I soon observ'd of Riches,
Inclin'd me to enquire into their worth:
I found their value was not in themselves,
But in their power to grant what we cou'd ask.
I then proceeded to my own Desires,
To know what state of Life wou'd suit with them:
I found 'em Moderate in their Demands;
They neither ask'd for Title, State or Power;
They slighted the Aspiring Post of Envy:
'Tis true they trembled at the Name Contempt;
A general Esteem was all they wish'd;
And that I did not doubt might be obtain'd,
If furnisht but with Virtue and good Nature;
My Fortune prov'd sufficient to afford me
Conveniencies of Life, and Independence.
This, Sir, was the result of my Enquiry;
And by this Scheme of Happiness I build,
When I prefer the Man I Love to you.

Æs. How wise, how witty, and how cleanly young Women grow, as soon as ever they are in Love?

Eu. How foppish, how impertinent, and how nauseous are old Men, when they pretend to be so too?

Æs. How Pert is Youth?

Eu. How Dull is Age?

Æs. Why so Sharp, young Lady?

Eu. Why so blunt, old Gentleman?

Æs. 'Tis enough; I'll to your Father, I know how to deal with him, tho' I don't know how to deal with you. Before to Morrow Noon, Damsel, Wife shall be written on your Brow.   [*Exit Æs.*

Eu. Then before to Morrow Night, Statesman, Husband shall be ſtampt upon your Forehead.   [*Exit Eu.*

End of the Third Aƈt.

ACT IV

Enter Oronces *and* Doris.

Do. PAtience, I beseech you.

Or. Patience? What, and see that lovely Creature thrown into the Arms of that Pedantick Monſter; 'Sdeath, I'd rather see the World reduc'd to Atoms, Mankind turn'd into Craw-fish, and my self an old Woman.

Do. So you think an old Woman a very unfortunate thing I find; but you are miſtaken Sir; she may plague other Folks, but she's as Entertaining to her self, as any one part of the Creation.

Or. [*walking to and fro.*] She's the Devil,——And I'm one of the Dam'd, I think. But I'll make some Body howl for't, I will so.

Do. You'll e'en do as all the young Fellows in the Town do, spoil your own Sport; ah——had young Mens Shoulders, but old Courtiers heads upon 'em, what a delicious time wou'd they have on't. For shame be wise; for your Miſtress's sake, at leaſt, use some Caution.

Or. For her sake I'll respeƈt, even like a Deity, her Father. He shall ſtrike me; he shall tread upon me, and find me humbler, even than a crawling Worm; for I'll not turn again; but for *Æsop*, that unfinish'd Lump; that Chaos of Humanity. I'll use him,——nay expeƈt it, for I'll do't——the firſt Moment that I see him, I'll——

Do. Not Challenge him, I hope;——'Twou'd be a pretty sight truly, to see *Æsop* drawn up in Battalia: Fie for shame, be wise once in your Life, think of gaining time, by putting off the Marriage for a Day or two, and not of waging War with Pigmy. Yonder's the old Gentleman walking by himself in the Gallery; go and wheedle him, you know his weak side; he's good natur'd in the bottom. Stir up his old Fatherly Bowels a little,

I'll warrant you'll move him at laſt, go get you gone, and play your Part discreetly.

Or. Well; I'll try; but if Words won't do with one, Blows shall with t'other, by Heavens they shall.   [*Exit Or.*

Do. [*Solus.*] Nay, I reckon we shall have rare work on't, by and by. Shield us kind Heaven; what things are Men in Love? Now they are Stocks and Stones; then they are Fire and Quicksilver; firſt whining and crying, then Swearing and Damning; this Moment they are in Love, and next Moment they are out of Love; ah——cou'd we but live without 'em——but it's in vain to think on't.   [*Exit Do.*

Enter Æsop at one side of the Stage, Mrs. Forge-Will *at t'other.*

For. Sir, I am your moſt devoted Servant: what I say is no Complement, I do assure you.

Æs. Madam, as far as you are really mine, I believe I may venture to assure you, I am yours.

For. I suppose, Sir, you know that I'm a Widow?

Æs. Madam, I don't so much as know you are a Woman.

For. O Surprising! why I thought the whole Town had known it. Sir, I have been a Widow this Twelve-Month.

Æs. If a Body may guess at your Heart by your Petticoat, Lady, you don't design to be so a Twelve-Month more.

For. O bless me, not a Twelve-Month? why my Husband has left me four squaling Brats. Besides, Sir, I'm undone.

Æs. You seem as chearful an undone Lady, as I have met with.

For. Alas, Sir, I have too great a Spirit ever to let Afflictions spoil my Face. Sir, I'll tell you my Condition; and that will lead me to my Business with you. Sir, my Husband was a Scrivener.

Æs. The *Deux* he was? I thought he had been a Count at leaſt.

For. Sir, 'Tis not the firſt time I have been taken for a Countess; my Mother us'd to say, as I lay in my Cradle, I had the Air of a Woman of Quality; and truly I have always liv'd like such. My Husband, indeed, had something Sneaking in him (as moſt Husbands have, you know Sir) but from the Moment I set foot in his House, bless me, what a Change was there. His Pewter was turn'd into Silver; his Goloshoes into a Glass Coach, and his little Travelling Mare, into a pair of *Flanders* Horses. Inſtead of a greasie Cook-maid to wait at Table, I had four tall Foot-men, in clean Linnen; all things became new and fashionable, and nothing look'd awkward in my Family. My Furniture was the wonder of my Neighbourhood, and my Cloaths the admiration of the whole Town; I had a Neck-lace that was envy'd by the Queen; and a pair of Pendants that set a Dutchess a crying. In a word, I saw nothing I lik'd, but I bought it; and my Husband, good Man, durſt ne'er refuse paying for't.

Thus I liv'd and I Flourish'd, 'till he sickned, and dy'd; but e'er he was cold in his Grave, his Creditors plunder'd my House. But what pity it was to see Fellows with dirty Shooes, come into my beſt Rooms, and touch my Hangings with their filthy Fingers. You won't blame me, Sir, if with all my Courage, I weep at this sensible part of my Misfortune.

Æs. A very sad Story, truly.

For. But now Sir, to my Business. Having been inform'd this Morning, That the King has appointed a great Sum of Money, for the Marriage of young Women who have liv'd well, and are fallen to decay: I am come to Acquaint you, I have two ſtrapping Daughters juſt fit for the Matter; and to desire you'll help 'em to Portions out of the King's Bounty, that they mayn't whine and pine, and be eaten up with the Green Sickness, as half the young Women in the Town are, or wou'd be, if there were not more helps for a Disease than one. This Sir, is my Business.

Æs. And this, Madam, is my Answer.

> A crawling Toad, all speckled o'er,
> Vain, gaudy, painted, patch'd,—a Whore,
> Seeing a well-fed Ox hard by,
> Regards him with an envious Eye,
> And (as the Poets tell;)
> Ye Gods I cannot bear't, quoth she,
> I'll burſt, or be as big as he,
> And so began to Swell.
>
> Her Friends and Kindred round her came,
> They shew'd her she was much to blame,
> The thing was out of reach.
> She told 'em they were busie Folks,
> And when her Husband wou'd have spoke,
> She bid him kiss her B——
> With that they all e'en gave her o'er,
> And She persiſted as before,
> 'Till with a deal of ſtrife,
> She swell'd at laſt, so much her Spleen,
> She burſt, like one, that we have seen,
> Who was a Scrivener's Wife.

This, Widow, I take to be your Case, and that of a great many others; for this is an Age, where moſt People get falls, by clambering too high, to reach at what they should not do. The Shooemaker's Wife reduces her Husband to a Cobler, by endeavouring to be as Spruce as the Taylors: The Taylor's brings hers to a Botcher, by going as fine as the Mercers;

The Mercer's lowers hers to a Foreman, by perking up to the Merchants; The Merchant's wears hers to a Broaker, by strutting up to Quality; and Quality bring theirs to nothing, by striving to out-do one another. If Women were humbler, Men wou'd be honester. Pride brings want, want makes Rogues, Rogues come to be hang'd, and the Devil alone's the Gainer. Go your ways home, Woman; and as your Husband maintain'd you by his Pen, maintain your Self by your Needle; put your great Girles to Service; Employment will keep 'em Honest; much work, and plain Diet, will cure the Green Sickness as well as a Husband.

For. Why you pitiful Pigmy, preaching, canting, Pick-thank; you little, sorry, crooked, dry, withered Eunuch; do you know that——

Æs. I know that I am so deform'd you han't Wit enough to describe me; but I have this good quality, That a foolish Woman can never make me angry.

For. Can't she so; I'll try that, I will.   [*She falls upon him,*
Æs. Help, help, help.   *holds his hands, and*
                                                                       boxes his Ears.

Enter Servants.   She runs off, they after her.

Æs. Nay, e'en let her go——let her go——don't bring her back again ——I'm for making a Bridge of Gold——for my Enemy to retreat upon ——I'm quite out of Breath,——a terrible Woman, I protest.

Enter a Country Gentleman drunk, in a Hunting Dress, with a Huntsman, Groom, Faulkner, and other Servants: one leading a couple of Hounds, another Grey-hounds, a Third a Spaniel, a Fourth a Gun upon his Shoulder, the Faulkner, a Hawk upon his Fist, &c.

Gen. Haux, haux, haux, haux, haux: Joular, there Boy, Joular, Joular, Tinker, Pedlar, Miss, Miss, Miss, Miss, Miss——Blood——Blood and Oons——O there he is; that must be he, I have seen his Picture. [*Reeling up to Æsop.*]——Sir—if your Name's *Æsop*——I'm your humble Servant.

Æs. Sir, My Name is *Æsop*, at your Service.

Gent. Why then Sir——Complements being past on both sides—— with your leave——we'll proceed to Business.
Sir, I am, by Profession——a Gentleman of——Three Thousand Pounds a Year——Sir, I keep a good Pack of Hounds, and a good Stable of Horses.
[*To his Groom.*] How many Horses have I, Sirrah?——Sir, this is my Groom.   [*Presenting him to Æsop.*

Groom. Your Worship has six Coach-Horses, (Cut and Long-Tail) two Runners, half a dozen Hunters, four breeding Mares, and two blind Stallions, besides Pads, Routs, and Dog-Horses.

Gen. Look you there Sir, I scorn to tell a Lye. He that questions my Honour——He's a Son of a Whore. But to Business——Having heard Sir, that, you were come to this Town; I have taken the Pains to come hither too, tho', I had a great deal of Business upon my Hands, for, I had appointed three *Justices* of the *Peace* to Hunt with 'em this Morning ——and be Drunk with 'em in the Afternoon. But the main Chance, must be lookt to——and that's this——I desire Sir, you'll tell the King from me——I don't like these Taxes——In one word as well as in Twenty——I don't like these Taxes.

Æs. Pray, Sir, how high may you be Tax't.

Gen. How high may I be Tax't Sir,——Why, I may be Tax't Sir, ——four Shillings in the Pound, Sir, one half I pay in Money——and t'other half I pay in Perjury, Sir. Hey, Joular, Joular, Joular. Haux, haux, haux, haux, haux. Who, hoo——Here's the best Hound Bitch in *Europe*, Zoons is she. And I had rather kiss her, then kiss my Wife—— Rot me if I had not——But, Sir, I don't like these Taxes.

Æs. Why how wou'd you have the War carry'd on?

Gent. War carry'd on Sir?——Why I had rather have no War carry'd on at all Sir, than pay Taxes. I don't desire to be ruin'd Sir.

Æs. Why you say you have Three Thousand Pounds a Year.

Gent. And so I have, Sir—— *Lett-Acre.* Sir, this is my Steward. How much Land have I, *Lett-Acre*?

Lett-Acre. Your Worship has Three Thausand Paunds a Year, as good Lond as any's i'th' Caunty; and two Thausand Paunds worth of Wood, to cut dawne at your Worship's pleasure, and put the Money in your Pocket.

Gent. Look you there, Sir, what have you to say to that?

Æs. I have to say, Sir, that you may pay your Taxes in Money, instead of Perjury, and still have a better Revenue, than I'm afraid you deserve. What Service do you do your King Sir?

Gent. None at all Sir——I'm above it.

Æs. What Service may you do your Country pray?

Gent. I'm Justice of the Peace—and Captain of the Militia.

Æs. Of what use are you to your Kindred?

Gent. I'm the Head of the Family, and have all the Estate.

Æs. What Good do you do your Neighbours?

Gent. I give 'em their Bellies full of Beef, every time they come to see me; and make 'em so drunk they Spew it up again, before they go away.

Æs. How do you use your Tenants?

Gent. Why I Skrew up their Rents 'till they break and run away, and if I catch 'em again; I let 'em Rot in a Goal.

Æs. How do you Treat your Wife?

Gent. I treat her all Day with ill Nature and Tobacco; and all Night with Snoring, and a dirty Shirt.

Æs. How do you Breed your Children?

Gent. I breed my Eldest Son—a Fool; my Youngest breed themselves; and my Daughters——have no Breeding at all.

Æs. 'Tis very well Sir, I shall be sure to speak to the King of you; or if you think fit to Remonstrance to him, by way of Petition or Address, how reasonable it may be to let Men of your Importance go Scot-free, in the time of a necessary War, I'll deliver it in Council, and speak to it as I ought.

Gent. Why, Sir, I don't disapprove your Advice, but my Clerk is not here, and I can't Spell well.

Æs. You may get it writ at your Leisure, and send it me. But because you are not much us'd to draw up Addresses perhaps; I'll tell you in general, what kind of one this ought to be.

May it please Your Majesty——

[*To the Gent.*] You'll excuse me if I don't know your Name and Title.

Gent. Sir *Polidorus Hogstye*, of *Beast-Hall*, in *Swine County*.

Æs. Very well.

May it please your Majesty; Polidorus Hogstye, *of* Beast-Hall, *in* Swine County, *most humbly represents, That he hates to Pay Taxes, the dreadful Consequences of 'em being inevitably these; That he must retrench two Dishes in Ten, where not above six of 'em are design'd for Gluttony.*

Four Bottles out of Twenty; where not above fifteen of 'em are for Drunkenness.

Six Horses out of Thirty; of which not above Twenty are kept for State.

And four Servants out of a Score; where one half do nothing but make Work for t'other.

To this deplorable Condition must your Important Subject be reduc'd, or forc't to cut down his Timber, which he wou'd willingly preserve, against an ill run at Dice.

And as to the necessity of the War, for the Security of the Kingdom; he neither knows, nor cares, whether it be necessary, or not.

He concludes, with his Prayers for Your Majesty's Life, upon condition, you will Protect him and his Fox-hounds, at Beast-Hall, *without e'er a Penny of Money.*

[*To the Gent.*] This Sir, I suppose, is much what you wou'd be at.

Gent. Exactly, Sir, I'll be sure to have one drawn up, to the self same purpose; and next Fox-Hunting, I'll engage half the Company shall set their Hands to't.

Sir I am your—most devoted Servant; and if you please to let me see you at *Beast-Hall*, here's my Huntsman *Hounds-foot* will shew you a Fox, shall lead you through so many Hedges and Bryers, you shall have no more Cloaths on your Back in half an Hours time——then you had—— in the Womb of your Mother. Haux, haux, haux, &c.　　　[*Ex. Shout.*

Æs. O Tempora, O Mores!

Enter Mr. Fruitful, *and his Wife.*

Mr. F. Heavens preserve the Noble *Æsop*; grant him long Life and happy Days.

Mrs. F. And send him a fruitful Wife, with a hopeful Issue.

Æs. And what is it I'm to do for you good People, to make you amends for all these friendly wishes?

Mr. F. Sir, here's my self and my Wife——

Mrs. F. Sir, here's I, and my Husband——

[*To her Husband.*] Let me speak in my turn, Goodman Forward.

[*To Æs.*] Sir, here's I, and my Husband, I say, think we have as good Pretensions to the King's Favour, as ever a Lord in the Land.

Æs. If you have no better then some Lords in the Land, I hope you won't expect much for your Service.

Mr. F. An't please you, you shall be Judge your self.

Mrs. F. That's as he gives Sentence, Mr. Little-wit; who gave you power to come to a Reference. If he do's not do us Right, the King himself shall; what's to be done here?

[*To Æs.*] Sir, I'm forc't to Correct my Husband a little; poor Man, he is not us'd to Court Business; but to give him his due, he's ready enough at some things: Sir, I have had twenty fine Children by him; fifteen of 'em are alive, and alive like to be; five tall Daughters are wedded and bedded, and ten proper Sons serve their King and their Country.

Æs. A goodly Company upon my word.

Mrs. F. Wou'd all Men take as much pains for the Peopling the Kingdom, we might tuck up our Aprons, and cry a Fig for our Enemies; but we have such a parcel of Drones amongst us——Hold up your Head, Husband——He's a little out of Countenance, Sir, because I chid him; but the Man's a very good Man at the bottom. But to come to my Business, Sir; I hope His Majesty will think it reasonable to allow me something for the Service I have done him; 'tis pity but Labour shou'd be encourag'd, especially when what one has done, one has don't with a good will.

[*To Mr. F.*] What Profession are you of, good People?

Mrs. F. My Husband's an Inn-keeper, Sir; he bears the Name, but I govern the House.

Æs. And what Posts are your Sons in, in the Service?

Mrs. F. Sir, there are four Monks.

Mr. F. Three Attorneys.

Mrs. F. Two Scriveners.

Mr. F. And an Excise-man.

Æs. The deux o'the Service; why I thought they had been all in the Army.

Mrs. F. Not one, Sir.

Æs. No, so it seems, by my Troth: Ten Sons that serve their Country, quoth a, Monks, Attorneys, Scriveners and Excise-men, Serve their Country with a Vengeance; you deserve to be rewarded, truly; you deserve to be hang'd, you wicked People you.

Get you gone out of my sight;

I never was so angry in my Life.   [*Exit Æs.*

[*Mr. F. to his Wife.*] So; who's in the right now; you or I; I told you what wou'd come on't; you muſt be always a Breeding, and Breeding, and the King wou'd take care of 'em, and the Queen wou'd take care of 'em. And always some pretence or other there was. But now we have got a great Kennel of Whelps, and the Devil will take care of 'em, for ought I see. For your Sons are all Rogues, and your Daughters are all Whores, you know they are.

Mrs. F. What, you are a grudging of your Pains now, you Lazy, Sluggish, Flegmatick Drone. You have a mind to die of a Lethargy, have you? but I'll raise your Spirits for you, I will so. Get you gone home, go; go home you Idle Sot, you, I'll raise your Spirits for you.

[*Exit, pushing him before her.*

Re-enter Æsop.

Æs. Solus. Monks, Attorneys, Scriveners, and Excise-men.

Enter Oronces.

Or. O here he is: Sir, I have been searching you, to say two Words to you.

Æs. And now you have found me Sir, what are they?

Or. They are, Sir——that my Name's *Oronces;* you comprehend me.

Æs. I comprehend your Name.

Or. And not my Business?

Æs. Not I, by my Troth.

Or. Then I shall endeavour to teach it you, Monsieur *Æsop.*

Æs. And I to learn it, Monsieur *Oronces.*

Or. Know Sir——that I admire *Euphronia.*

Æs. Know Sir——that you are in the right on't.

Or. But I pretend, Sir, that no Body else shall admire her.

Æs. Then I pretend, Sir, she won't admire you.

Or. Why so Sir?

Æs. Because, Sir.

Or. What Sir?

Æs. She's a Woman, Sir.

Or. What then Sir?

Æs. Why then Sir, she desires to be admir'd by every Man she meets.

Or. Sir, You are too familiar.

Æs. Sir, You are too haughty; I must soften that harsh tone of yours: It don't become you, Sir; it makes a Gentleman appear a Porter, Sir: And that you may know the use of good Language, I'll tell you what once happen'd.

Once on a Time——

Or. I'll have none of your old Wives Fables, Sir: I have no Time to lose; therefore, in a word——

Æs. In a word, be mild. For nothing else will do you Service. Good Manners and soft words have brought many a difficult thing to pass. Therefore hear me patiently.

> *A Cook one Day, who had been drinking,*
> *(Only as many times you know,*
> *You spruce young witty Beaux will do,*
> *T'avoid the dreadful pain of Thinking)*
> *Had Orders sent him to behead*
> *A Goose, like any Chaplain fed.*
> *He took such Pains, to set his Knife right,*
> *'T had done one good t'have lost ones Life by't.*
> *But many Men, have many Minds,*
> *There's various Tasts, in various Kinds,*
> *A Swan (who by mistake he seiz'd)*
> *With wretched Life was better pleas'd.*
> *For as he went to give the Blow,*
> *In tuneful Notes, she let him know,*
> *She neither was a Goose, nor wisht*
> *To make her* Exit *so.*
>
> *The Cook (who thought of nought but Blood,*
> *Except it were the Grease,*
> *For that you know's his Fees).*
> *To hear her Sing, in Great Amazement stood.*
> *Cods Fish, Quoth he, 'twas well you spoke*
> *For I was just, upon the Stroke.*
> *Your Feathers have so much of Goose,*
> *A Drunken Cook, cou'd do no less,*
> *Then think you one: That you'll Confess.*
> *But y'ave a Voice, so soft, so sweet,*
> *That rather then you shall be eat,*
> *The House shall Starve, for want of Meat*
> *And so he turn'd her loose.*

To Or.] Now Sir; what say you? Will you be the Swan, or the Goose?

Or. The Choice can't, sure, be difficult to make,
I hope, you will excuse my Youthful heat,
Young Men and Lovers, have a Claim to Pardon
But since the faults of Age, have no such Plea,
I hope, you'll be more Cautious of offending.
The Flame that warms *Euphronia's* heart and mine
Has long, alas! been kindled in our Breasts,
Even years are past, since our two Souls were wed,
'Twou'd be Adultery, but to wish to part 'em,
And wou'd a Lump of Clay alone content you,
A Mistress Cold and Senseless in your Arms,
Without the least remains, or Signs of Life
Except her Sighs, to Mourn her Absent Lover.
Whilst you shou'd press her, in your eager Arms,
With fond desire, and extasie of Love,
Wou'd it not pierce you, to the very Soul;
To see her Tears, run trickling down her Cheeks,
And know their Fountain, meant 'em all to me?
Cou'd you bear this?
Yet thus the Gods revenge themselves on those
Who stop the Happy Course of mutual Love.
If you must be unfortunate One way
Chuse that, where Justice may support your Grief
And shun the weighty Curse, of Injur'd Lovers.
Æs. Why this is pleading, like a Swan indeed——
Were any thing at Stake, but my *Euphronia.* . . .
Or. Your *Euphronia* Sir,——
Æs. The Goose——take heed——
Were any thing, I say, at stake but her;
Your Plea wou'd be too strong to be refus'd.
But our Debate's about a Lady, Sir,
That's Young, that's Beautiful, that's made for Love
——So am not I you'll say? But y'are mistaken Sir; I'm made to Love,
tho' not to be belov'd. I have a heart like yours: I've folly too: I've
every Instrument of Love like others.
Or. But Sir, you have not been so long a Lover,
Your Passion's young and tender,
'Tis easie for you to become its Master.
Whilst I shou'd strive in Vain, mine's Old and Fixt.
Æs. The older 'tis, the easier to be govern'd,
Were mine of as long a standing, 'twere possible I might get the better

on't. Old Passions are like Old Men; Weak, and soon jostled into the Channel.

Or. Yet Age sometimes is strong, even to the Verge of Life.

Æs. Ay, but there our Comparison don't hold.

Or. You are too merry, to be much in Love,

Æs. And you too sad, to be so long.

Or. My Grief may end my days, so Quench my Flame; But nothing else can e'er extinguish it.

Æs. Don't be Discourag'd Sir; I have seen many a Man out live his Passion Twenty years.

Or. But I have Sworn, to dye *Euphronia*'s Slave.

Æs. A Decay'd Face, always absolves a Lovers Oath.

Or. Lovers, whose Oaths are made to Faces then? But 'tis *Euphronia*'s Soul that I adore, which never can decay.

Æs. I wou'd fain see a young Fellow in Love with a Soul of Threescore.

Or. Quit but *Euphronia* to me, and you shall,
At least if Heaven's Bounty will afford us,
But Years enough to prove my Constancy,
And this is all I ask the Gods and you.   [*Exit Or.*

Æsop solus.

A good pretence however, to beg a long Life.
How grosly do the Inclinations of the Flesh,
Impose upon the simplicity of the Spirit?
Had this young Fellow but studied Anatomy, he'd have found the Source
of his Passion, lay far from his Mistress's Soul.
Alas, Alas!
Had Women no more Charms in their Bodies,
Than what they have in their Minds,
We shou'd see more wise Men in the World,
Much fewer Lovers and Poets.   [*Exit.*

End of the Fourth Act.

ACT V.

Enter Euphronia *and* Doris.

Eu. HEavens, what is't you make me do, *Doris?* Apply myself to the Man I loath; beg Favours from him I hate; seek a Reprieve from him I abhor? 'Tis low, 'tis mean, 'tis base in me.

Do. Why, you hate the Devil as much as you do *Æsop*, (or within a small matter) and shou'd you think it a scandal to pray him to let you alone a day or two, if he were a going to run away with you; ha?

Eu. I don't know what I think, nor what I say, nor what I do: But sure th'art not my Friend, thus to advise me.

Do. I advise? I advise nothing; e'en follow your own way, marry him and make much of him. I have a mind to see some of his Breed; if you like it, I like it: He shan't breed out of me only; that's all I have to take care of.

Eu. Prithee don't diſtract me.

Do. Why, to morrow's the day, fix'd and firm, you know it; Much Meat, little Order, a great many Relations, few Friends, Horse-play, Noise, and bawdy Stories; all's ready for a Compleat Wedding.

Eu. Oh, what shall I do?

Do. Nay, I know this makes you tremble; and yet your tender Conscience scruples to drop one Hypocritical Curtsy, and say, ' pray ', Mr. *Æsop*, be so kind to defer it a few days longer.

Eu. Thou know'ſt I cannot dissemble.

Do. I know you can dissemble well enough when you shou'd not do't. Do you remember how you us'd to plague your poor *Oronces;* make him believe you loath'd him, when you cou'd have kiss'd the ground he went on; affront him in all publick Places; ridicule him in all Company; abuse him where-ever you went; and when you had reduc'd him within an Ace of hanging or drowning, then come home with Tears in your Eyes, and cry, now, *Doris*, let's go lock our selves up, and talk of my dear *Oronces*. Is not this true?

Eu. Yes, yes, yes. But, prithee, have some Compassion on me. Come, I'll do any thing thou bidd'ſt me——What shall I say to this Monſter? Tell me, and I'll obey thee.

Do. Nay, then there's some hopes of you.

Why, you muſt tell him——'Tis natural to you to dislike Folks at firſt sight: That since you have consider'd him better, you find your Aversion abated: That though perhaps it may be a hard matter for you ever to think him a Beau, you don't despair in time of finding out his *Je ne sçai quoy*. And that on t'other side; tho' you have hitherto thought (as moſt young Women do) that nothing cou'd remove your firſt Affection, yet you have very great hopes in the natural Inconſtancy of your Sex.

Tell him, 'tis not impossible a change may happen, provided he gives you time: But that if he goes to force you, there's another piece of Nature peculiar to Woman, which may chance to spoil all, and that's Contradiction: Ring that Argument well in his Ears: He's a Philosopher, he knows it has weight in't.

In short, Wheedle, whine, flatter, lye, weep, spare nothing, it's a moiſt Age, Women have Tears enough; and when you have melted him down, and gain'd more time, we'll employ it in Closet-Debates how to cheat him to the end of the Chapter.

Eu. But you don't consider, *Doris*, that by this means I engage my self to him; and can't afterwards with Honour retreat.

Do. Madam, I know the World——Honour's a Jest, when Jilting's useful.

Besides, he that wou'd have you break your Oath with *Oronces,* can never have the Impudence to blame you for cracking your Word with himself. But who knows what may happen between the Cup and the Lip. Let either of the Old Gentlemen dye, and we ride triumphant. Wou'd I cou'd but see the Statesman sick a little, I'd recommend a Doctor to him, a Cousin of mine, a Man of Conscience, a wise Phisician; tip but the Wink, he understands you.

Eu. Thou wicked Wench, woud'st poison him?

Do. I don't know what I wou'd do, I think, I study, I invent, and some how I will get rid of him. I do more for you, I'm sure, than you and your Knight-Errant do together for your selves.

Eu. Alas, both he and I do all we can; thou know'st we do.

Do. Nay, I know y'are willing enough to get together; but y'are a couple of helpless Things, Heaven knows.

Eu. Our Stars, thou see'st, are bent to Opposition.

Do. Stars!——I'd fain see the Stars hinder me from running away with a Man I lik'd.

Eu. Ay, But thou know'st, shou'd I disoblige my Father, he'd give my Portion to my younger Sister.

Do. Ay, there the Shooe pinches; there's the Love of the Age: Ah! ——to what an Ebb of Passion are Lovers sunk in these days. Give me a Woman that runs away with a Man, when his whole Estate's pack'd up in his Snap-sack. That tucks up her Coats to her Knees; and through thick and through thin, from Quarters to Camp trudges heartily on, with a Child at her Back, another in her Arms, and a brace in her Belly: There's Flame with a Witness, where this is the Effects on't. But we must have Love in a Feather-bed, Forsooth, a Coach and Six Horses, Clean Linnen and a Cawdle; Fie, for shame.

O ho, here comes our Man. Now shew your self a Woman, if you are one.

Enter Æsop.

Æs. I'm told, fair Virgin, you desire to speak with me. Lovers are apt to flatter themselves: I take your Message for a Favour. I hope 'twas meant so.

Eu. Favours from Women are so cheap of late, Men may expect 'em truly without Vanity.

Æs. If the Women are so liberal, I think the Men are generous too on their side: 'Tis a well-bred Age, thank Heaven; and a deal of Civility there passes between the two Sexes. What Service is't, that I can do you, Lady?

Eu. Sir, I have a small Favour to intreat you.

Æs. What is't? I don't believe I shall refuse you.

Eu. What, if you shou'd promise me you won't.

Æs. Why, then I shou'd make a Divorce between my good Breeding and my Sence, which ought to be as sacred a Knot as that of Wedlock.

Eu. Dare you not trust then, Sir, the thing you love?

Æs. Not when the thing I love don't love me; never.

Do. Trust is sometimes the way to be belov'd.

Æs. Ay, but 'tis oftner the way to be cheated.

Eu. Pray promise me you'll grant my suit.

Do. 'Tis a reasonable one, I give you my word for't.

Æs. If it be so, I do promise to grant it.

Do. That's still leaving your self Judge.

Æs. Why, who's more concern'd in the Tryal?

Do. But no body ought to be Judge in their own Cause.

Æs. Yet he that is so, is sure to have no wrong done him.

Do. But if he do's wrong to others, that's worse.

Æs. Worse for them, but not for him.

Do. True Politician by my troth!

Æs. Men must be so, when they have to do with Sharpers.

Eu. If I should tell you then, there were a possibility I might be brought to Love you; you'd scarce believe me?

Æs. I shou'd hope as a Lover, and suspect as a Statesman.

Do. aside.] Love and Wisdom! There's the Passion of the Age again.

Eu. You have liv'd long, Sir, and observ'd much: Did you never see Time produce strange Changes?

Æs. Amongst Women I must confess I have.

Eu. Why I'm a Woman, Sir.

Æs. Why truly that gives me some hopes.

Eu. I'll encrease 'em, Sir; I have already been in Love two years.

Do. And time you know, wears all things to tatters.

Æs. Well observ'd.

Eu. What if you shou'd allow me some, to try what I can do?

Æs. Why truly, I wou'd have patience a day or two, if there were as much probability of my being your new Gallant, as perhaps there may be of your changing your old one.

Do. She shall give you fair play for't, Sir; Opportunity and leave to prattle, and that's what carries most Women in our days. Nay, she shall do more for you. You shall play with her Fan; squeese her little Finger;

buckle her Shooe; read a Romance to her in the Arbour; and saunter in the Woods, on a Moon-shiny night. If this don't melt her, she's no Woman; or you no Man——

Æs. I'm not a Man to melt a Woman that way: I know my self, and know what they require. 'Tis through a Womans Eye you pierce her Heart. And, I've no Darts can make their entrance there.

Do. You are a great Statesman, Sir; but I find you know little of our matters. A Womans Heart's to be enter'd fourty ways. Every Sence she has about her, keeps a door to't. With a Smock-face, and a Feather, you get in at her Eyes. With powerful Nonsense, in soft words; you creep in at her Ears. An Essenc'd Peruke, and a Sweet Handkerchief; let's you in at her Nose. With a Treat and a Box full of Sweet-Meats, you slip in at her Mouth: And if you would enter by her Sense of Feeling, 'tis as beaten a Road as the rest. What think you now, Sir? *There are more ways to the Wood than one,* you see.

Æs. Why, y'are an admirable Pilot: I don't doubt but you have steer'd many a Ship safe to Harbour: But I'm an old stubborn Sea-man; I must Sail by my own Compass still.

Eu. And by your Obstinacy, lose your Vessel.

Æs. No: I'm just entring into Port; we'll be Marryed to morrow.

Eu. For Heaven's sake, defer it some days longer: I cannot Love you yet, indeed I cannot.

Æs. Nor never will, I dare swear.

Eu. Why then will you Marry me?

Æs. Because I Love you.

Eu. If you Lov'd me, you wou'd never make me miserable.

Æs. Not if I Lov'd you for your sake; but I Love you for my own.

Do. [*aside.*] There's an old Rogue for you.

Eu. [*weeping.*] Is there no way left? Must I be wretched?

Æs. 'Tis but resolving to be pleas'd. You can't imagine the strength of Resolution. I have seen a Woman resolve to be in the wrong, all the days of her life: And by the help of her Resolution, she has kept her word to a tittle.

Eu. Methinks the Subject we're upon, shou'd be of weight enough to make you serious.

Æs. Right: To morrow morning pray be ready: You'll find me so: I'm serious: Now I hope you are pleas'd.   [*Turning away from her.*

Eu. [*Going off weeping, and leaning upon* Doris.] Break Heart! For if thou hold'st, I'm miserable.

Do. to *Æs.* Now may the Extravagance of a lewd Wife, with the Insolence of a Vertuous one, join hand in hand to bring thy Gray Hairs to the Grave.   [*Exeunt* Eu. *and* Do.

Æs. My old Friend wishes me well to the last I see.

Enter Learchus *hastily, followed by* Oronces.

Or. Pray hear me, Sir.

L. 'Tis in vain: I'm resolv'd, I tell thee.
Most Noble *Æsop*, Since you are pleas'd to accept of my poor Off-spring
for your Consort, be so Charitable to my Old Age, to deliver me from the
Impertinence of Youth, by making her your Wife this Instant, for there's
a Plot against my Life, they have resolv'd to teaze me to Death to night,
that they may break the Match to morrow morning. Marry her this
Instant, I intreat you.

Æs. This Instant, say you?

L. This Instant; this very Instant.

Æs. 'Tis enough; get all things ready; I'll be with you in a moment.
[*Exit Æs.*

L. Now what say you, Mr. *Flame-Fire?* I shall have the whip hand
of you presently.

Or. Defer it but till to morrow, Sir.

L. That you may run away with her to night, ha?——
Sir, your most Obedient Humble Servant.
Hey; who waits there? Call my Daughter to me: quick.
I'll give her her dispatches presently.

Enter Euphronia.

Eu. D'ye call, Sir?

L. Yes; I do Minx. Go Shift your self, and put on your best Cloaths.
You are to be Marry'd.

Eu. Marry'd, Sir?

L. Yes, Marry'd Madam; and that this Instant too.

Eu. Dear Sir!——

L. Not a word: Obedience and a clean Smock. Dispatch.
[*Exit Eu. weeping.*

Learchus *going off, turns to* Oronces.

Sir, your most Obedient Humble Servant.

Or. Yet hear what I've to say.

L. And what have you to say, Sir?

Or. Alas! I know not what I have to say!

L. Very like so. That's a sure sign he's in Love now.

Or. Have you no Bowels?

L. Ha, ha! Bowels in a Parent! Here's a young Fellow for you.
Hark thee, Stripling. Being in a very merry humour, I don't care if I
discover some Paternal Secrets to thee.

Know then; that how humoursome, how whimsical soever we may

appear, there's one fixt Principle that runs through almost the whole Race of us; and that's to please our selves. Why, do'st think I got my Daughter? Why there was something in't that pleas'd me. Why do'st think I Marry my Daughter? Why, to please my self still. And what is't that pleases me? Why my Interest, what do'st think it shou'd be? If *Æsop*'s my Son in Law, he'll make me a Lord: If thou art my Son in-Law———thou'lt make me a Grand-father. Now I having more mind to be a Lord than a Grand-father, give my Daughter to him, and not to thee.

Or. Then shall her Happiness weigh nothing with you?

L. Not this: If it did, I'd give her to thee, and not to him.

Or. Do you think forc'd Marriage the way to keep Women Vertuous?

L. No; nor I don't care whether Women are Vertuous or not.

Or. You know your Daughter Loves me.

L. I do so.

Or. What if the Children that *Æsop* may happen to Father, shou'd chance to be begot by me?

L. Why then *Æsop* wou'd be the Cuckold, not I.

Or. Is that all you care?

L. Yes: I speak as a Father.

Or. What think you of your Childs concern in t'other World?

L. Why, I think it my Childs concern; not mine. I speak as a Father.

Or. Do you remember you once gave me your Consent to Wed your Daughter?

L. I did.

Or. Why did you so?

L. Because you were the best Match that offer'd at that time. I did like a Father.

Or. Why then, Sir, I'll do like a Lover. I'll make you keep your Word, or cut your Throat.

L. Who waits there? Hey?

Enter Servants.

Seize me that Bully there. Carry him to Prison, and keep him safe.
[*They seize him.*

Or. Why, you won't use me thus?

L. Yes, but I will tho'. Away with him. Sir, your most Humble Servant. I wish you a good Nights Rest, and as far as a Merry Dream goes, my Daughter's at your Service.   [*Exeunt Servants with* Oronces.

Or. Death and Furies.

L. Singing.] *Dol, de tol dol, dol dol, de tol dol:*
Lilly Burleighre's lodg'd in a Bough.

Enter a Troop of Musicians, Dancers, &c.

L. How now? What have we got here?

Mus. Sir, we are a Troop of Trifling Fellows, Fidlers and Dancers, come to Celebrate the Wedding of your Fair Daughter: If your Honour pleases to give us leave.

L. With all my Heart. But who do you take me for, Sir; Ha?

Mus. I take your Honour for our Noble Governour of *Sysicus*.

L. Governour of *Sysicus*; Governour of a Cheese-Cake. I'm Father-in-law to the Great *Æsop*, Sirrah.

All bow to him.

Aside.]——I shall be a Great Man.
Come, Tune your Fiddles; Shake your Legs. Get all things ready. My Son-in-law will be here presently——I shall be a great Man.   [*Exit.*

Mus. A great Marriage Brother. What do'st think will be the end on't?

2. *Mus.* Why, I believe we shall see three turns upon't. This Old Fellow here, will turn Fool; his Daughter will turn Strumpet; and his Son-in-law will turn 'em both out of doors. But that's nothing to thee nor me, as long as we are paid for our Fidling. So tune away, Gentlemen.

1. *Mus.* D'ye hear Trumpets? When the Bride appears, Salute her with a Melancholly Waft. 'Twill suit her humour; for I guess she mayn't be over well pleas'd.

Enter Learchus *with several Friends and a Priest.*

L. Gentlemen and Friends, y'are all welcome. I have sent to as many of you, as our short time wou'd give me leave, to desire you wou'd be Witnesses of the Honour the Great *Æsop* designs our self and Family. Hey; who attends there?
Go, let my Daughter know I wait for her.   [*Exit Servants.*
——'Tis a vast Honour that is done me, Gentlemen.

2. *Gent.* It is indeed, my Lord.

L. Aside.] Look you there; if they don't call me my Lord already.
——I shall be a great Man.

Enter Euphronia *weeping, and leaning upon* Doris,
both in deep Mourning.

L. How now? What's here? All in deep Mourning? Here's a provoking Baggage for you.

The Trumpets sound a Melancholly Air till *Æsop* appears; and
then the Violins and Hautbois strike up a *Lancashire Hornpipe.*

Enter Æsop *in a Gay Foppish Dress, Long Peruke, &c. a Gaudy Equipage
of Pages and Footmen, all enter, in an Airy Brisk manner.*

(59)

Æsop in an affected tone, to Euphronia.

Gad take my Soul, Mame, I hope I shall please you now——Gentlemen all; I'm your Humble Servant. I'm going to be a very happy Man you see.

To Eu.] When the heat of the Ceremony's over, if your Ladyship pleases, Mame; I'll wait upon you to take the Air in the Park. Hey, Page. Let there be a Coach and six Horses ready instantly.

Observing her Dress.]——I vow to Gad, Mame; I was so taken up with my good Fortune, I did not observe the extream fancy of your Lady-ships Wedding-Cloaths——Infinitely pretty, as I hope to be sav'd: a World of Variety, and not at all Gawdy.

To L.]——My Dear Father-in-Law. Embrace me.

L. Your Lordship does me too much Honour.

Aside.]——I shall be a Great Man.

Æs. Come Gentlemen; Are all things ready? Where's the Priest?

Pr. Here, my Noble Lord.

Æs. Most Reverend—Will you please to say Grace that I may fall to; for I'm very hungry, and here's very good Meat. But where's my Rival all this while? The least we can do, is to invite him to the Wedding.

L. My Lord he's in Prison.

Æs. In Prison! how so?

L. He wou'd have murder'd me.

Æs. A bloody Fellow! But let's see him however. Send for him quickly.

Ha, Governor——that handsome Daughter of yours, I will so mumble her——

L. I shall be a great Man.

Enter Oronces *pinion'd and guarded.*

Æs. O ho: Here's my Rival: Then we have all we want. Advance, Sir, if you please. I desire you'll do me the Favour to be a Witness to my Marriage, lest one of these days you shou'd take a Fancy to dispute my Wife with me.

Or. Do you then send for me to insult me: 'Tis base in you.

Æs. I have no time now to throw away upon Points of Generosity; I have hotter Work upon my hands. Come, Priest, advance.

L. Pray hold him fast there; he has the Devil and all of Mischief in's Eye.

Æs. to Eu.] Will you Ladyship please, Mame, to give me your fair hand——hey-day. [*She refuses her Hand.*

L. I'll give it you, my Noble Lord, if she won't.

Aside.] A stubborn, self-will'd, stiff-necked Strumpet.

Learchus *holds out her Hand to* Æsop, *who takes it;* Oronces *stands on* Æsop's *left hand, and the Priest before 'em.*

Æs. Let my Rival stand next me: Of all Men I'd have him be satisfy'd.
Or. Barbarous Inhumane Monster.
Æs. Now, Priest do thy Office.

Flourish with the Trumpets.

Pr. Since the Eternal Laws of Fate decree,
That He, thy Husband; She, thy Wife shou'd be.
May Heaven take you, to its Care.
May *Jupiter* look kindly down,
Place on your Heads Contentments Crown;
And may his Godhead never frown
Upon this Happy Pair.   *[Flourish again of Trumpets.*
          [*As the Priest pronounces the last Line,* Æsop *joins* Oronces
                and Euphronia's *hands.*
Or. O happy Change: Blessings on Blessings wait on the Generous
Æsop.
Æs. Happy, thrice happy may you ever be.
And if you think, there's something due to me,
Pay it in mutual Love and Constancy.
Eu. to Æs.] You'll pardon me, most Generous Man, if in the present
Transports of my Soul, which you your self have by your Bounty caus'd,
my willing Tongue is ty'd from uttering the Thoughts that flow from a
most grateful Heart.
Æs. For what's I've done, I merit little Thanks,
Since what I've done, my Duty bound me to.
I wou'd your Father had acquitted his:
But he who's such a Tyrant o'er his Children,
To sacrifice their Peace to his Ambition,
Is fit to govern nothing but himself.
To L.] And therefore, Sir, at my return to Court,
I shall take Care this City may be sway'd
By more Humanity than dwells in you.
Lea. aside.] I shall be a great Man.
Eu. to Æs.] Had I not reason, from your Constant Goodness,
To judge your Bounty, Sir, is infinite,
I shou'd not dare to sue for farther Favours.
But pardon me; if imitating Heaven and you,
I easily forgive my aged Father,
And beg that *Æsop* wou'd forgive him too.   *[Kneeling to him.*

Æs. The Injury he wou'd have done to you, was great indeed: But 'twas a Blessing he design'd for me; if therefore you can pardon him, I may.

To L.] Your injur'd Daughter, Sir, has on her Knees intreated for her cruel, barbarous Father; and by her Goodness has obtain'd her Suit. If in the Remnant of your days, you can find out some way to recompence her, do it, that Men and Gods may pardon you, as she and I have done. But let me see, I have one Quarrel still to make up. Where's my old Friend, *Doris.*

Do. She's here, Sir, at your Service; and as much your Friend as ever: True to her Principles, and firm to her Mistress. But she has a much better Opinion of you now than she had half an hour ago.

Æs. She has reason: For my Soul appear'd then as deform'd as my Body. But I hope now, one may so far mediate for t'other, that, provided I don't make Love, the Women won't quarrel with me; for they are worse Enemies even than they are Friends.

Come, Gentlemen, I'll humour my Dress a little longer, and share with you in the Diversions these Boon Companions have prepar'd us. Let's take our Places, and see how they can divert us.

Æsop leads the Bride to her Place. All being seated, there's a short Consort of Hautboys, Trumpets, &c. After which a Dance between an Old Man and a young Woman, who shuns him still as he comes near her. At last he stops, and begins this Dialogue; which they sing together.

Old Man.

Why so Cold, and why so Coy.
What I want in Youth and Fire,
I have in Love and in Desire:
To my Arms, my Love, my Joy·
Why so Cold, and why so Coy?

Woman.

'Tis Sympathy perhaps with you;
You are Cold, and I'm so too.

Old Man.

My Years alone have froze my Blood;
Youthful Heat in Female Charms,
Glowing in my Aged Arms,
Wou'd melt it down once more into a Flood.

Woman.

Women, alas, like Flints, ne'er burn alone,
To make a Virgin know,
There's Fire within the Stone,
Some Manly Steel must boldly strike the Blow.

Old Man.

Assist me only with your Charms,
You'll find I'm Man, and still am bold;
You'll find I still can strike, tho' old:
I only want your Aid to raise my Arm.

Enter a Youth who seizes on the young Woman.

Youth.

Who talks of Charms, who talks of Aid.
I bring an Arm
That wants no Charm,
To rouse the Fire that's in a Flinty Maid.
Retire Old Age.

Woman.

——Winter be gone:
Behold the Youthful Spring comes gayly on.
Here, here's a Torch, to light a Virgin's Fire:
To my Arms, my Love, my Joy;
When Women have what they desire,
They're neither Cold nor Coy.

[She takes him in her Arms.

The Song and Dance ended, Æsop takes Euphronia *and* Oronces *by the Hands, leading them forwards.*

Æs. By this time, my young eager Couple, 'tis probable you wou'd be glad to be alone; perhaps you'll have a mind to go to Bed even without your Supper; for Brides and Bridegrooms eat little on their Wedding-night. But since if Matrimony were worn as it ought to be, it wou'd perhaps sit easier about us than usually it does, I'll give you one Word of Council, and so I shall release you.

When one is out of Humour, let the other be dumb.
Let your Diversions be such, as both may have a share in 'em.

Never let Familiarity exclude Respect.

Be clean in your Cloaths, but nicely so in your Persons: Eat at one Table: Lye in one Room, but sleep in two Beds.

I'll tell the Ladies why.

Turning to the Boxes.

In the sprightly Month of *May*,
When Males and Females, sport and play,
And Kiss and Toy away the Day.
An eager Sparrow, and his Mate,
Chirping on a Tree were sate,
Full of Love——and full of Prate.
They talk't of nothing, but their Fires,
Of Raging Heats, and Strong Desires,
Of Eternal Constancy;
How true and faithful, they wou'd be,
Of this and that, and endless Joys,
And a thousand more such Toys.
The only thing they apprehended,
Was that their Lives wou'd be so short,
They cou'd not finish, half their Sport
Before their Days were ended.
 But, as from Bow to Bow they rove,
  They chanc'd at last
  In furious haste,
On a Twigg, with Birdlime spread;
(Want of a more Downy Bed)
  To act a Scene of Love.
Fatal it prov'd, to both their Fires.
For tho' at length, they broke away,
And baulk'd the School-Boy of his Prey,
Which made him weep, the live-long day.
The Bridegroom, in the hasty strife,
Was stuck so fast, to his Dear Wife;
That tho' he us'd, his utmost Art,
He quickly found, it was in vain,
To put himself, to farther pain,
They never more must part.
A gloomy Shade, o'recast his Brow;
He found himself——I know not how,
He lookt——as Husbands often do.
Wheree'er he mov'd, he felt her still,
She kiss'd him oft, against his will:

(64)

Abroad, at Home; at Bed and Board;
With favours, she o'rewhelm'd her Lord.
Oft he turn'd his Head away,
And seldom had a word to say,
Which absolutely spoyl'd her Play,
For she was better ſtor'd.
Howe'er, at length her Stock was spent,
(For Female Fires, sometimes may be
Subject to Mortality;)
So Back to Back they sit, and sullenly Repent,
But the Mute Scene, was quickly ended,
The Lady, for her share pretended,
The want of Love, lay at his Door,
For her part, she had ſtill in ſtore
Enough for him, and twenty more,
Which cou'd not be contended.
He answer'd her, in homely words,
(For Sparrows are but ill bred Birds)
That he already had enjoy'd
So much, that truly he was Cloy'd.
Which so provok'd her Spleen,
That after some good hearty Prayers,
A Joſtle, and some spightful Tears.
They fell together, by the Ears,
And ne'er were fond again.

FINIS.

ÆSOP

PART II.

Enter Players.

Æs. WELL, good People, who are all you?
    Omnes. Sir, we are Players——
Æs. Players? What Players?
Play. Why, Sir, we are Stage-Players,
That's our Calling:
Tho' we play upon other things too; some of us play
Upon the Fiddle; some play upon the Flute;
We play upon one another, we play upon the Town,
And we play upon the Patentees.
    Æs. Patentees! Prithee, what are they?
    Play. Why, they are, Sir——Sir, they are——I Cod I don't know
What they are——Fish or Flesh——Masters or Servants
——Sometimes one——Sometimes t'other, I think——
Just as we are in the Mood.
    Æs. Why, I thought they had a lawful Authority over you.
    Play. Lawful Authority, Sir—Sir, we are freeborn Englishmen,
We care not for Law nor Authority neither,
When we are out of Humour.
    Æs. But I think they pretended at least to an Authority
Over you; 'pray' upon what Foundation was it built?
    Play. Upon a rotten one——if you'll believe us?
Sir, I'll tell you what the Projectors did:
They imbark'd Twenty thousand pound upon a Leaky
Vessel——She was built at *Whitehall;*
I think they call'd her——the Patent——ay, the Patent;
Her Keel was made of a Broad Seal——and the King
Gave 'em a White Staff for their Main Mast.
She was a pretty tight Frigat to look upon, indeed:
They spar'd nothing to set her off; they Guilded her,
And Painted her, and Rigg'd, and Gunn'd her;
And so sent her a Privateering.
But the first Storm that blew,
Down went the Mast, a-shore went the Ship——

Crack says the Keel, mercy cry'd the Pilot;
But the Wind was so high, his Prayers cou'd not
Be heard——so they split upon a Rock——
That lay hid under a Petticoat.

    Æs. A very sad Story, this: but what became of the
Ship's Company?

    Play. Why, Sir, your humble Servants here, who were
The Officers and the best of the Sailors——
(Little *Ben* amongst the rest) seiz'd on a small
Bark that lay to our hand, and away we put to sea again.
To say the Truth, we were better Man'd than
Rigg'd, and Ammunition was plaguy scarce amongst
Us——However, a-Cruising we went, and some petty
Small Prizes we have made; but the Blessing
Of Heaven not being among us——
Or how the Devil 'tis, I can't tell; but we are not rich.

    Æs. Well, but what became of the rest of the Crew?

    Play. Why, Sir, as for the Scoundrels, they, poor Dogs,
Stuck by the Wrack. The Captain gave 'em Bread,
And Cheese, and good Words——He told them, if they
Wou'd patch her up, and venture t'other Cruise;
He'd prefer 'em all; so to work they went,
And to Sea they got her.

    Æs. I hope he kept his Word with 'em.

    Play. That he did; he made the Boat-Swain's Mate,
Lieutenant; he made the Cook, Doctor: He was
Forc'd to be Purser, and Pilot, and Gunner himself;
And the Swabber took Orders to be Chaplain.

    Æs. But with such unskilful Officers I'm afraid
They'll hardly keep above Water long.

    Play. Why truly, Sir, we care not how soon they are under:
But Curst Folks, thrive, I think. I know nothing else
That makes 'em swim.
I'm sure, by the Rules of Navigation, they ought to
Have over-set long since; for they carry a great deal
Of Sail, and have very little Ballast.

    Æs. I'm afraid you ruine one another. I fancy if you
Were all in a Ship together again, you'd have less
Work and more Profit.

    Play. Ah, Sir——we are resolv'd we'll never sail under
Captain Patentee again.

    Æs. Prithee, why so?

    Play. Sir, he has us'd us like Dogs.

Wom. ——And Bitches too, Sir.

Æs. I'm sorry to hear that; 'pray' how was't he treated you?

Play. Sir, 'tis impossible to tell; he us'd us like the *English*
At *Amboyna*——

Æs. But I wou'd know some Particulars; tell me what
'Twas he did to you.

Play. What he did, Sir——why, he did in the first place, Sir——
——In the first place, Sir, he did——I Cod I don't know what
He did——Can you tell, Wife?

Wom. Yes, marry can I; and a Burning Shame it was too.

Play. O, I remember now, Sir, he wou'd not give us Plumbs
Enough in our Pudding.

Æs. That indeed was very hard; but did he give you as
Many as he promis'd you.

Play. Yes, and more; but what of all that, we had not as
Many as we had a Mind to——

1 *Wom.* Sir, my Husband tells you Truth——

Æs. I believe he may; but what other wrongs did he do you?

1 *Wom.* Why, Sir, he did not treat me with respect; 'twas not
One Day in three, he wou'd so much as bid me good Morrow——

2 *Wom.* Sir, he invited me to Dinner, and never drank my health.

1 *Wom.* Then he cock'd his Hat at Mrs. *Pert.*

2 *Wom.* Yes, and told Mrs. *Slippery* he had as good a Face
As she had.

Æs. Why, these were insufferable Abuses——

2 *Play.* Then, Sir, I did but come to him one day——
And tell him I wanted Fifty Pound, and what do you
Think he did by me, Sir——
Sir he turn'd round upon Heel like a Top——

1 *Play.* But that was nothing to the Affront he put upon me, Sir.
I came to him, and in very civil Words, as I thought,
Desir'd him to double my Pay: Sir, wou'd you believe it,
He had the Barbarity to ask me, if I intended
To double my Work; and because I told him, No,
Sir——he did use me, good Lord, how he did use me.

Æs. Prithee how?

1 *Play.* Why, he walk'd off, and answer'd me never a Word.

Æs. How had you Patience.

1 *Play.* Sir, I had not Patience. I sent him a Challenge;
And what do you think his Answer was——he sent me Word
I was a Scoundrel Son of a Whore,
And he wou'd only fight me by Proxy——

Æs. Very fine.

1 *Play.* At this rate, Sir, were we poor Dogs us'd——till one
Frosty Morning down he comes amongst us——and
Very roundly tells us——That for the Future,
No Purchase, no Pay.   They that wou'd not work shou'd
Not eat———
Sir, we at first ask'd him coolly and civilly——Why?
His Answer was, because the Town wanted
Diversion, and he wanted Money——
Our Reply to this, Sir, was very short; but I think
To the purpose.
    Æs. What was it?
    1 *Play.* It was, Sir, that so we wallow'd in Plenty——and Ease
The Town and he might be damn'd——
This, Sir, is the true History of Separation——and we
Hope you'll stand our Friend——
    Æs. I'll tell you what, Sirs——
I once a Pack of a Beagles knew——
That much resembled, I know who:
With a good Huntsman at their Tail,
In full Command,
With Whip in Hand.
They'd run apace
The Chearful Chace,
And of their Game were seldom known to fail.
But being at length their chance to find
A Huntsman of a gentler Kind,
They soon perceiv'd the Rein was slack,
The Word went quickly through the Pack——
They one and all cry'd Liberty:
This happy Moment we are free.
We'll range the Woods,
Like Nymphs and Gods,
And spend our Mouths in praise of Mutiny.
With that old *Jowler* trots away,
And *Bowman* singles out his Prey.
Thunder bellow'd through the Wood,
And swore he'd burst his Guts with Blood.
Venus tript it o'er the Plain,
With boundless Hopes of boundless Gain.
——*Juno*, she slipt down the Hedge,
But left her Sacred Word for Pledge;
That all she pickt up by the by——
Shou'd to the Publick Treasury.

And well they might rely upon her;
For *Juno* was a Bitch of Honour.
In short, they all had hopes to see
A Heavenly Crop of Mutiny,
And so to Reaping fell:
But in a little time they found,
It was the Devil had Till'd the ground,
And brought the Seed from Hell.
The Pack divided, nothing throve;
Discord seiz'd the Throne of Love.
Want and Misery all endure,
All take pains, and all grow poor.
When they had toyl'd the live-long day,
And came at night, to view their Prey.
Oft alas so ill they'd sped,
That half went supperless to Bed.
At length they all in Council sate,
Where at a very fair Debate,
It was agreed at laſt,
That Slavery, with Ease and Plenty,
When Hounds were something turn'd of twenty,
Was much a better Fate,
Than 'twas to work and Faſt.

    1 *Play*. Well, Sir——and what did they do then?

    Æs. Why they all went home to their Kennel again.
If you think they did wisely, you'll do well to follow their Example.

[Exit Æsop.

    1 *Play*. Well Beagles; What think you of the little Gentleman's Advice.

    2 *Wom*. I think he's a little ugly Philosopher, and talks like a Fool.

    1 *Play*. Ay, why there's it now! If he had been a tall handsome Blockhead, he had talk'd like a Wise Man.

    2 *Wom*. Why, do you think, Mr. *Jowler*, that we'll ever joyn again?

    1 *Play*. I do think, sweet Mrs. *Juno*, that if we do not joyn again, you muſt be a little freer of your Carcass than you are, or you muſt bring down your Pride to a Serge Petticoat.

    1 *Wom*. And do you think, Sir, after the Affronts I have receiv'd, the Patent and I can ever be Friends?

    1 *Play*. I do think, Madam, that if my Intereſt had not been more affronted than your Face, the Patent and you had never been Foes.

    1 *Wom*. And so, Sir, then you have serious thoughts of a Reconciliation!——

    1 *Play*. Madam, I do believe I may.

1 *Wom.* Why then Sir, give me leave to tell you, that——make it my Interest, and I'll have serious thoughts on't too.

2 *Wom.* Nay, if you are thereabouts, I desire to come into the Treaty.

3 *Play.* And I.

4 *Play.* And I.

2 *Play.* And I, no separate Peace.   None of your *Turin* Play, I beseech you.

1 *Play.* Why then, since you are all so Christianly dispos'd——
I think we had best Adjourn immediately to our Council-
Chamber; chuse some Potent Prince for Mediator,
And Guarantee——Fix upon the place of Treaty,
Dispatch our Plenipos, and whip up the Peace
Like an Oyster.   For under the Rose, my Confederates,
Here is such a damn'd Discount upon our Bills,
I'm afraid, if we stand it out another Campaign,
We must live upon slender Subsistance.   [*Exeunt.*

*Enter Æsop.   And a little after A Country Gentleman, who
walks to and fro, looking angerly upon Æsop.*

Æs. Have you any business with me, Sir?

G. ——I can't tell whether I have or not.

Æs. You seem disturb'd, Sir.

G. I'm always so, at the sight of a Courtier.

Æs. Pray what may it be, that gives you so great an Antipathy to 'em?

G. My Profession.

Æs. What's that?

G. Honesty.

Æs. ——'Tis an honest Profession.
I hope, Sir, for the general good of Mankind, you are in some Publick
Employment.

G. So I am, Sir,——no thanks to the Court.

Æs. You are then, I suppose, Employ'd by——

G. My Country.

Æs. Who have made you——

G. A Senator.

Æs. Sir, I Reverence you.   [*Bowing.*

G. Sir, you may Reverence as low as you please. But I shall spare none
of you. Sir, I am intrusted by my Country with above ten thousand of
their Grievances, and in order to Redress 'em, my design is, to hang ten
thousand Courtiers.

Æs. Why, 'tis making short work, I must confess.
But are you sure, Sir, that wou'd do't?

G. Sure.——Ay, sure.

Æs. How do you know?

G. Why the whole Country says so, and I at the Head of 'em. Now, let me see who dares say the Contrary.

Æs. Not I truly. But Sir, if you won't take it ill, I'll ask you a Question or two.

G. Sir, I shall take ill what I please. And if you, or e'er a Courtier of you all, pretend the contrary, I say, it's a breach of Priviledge—— Now put your Question if you think fit.

Æs. Why, then Sir, with all due regard to your Character, and your Priviledge too. I wou'd be glad to know, what you chiefly complain of?

G. Why, Sir, I do chiefly complain, That we have
A great many Ships, and very little Trade:
A great many Tenants, and very little Money:
A great many Souldiers, and very little Fighting.
A great many *Gazettes*, and little good News.
A great many States-Men, and very little Wisdom.
A great many Parsons, and not an ounce of Religion.

Æs. Why, truly Sir, I do confess these are Grievances very well worth your Redressing. I perceive you are truly sensible of our Diseases, but I'm afraid you are a little out in the Cure.

G. Sir, I perceive you take me for a Country-Physician: But you shall find, Sir, that a Country-Doctor, is able to deal with a Court-Quack; and to shew you, that I do understand something of the State of the Body Politick, I will tell you, Sir, that I have heard a Wise Man say, The Court is the Stomach of the Nation, in which, if the business be not thoroughly digested, the whole Carcass will be in disorder. Now, Sir, I do find by the Latitude of the Members, and the Vapours that fly into the Head, that this same Stomach is full of Indigestions, which must be remov'd. And therefore, Sir, I am come Post to Town with my Head full of *Crocus Me^m*. and design to give the Court a Vomit.

Æs. Sir, the Physick you mention, tho' necessary sometimes, is of too violent a Nature, to be us'd without a great deal of Caution. I'm afraid you are a little too rash in your Prescriptions. Is it not possible you may be mistaken in the Cause of the Distemper?

G. Sir, I do not think it possible, I shou'd be mistaken in any thing.

Æs. Pray, Sir, have you been long a Senator?

G. No, Sir.

Æs. Have you been much about Town?

G. No, Sir.

Æs. Have you Convers'd much with Men of Business?

G. No, Sir.

Æs. Have you made any serious enquiry into the present Disorders of the Nation?

G. No, Sir.

Æs. Have you ever heard what the Men now employ'd in business, have to say for themselves?

G. No, Sir.

Æs. How then do you know they deserve to be punish'd, for the present disorders in your Affairs?

G. I'll tell you how I know.

Æs. I wou'd be glad to hear.

G. Why, I know by this——I know it I say, by this—— That I'm sure on't.——

And to give you demonstration that I'm sure on't, there is not one Man in a good Post in the Nation——but I'd give my Vote to hang him: Now I hope you are convinc'd.

Æs. As for Example. The first Minister of State: Why wou'd you hang him?

G. Because he gives bad Council.

Æs. How do you know?

G. Why they say so.

Æs. And who wou'd you put in his room?

G. One that wou'd give better.

Æs. Who's that?

G. My self.

Æs. The Secretary of State: Why wou'd you hang him?

G. Because he has not good intelligence.

Æs. How do you know?

G. I have heard so.

Æs. And who wou'd you put in his Place?

G. My Father.

Æs. The Treasurer, why would you hang him?

G. Because he doesn't understand his Business.

Æs. How do you know?

G. I dreamt so.

Æs. And who would you have succeed him?

G. My Uncle.

Æs. The Admiral: why would you hang him?

G. Because he has not destroyed the Enemies.

Æs. How do you know he could do it?

G. Why, I believe so.

Æs. And who would you have Command in his stead?

G. My Brother.

Æs. And the General: why would you hang him?

G. Because he took ne'er a Town last Campaign.

Æs. And how do you know 'twas in his power?

G. Why I don't care a Sous whether it was in's power or not. But I have a Son at home, a brave chapping Lad; he has been Captain in the *Militia* this twelve months, and I'd be glad to see him in his Place. What do you ſtare for, Sir? ha? I gad I tell you he'd scour all the Devils. He's none of your Fencers; none of your *Sa, Sa* men. *Numphs* is down-right; that's his Play. You may see his Courage in his Face. He has a pair of Cheeks like two Bladders; a Nose as flat as your Hand, and a Forehead like a Bull.

Æs. In short, Sir, I find if you and your Family were provided for, things would soon grow better than they do.

G. And so they wou'd, Sir. Clap me at the Head of the State, and *Numphs* at the Head of the Army; He with his Club Musquet, and I with a Club Head peice, we'd soon put an end to your business.

Æs. I believe you wou'd indeed. And therefore since I happen to be acquainted with your extraordinary Abilities, I am resolv'd to give the King an account of you, and employ my Intereſt with him, that you and your Son may have the Poſts you desire.

G. Will you by the Lord?——Give me your fiſt, Sir——the only honeſt Courtier that ever I met with in my Life.

Æs. But, Sir, when I have done you this mighty peice of Service, I shall have a small requeſt to beg of you, which I hope you won't refuse me.

G. What's that?

Æs. Why 'tis in behalf of the two Officers who are to be displac'd, to make room for you and your Son.

G. The Secretary and the General?

Æs. The same. 'Tis pity they should be quite out of business; I muſt therefore desire you'll let me recommend one of 'em to you for your Bailiff, and t'other for your Huntsman.

G. My Bailiff and my Huntsman?——Sir, that's not to be granted.

Æs. Pray why?

G. Why?—Because one wou'd ruin my Land, and t'other wou'd spoil my Fox-Hounds.

Æs. Why do you think so?

G. Why do I think so?——These Courtiers will ask the ſtrangeſt Queſtions——
Why Sir, do you think that Men bred up to the State, and the Army, can underſtand the business of Ploughing and Hunting.

Æs. I did not know but they might.

G. How cou'd you think so?

Æs. Because I see men bred up to Ploughing and Hunting, underſtand the business of the State and the Army.

G. I'm shot——I han't one word to say for my self——I never was so caught in my Life.

Æs. I perceive, Sir, by your Looks, what I have said has made some impression upon you; and wou'd perhaps do more if you wou'd give it leave.

Taking his Hand.] Come Sir, tho' I am a ſtranger to you, I can be your Friend: My Favour at Court does not hinder me from being a Lover of my Country. 'Tis my Nature, as well as Principles, to be pleas'd with the prosperity of Mankind. I wish all things happy, and my ſtudy is to make 'em so.

The Diſtempers of the Government (which I own are great) have employ'd the ſtretch of my Underſtanding, and the deepeſt of my thoughts, to penetrate the Cause, and to find out the Remedy. But alas! all the product of my ſtudy is this; That I find there is too near a Resemblance between the Diseases of the State and those of the Body; for the moſt expert Miniſter to become a greater Maſter in one than the College is in t'other. And how far their Skill extends, you may see by this Lump upon my Back. Allowances in all Professions there muſt be, since 'tis weak Man that is the weak Professor. Believe me, Senator, for I have seen the Proof on't. The longeſt Beard amongſt us is a Fool. Cou'd you but ſtand behind the Curtain, and there observe the secret Springs of State; you'd see in all the Good or Evil that attends it, Ten Ounces of Chance for One Grain either of Wisdom or Roguery.

You'd see perhaps, a Venerable Statesman, sit faſt asleep in a great Downy Chair; whilſt in that soft Vacation of his thought, Blind Chance (or what at leaſt we blindly call so) shall so dispose a thousand secret Wheels, that when he wakes, he needs but write his Name, to publish to the World some bleſt Event, for which his Statue shall be rais'd in Brass.

Perhaps a moment thence, you shall behold him torturing his Brain: His thoughts all ſtretcht upon the Rack for Publick Service. The livelong Night, when all the World's at reſt, consum'd in Care, and watching for their safety, when by a Whirlwind in his Fate, in spight of him, some mischief shall befall 'em, for which a furious Sentence ſtrait shall pass, and they shall Vote him to the Scaffold. Even thus uncertain are Rewards and Punishments; and even thus little do the People know when 'tis the Statesman merits one or t'other.

G. Now do I believe I am beginning to be a wise man; for I never till now perceiv'd I was a Fool. But do you then really believe Sir, our Men in Business do the beſt they can?

Æs. Many of 'em do: some perhaps do not. But this you may depend upon; He that is out of business is the worſt Judge in the World of him that is in: Firſt, because he seldom knows any thing of the matter; and secondly, because he always desires to get his place.

G. And so Sir you turn the Tables upon the Plaintiff, and lay the Fool and Knave at his Door.

Æs. If I do him wrong I'm sorry for't. Let him Examine himself, he'll find whether I do or not.   [*Exit Æsop.*

G. ——Examine?——I think I have had enough of that already. There's nothing left, that I know of, but to give Sentence: And truly I think there's no great difficulty in that. A very pretty Fellow I am indeed. Here am I come bellowing and roaring, 200 miles Post, to find my self an Ass; when with one quarter of an hours consideration, I might have made the self same Discovery; without going over my Threshold. Well: if ever they send me on their Errand, to reform the State again, I'll be damn'd. But this I'll do: I'll go home and reform my Family if I can: Them I'm sure I know: There's my Father's a peevish Old Coxcomb. There's my Uncle's a Drunken Old Sot: There's my Brother's a Cowardly Bully, Son *Numphs* is a Lubberly Whelp: I've a great Ramping Daughter, that stares like a Heifer, and a Wife that's a Slatternly Sow.   [*Exit.*

Enter a Young Gay Airy Beau, who stands smiling contemptibly upon Æsop.

Æs. Well Sir, what are you?

B. A Fool.

Æs. That's impossible;——for if thou wer't, thoud'st think thy self a Wise Man.

B. So I do——This is my own Opinion——the t'other's my Neigh-bours.   [*Walking Airily about.*

Æsop gazing after him.] Have you any business with me, Sir?

B. Sir, I have Business with no body——Pleasure's my study.

Æs. Aside.] An Odd Fellow this——Pray Sir, who are you?

B. I can't tell——

Æs. ——Do you know who I am?

B. No Sir: I'm a Favourite at Court, and I neither know my self, nor any body else.

Æs. Are you in any Imployment?

B. Yes——

Æs. What is it?

B. I don't know the Name on't.

Æs. You know the Business on't I hope?

B. That I do——the Business of it is——to——put in a Deputy, and receive the Money.

Æs. ——Pray what may be your Name?

B. Empty.

Æs. Where do you live?

B. In the Side-Box.

Æs. What do you do there?

B. I Ogle the Ladies.

Æs. To what purpose?

B. To no purpose.

Æs. Why then do you do it?

B. Because they like it, and I like it.

Æs. Wherein consists the Pleasure?

B. In Playing the Fool.

Æs. ——Pray Sir, what Age are you?

B. Five and Twenty——my Body——my Head's about Fifteen.

Æs. Is your Father living?

B. Dead, thank God.

Æs. Has he been long so?

B. Positively yes.

Æs. Where were you brought up?

B. At School.

Æs. What School?

B. The School of *Venus.*

Æs. Were you ever at the University?

B. Yes.

Æs. What study did you follow there?

B. My Bed-maker.

Æs. How long did you stay?

B. Till I had lost my Maiden-head.

Æs. Why did you come away?

B. Because I was expell'd.

Æs. Where did you go then?

B. To Court.

Æs. Who took care of your Education there?

B. A Whore and a Dancing-Master.

Æs. What did you gain by them?

B. A *Minuet,* and the *Pox.*

Æs. Have you an Estate?

B. I had.

Æs. What's become on't?

B. Spent.

Æs. In what?

B. In a Twelvemonth.

Æs. But how?

B. Why, In Dressing, Drinking, Whoring, Claps, Dice and Scriveners. What do you think of me now, Old Gentleman?

Æs. Pray what do you think of your self?

B. I don't think at all: I know how to bestow my time better.

Æs. Are you Married?

B. No——have you ever a Daughter to bestow upon me?

Æs. She wou'd be well bestow'd.

B. Why, I'm a strong young Dog, you Old Putt you; she may be worse coupled——

Æs. Have you then a mind to a Wife, Sir?

B. *Yaw myn Heer.*

Æs. What wou'd you do with her?

B. Why, I'd take care of her Affairs, rid her of all her troubles, her Maidenhead and her Portion.

Æs. And pray what sort of Wife wou'd you be willing to throw your self away upon?

B. Why, upon one that has Youth, Beauty, Quality, Vertue, Wit and Money.

Æs. And how may you be qualified your self, to back you in your Pretensions to such a one?

B. Why, I am qualified, with——a Periwig——a Snuff-box,——a Feather,——a——Smooth Face,——a Fool's Head——and a Patch.

Æs. But One Question more: What Settlements can you make?

B. Settlements?——Why, if she be a very Great Heiress indeed, I believe I may settle——my self upon her for Life, and my Pox upon her Children for ever.

Æs. 'Tis enough; you may expect I'll serve you, If it lies in my way. But I wou'd not have you relie too much upon your Success, because People sometimes are mistaken——As for Example——

An Ape there was of Nimble Parts,
A great Intruder into Hearts,
As Brisk, and Gay, and full of Air,
As you, or I, or any here;
Rich in his Dress, of splendid shew,
And with an Head like any Beau.
Eternal Mirth was in his Face;
Where'er he went,
He was content,
So Fortune had but Kindly sent
Some Ladies——and a Looking-glass.
Encouragement they always gave him,
Encouragement to play the Fool;
For soon they found it was a Tool;
Wou'd hardly be so much in Love,
But that the Mumbling of a Glove,
Or tearing of a Fan, wou'd save him.

These Bounties he accepts as Proof,
Of feats done by his Wit and Youth,
He gives their freedom gone for ever;
Concludes each Female heart undone,
Except that very happy one:
To which he'd please to do the favour.
In short, so smooth his matters went,
He guest, where'er his thoughts were bent,
The Lady he must carry.
So put on a fine New Cravat,
He comb'd his Wig, he cock't his Hat,
And gave it out, He'd Marry;
But here, alas! he found to's Cost,
He had reckon'd long without his Host;
For where soe'er he made th' Attack,
Poor Pug with shame was beaten back.

The first Fair she he had in Chace,
Was a Young Cat, extreamly Rich,
Her Mother was a Noted Witch;
So had the Daughter prov'd but Civil,
He had been related to the Devil.
But when he came
To urge his Flame,
She scratch'd him o'er the Face.

With that he went among the Bitches,
Such as had Beauty, Wit and Riches,
And swore Miss *Maulkin*, to her Cost,
Shou'd quickly see what she had lost:
But the poor Unlucky Swain
Miss'd his Shepherdess again;
His Fate was to miscarry,
It was his Destiny to find,
That Cats and Dogs are of a mind,
When Monkeys come to Marry.

B. 'Tis very well;——"Tis very well, Old Spark, I say, 'tis very well
——Because I han't a pair of Plod-Shooes, and a Dirty Shirt, you think
a Woman won't venture upon me for a Husband——Why now to shew
you, Old Father, how little you Philosophers know of the Ladies,——I'll
tell you an Adventure of a Friend of mine.

A Band, a Bob Wig, and a Feather.
Attack'd a Ladies heart together:
The Band in a most Learned Plea,
Made up of Deep Philosophy,
Told her, if she wou'd please to wed,
A Reverend Beard, and take instead
Of Vigorous Youth,
Old Solemn Truth,
With Books and Morals into Bed,
How happy she wou'd be.

The Bob, he talkt of Management,
What wond'rous Blessings Heaven sent
On Care, and Pains, and Industry,
And truly he must be so free,
To own, he thought your Airy Beaux,
With Powder'd Wigs and Dancing Shooes,
Were good for nothing (mend his soul),
But prate, and talk, and play the Fool.

He said 'twas *Wealth* gave Joy and Mirth,
And that to be the dearest Wife
Of one who labour'd all his Life,
To make a Mine of Gold his own,
And not spend 6 *pence* when he'ad done,
Was Heaven upon Earth.

When these two Blades had done, d'ye see,
The Feather, (as it might be me)
Steps out, Sir, from behind the Skreen,
With such an Air, and such a Mien,——
Look you, Old Gentleman, in short,
He quickly spoil'd the Statesmens sport.

It prov'd such Sun-shine weather,
That you must know, at the first Beck,
The Lady leapt about his Neck,
And off they went together.

To *Æsop.*] There's a Tale for your Tale, Old Dad; and so——
Serviteur.   [*Exit.*

The End of the Second Part.

THE
PILGRIM

A

COMEDY

As it is Acted at the

THEATRE-ROYAL,

IN

DRURY LANE

Written Originally by Mr. Fletcher, *and now very much Alter'd, with several Additions.*

LIKEWISE

A Prologue, Epilogue, Dialogue *and* Masque, *Written by the late great Poet* Mr. DRYDEN, *just* before his Death, being the last of his WORKS.

Source

THIS play is from Fletcher's *The Pilgrim*, acted at Court in 1621, though it may be of earlier date. Fletcher's play is partly original, but " Viele der Wunderlichkeiten dieser unruhigen Handlung werden uns erst durch das Studium der bis jetzt noch nicht bestimmten Quelle verstandlich: durch die Lektüre von Lope de Vega's Schlechtgeordneten, mit Ereignissen überfüllten Prosa-Roman, " El Peregrino en su Patria." Emil Koeppel. *Quellen-Studien zu den Drama....* Beaumont and Fletcher. Erlangen and Leipzig, 1895. The mad gentleman who sings the song (probably) is most likely from Cervantes (see Note on Song). Perhaps the plot owes something to *Two Gentlemen of Verona*, but women dressed as men were popular since Barnabe Rich's *Apolonius and Silla*, 1581.

Vanbrugh's play is a direct adaptation of Fletcher's play. Ward justified its omission from his edition by remarking that the alterations " which can hardly be said to improve the play," consist " in the reduction of Fletcher's blank verse to prose, and a few trivial additions to the dialogue." The additions, indeed, are not so important as the deletions, for all that is added comes to a very little space. This is taken up by the stuttering and drunken servants and the tailor. But the alterations cannot fail to be of interest as showing the difference in taste, not only in the audiences of the two periods, but also of the two authors. There is always a certain sentimentality in Fletcher, of which Vanbrugh is innocent, a sentimentality visible through the phrasing rather than in anything actually said, and in a long-windedness which is apt to become fatiguing as it is often incongruous. Fletcher is inclined to overdo an amusing point, and let it flag through sheer length. These assertions may be illustrated from the following comparison:

Vanbrugh. A handsome lusty young fellow, that will make such a bustle about you, he'll send your spleen to the *Devil*, Madam.

Fletcher. Madam, I think a lusty handsome fellow,
If he be kind and loving, and a right one,
Is even as good a pill to purge this melancholy,
As ever *Galen* gave, I am sure more natural:
And merrier for the heart, than Wine and Saffron:
Madam, wanton youth is such as Cataplasme.

The audiences of those days did not readily take to unadulterated, or untrimmed Fletcher, as Farquhar's adaptation of *The Wild Goose Chase* as *The Inconstant* serves with this play to show. But it is difficult to believe that Vanbrugh did not like Fletcher, especially in his use of words. He nearly always preserves the rich phrase where he can. Sometimes he even betters his original, as in the introduction of such a word as *keckle*, admirably introduced. It may also be mentioned that Vanbrugh treats this play to a certain amount of what we call bowdlerising, as was perhaps advisable under the circumstances; not the action, which is left unaltered, but the frankness of speech.

The real interest of the two versions can only reach its height by a line-for-line comparison between them, which is impossible here, but the reader may be referred to a very excellent structural digest given by Dr. A. C. Sprague in his *Beaumont and Fletcher on the Restoration Stage*. A reasonably long extract from the beginning is given, which may perhaps stimulate the reader to get down his Fletcher from his shelves. The 1788 edition attributes the alterations to Dryden, but as it prints neither the song nor the masque it may be that this was due to a wish to drag in Dryden's name somehow. The following is from the 1675 Folio edition of Beaumont and Fletcher:

> *Curio.* Seignor *Alphonso*, ye are too rugged to her,
> Believe too full of harshness.
> *Alph.* Yes, it seems so.
> *Seb.* A Father of so sweet a child, so happy,
> Fye, Sir, so excellent in all endowments,
> In blessedness of beauty, such a mirror.
> *Alph.* She is a fool, away.
> *Seb.* Can ye be angry?
> Can any wind blow rough, upon a blossom
> So fair, and tender? Can a Father's nature
> A noble Fathers too?
> *Alph.* All this is but prating:
> Let her be rul'd; let her observe my humour,
> With my eyes let her see; with my ears listen;
> I am her Father: I begot her, bred her,
> And I will make her——
> *Curio.* No doubt ye may compel her,
> But what a mischievous unhappy fortune
> May wait upon this will of yours, as commonly
> Such forcings ever end in hates and ruines.
> *Alph.* Is't not a man I wish her to? a strong man?
> What can she have? What could she have? a Gentleman?
> A young man? and an able man? a rich man?
> A handsome man? a valiant man? do you mark me?
> None of your pieced-companions, your pin'd-Gallants
> That flie to fitters, with every flaw of weather:
> None of your impt bravadoes; what can she ask more?
> Is not a metal'd man fit for a woman?
> A strong-chin'd man? I'le not be fool'd, nor flurted.
> *Seb.* I grant ye *Roderigo* is all these,
> And a brave Gentleman: must it therefore follow
> Upon necessity she must doat upon him?
> Will ye allow no liberty in choosing?
> *Curio.* Alas she is tender yet.
> *Alph.* Enough, enough, enough, Sir!
> She is malleable: she'll endure the hammer,
> And why not that strong workman that strikes deepest?

Let me know that? She is fifteen, with the vantage,
And if she be not ready now for mannage—
   Seb. You know he is a banish'd man; an outlaw;
And how he lives: his nature rough, and bloody
By customary Rapines: now, her sweet humour
That is as easie as a calm, and peaceful,
All her affections, like the dews on Roses,
Fair as the flower's themselves: as sweet and gentle:
How would you have these meet?
   Alph. A bed, a bed, Sir:
Let her be the fairest Rose, and the sweetest,
Yet I know this fair Rose must have her prickles.

It is curious to note how Vanbrugh changes the sense of the word *flurt* (or *flirt*) to one different from Fletcher's, but how later on he uses it in the same sense. See notes. The amusing change from *Enough, enough, enough,* to *Tough, tough, tough,* illustrates the gay spirit in which Vanbrugh undertook this adaptation.

Text

THE text is from the original quarto of 1700. The play occurs in none of the collected *Works* of Vanbrugh, and the next edition was not until 1753, to be followed in 1788 by one printed at Dublin from the Drury Lane prompt book. This last is woefully cut. These have therefore not been of much use in collating the text. On the other hand, some use has been made of the excellent Beaumont and Fletcher folio (F), printed by Mackock in 1679, which was possibly the text Vanbrugh used. Where the spelling of this is more modern than that of 1700 it has been adopted, and the folio has enabled one or two mistakes to be corrected. All deviations from 1700 are noted or notified, except for corrections of obvious misprints, such as *pend* for spend. Hardly any alterations in punctuation have been made, and these are justified by common sense and the folio.

A query arises as to the *Song of a Scholar and his Mistress,* and the *Secular Masque.* In the 1700 text the song follows immediately after the play; but the last words of the play are " let the Masque begin." In 1753 the song was printed after the masque. Artistically the song appears to have no business between the play and the masque, and it is possible that it should come in Act III, where the Scholar sings. After " I'll sing charms," 1753 prints (*Sings*), and (*Musick.*) where 1700 does, thus perhaps the duet goes in here, where Scott would have it put. On the other hand, it may have been necessary to interpolate something between the play and the masque to allow of stage setting and the grouping of the actors. Perhaps the scene closed over the altar for the song and was opened again for the masque when the altar was out of the way. As neither song nor masque appears in 1788, which ought with luck to have thrown some light on the affair, it has been thought better to leave them as printed in the original quarto.

I have been unable to see the unique, and hitherto entirely unknown copy of the *Secular Masque* "deliver'd Gratis at the Theatre," which appeared at the sale of the Britwell library early this year (1927).

Theatrical History

IT is not known upon what day *The Pilgrim* was first acted. The internal evidence of the *Secular Masque* made Genest suppose that it must have been produced on New Year's Day, 25 March. The masque is certainly written for that day, but the presumption is that it was written separately and tacked on to the play. This view is supported by Gildon in his *Comparison between the Two Stages*, 1702, in which Dryden is made to say in reference to the play: "if you'll let my son have the profits of the *Third Night*, I'll give you a *Secular Mask*." According to Egerton, in his life of Mrs. Oldfield, the profits of the third night went to Dryden's son only because Dryden died on the third night, which was May 1. The third night would not necessarily be the third successive night, but the earlier limits are set by a letter to which Dr. Sprague draws attention in his *Beaumont and Fletcher on the Restoration Stage*. In a letter to Mrs. Steward, dated Thursday, 11 April, 1700, Dryden wrote: "Within this moneth there will be play'd, for my profit, an old play of Fletcher's, call'd the 'Pilgrim' corrected by my good friend Mr. Vanbrook: and to which I have added a new masque; and am to write a new prologue and epilogue." Dr. Sprague's conclusion seems impeccable: "In view of the lack of evidence to the contrary, I believe that 29 April is probably as close to the actual date as we can reach."

Cibber, who was offered any part he liked, chose those of the Stuttering Cook and the Mad Englishman, "In which homely Characters, I saw more Matter for Delight, than those that might have a better Pretence to the Aimable." In this he was right, at least to judge from popular applause. To "make up his mess" he was offered the Epilogue, but when Dryden heard him speak this he was so pleased that he insisted upon his having the Prologue as well; so Cibber spoke them both, a very unusual circumstance. Johnson, who had much improved since the separation of the companies, played Alphonso. Powell and Wilks, who appear always to have been quarreling in private life, appropriately took the rivals, and no doubt played the parts with an undercurrent of real feeling. Powell was the more naturally gifted actor, but was unreliable owing to his manner of living, and was never so beloved of the audience as Wilks was. Haynes and "Pinkey," both gay, played minor parts.

The surprise of the performance was Mrs. Oldfield's Alinda. This was only the second part she had ever played, except for small ones, "almost mute" and certainly "unheeded," since the day, about a year before, that she had been rescued from a tavern by George Farquhar. She has an especial interest for us, for Arthur Maynwaring, Vanbrugh's friend, was passionately in love with her until he died. She was buried in Westminster Abbey beneath the monument to Congreve. Still, even after her triumph as Alinda, her advancement was slow, and it was not until 1704 that

> Engaging Oldfield who with grace and ease,
> Could join the arts to ruin and to please,

was thought highly enough of by Cibber for him to give her Lady Betty to play in

The Careless Husband. He had been impressed by her performance as Leonora in *Sir Courtly Nice*, when she acted it at Bath in the place of Mrs. Verbruggen, who was ill. Once at the Haymarket " Mrs. Oldfield's Voice, Figure and Manner of Playing soon made *her* shine out, even here, the *brightest Star.* Upon the Preference being given to her in the *Benefit-Plays*, and other disputes fomented among the Managers, Mrs. *Barrey* and Mrs. *Bracegirdle* entirely quitted the Business, and left Mrs. Oldfield *sole Empress* of the Stage " (Egerton). She is the Flavia of *Tatler*, No. 212. " Her beauty is full of attraction, but not of allurement," but Steele was particularly impressed by the genteel way she wore her clothes. The play was acted for her benefit on 6 July, 1700.

The *Pilgrim* was acted at Drury Lane five times in 1703, one on 3 July having " a new Epilogue by the little girl who played Queen Bess in Anna Bullen." It reappeared three times in 1704 and twice in 1706. In the next year it went over to the Haymarket, where it was acted six times, with Wilks, Johnson, Cibber and Mrs. Oldfield in their original parts; Mills played Lopez, and Bullock the Mad Scholar. Pack played the Mad Priest, a part in which he became famous, so that when he went over to Drury Lane in 1708 it was played for his benefit there on 24 May, with him in that part. Mrs. Moor played the part of Juletta at Drury Lane in 1709, 15 March, and in the autumn it reappeared at the Haymarket with Doggett as the Mad Welshman and Estcourt as the Mad Priest, the rest of the cast being much the original one. Four days later Mr. Bickerstaffe of *The Tatler* complained of gagging, for one of his acquaintance had expressed " a very becoming indignation against a practice which I myself have been very much offended at. 'There is nothing,' said he, ' more ridiculous than for an actor to insert words of his own in the part he is to act, so that it is impossible to see the poet for the player: you will have Pinkethman and Bullock helping out Beaumont and Fletcher.' " These two actors are again blamed for gagging in *Spectator*, 539, as though it were a common practice of theirs.

It was acted at least twice, often more, every year until 1733 inclusive, at Drury Lane, the Haymarket, at the new theatre in Lincoln's Inn Fields, for the first time in 1715; at Goodman's Fields, and finally in 1734 at Covent Garden. In 1712 Wilks resigned Pedro to Bullock junior, a favourite pupil of his, and on 19 July, 1716, Quin made his appearance as Pedro, with Mrs. Horton as Juletta. The part of Alinda was taken by Mrs. Willis and Mrs. Thurmond, who acted it for her benefit at Lincoln's Inn Fields on 24 April of that year. In 1726 Mrs. Bullock played Alinda to the Juletta of Mrs. Younger, who kept the part until 1733.

It was billed for Covent Garden on 24 April, 1738, as " not acted 4 years," when Mrs. Stevens played Juletta; Ryan Pedro; Bridgewater Roderigo; Yates the Mad Welshman; the part of Alinda being taken by Mrs. Vincent.

> Lo! Vincent comes—with simple grace array'd;
> She laughs at paltry arts, and scorns parade.
> Nature through her is by reflection shewn;
> Whilst Gay once more knows Polly for his own.

In 1740, as between the early and the late seasons at Drury Lane, the Stuttering Servant was played by Yates and Woodward. But in the revival at Covent Garden on 20 January, 1742, Woodward played the Mad Tailor; Ryan and Bridgewater their old parts; Hippisley Alphonso, which he had played in 1726; Mrs. Vincent

Alinda again; while Juletta was played by Mrs. Pritchard. This was evidently a favourite part of hers, but she unfortunately stuck to it for too long:

> In Comedy—" Nay, there," cries Critic, " hold.
> " Pritchard's for Comedy too fat and old.
> " Who can, with patience, bear the grey coquette,
> " Or force a laugh with over-grown Julett?
> " Her Speech, Look, Action, Humour, all are just;
> " But then, her age and figure give disgust."

Nevertheless Churchill defends her. The play was acted with the same cast on 21 December, 1744, was twice staged at Covent Garden in 1746, and once in 1748.

On 30 October, 1750, Drury Lane advertised the play as " not acted 10 years," ignoring performances at other theatres. Palmer played Pedro; Yates Alphonso; Woodward the Mad Tailor and his old part of the Stuttering Cook. Shuter played the Drunken Servant, and Mrs. Pritchard, not, we suppose, with universal approval, Juletta. In the Masque, Beard, the famous tenor, sang Momus. Genest says that it was ridiculous in Garrick to revive the Masque, as 1750 is as far as possible from the beginning of any century. It is possible that Garrick thought it a lovely thing: the setting was Boyce's. It was evidently a success, as it was revived on 9 November, Mrs. Clive taking part in the Masque as Diana.

It was acted again on 4 May, 1753, Drury Lane very erroneously declaring that it was " not acted 7 years." Ryan played Pedro; Sparks Roderigo; Macklin the Mad Englishman; and Dyer the Mad Scholar. At this date Arthur used to play Alphonso. Mrs. Vincent played the part of Alinda. In 1762, on 15 February, Covent Garden billed it as " not acted 10 years," with Smith as Pedro; Shuter Alphonso; Mrs. Green Juletta; and Mrs. Vincent in her old part of Alinda.

It was played at Liverpool on 19 August, 1777, with J. P. Kemble as Roderigo, Lewis as Pedro, and Mrs. Kniveton, for whose benefit it was performed, in the character of Alinda. It was played at Bath in 1783, and also at Covent Garden on 9 May, for the benefit of Wilson, Hayne's Epilogue (the new one of 1703 previously referred to?) " to be spoken by Wilson riding on an ass."

It was performed again six times odd, apparently for the last revival, by Kemble in the Drury Lane season of 1787, 1788, with a few alterations, but substantially Vanbrugh's version, though the omission of the meeting of Pedro and Alinda in the madhouse seems unfortunate. The character of the Mad Parson was also omitted. Kemble played Pedro; Baddeley Alphonso; Barrymore Roderigo; Suett Lopez; while the versatile Palmer played Cibber's original two parts of the Stuttering Cook and the Mad Englishman. Mrs. Jordan figured in these performances as Juletta. " Hers was not the school of Declamation: she thought of *acting* as Burke did of *writing*." There appear to have been no further revivals.

PROLOGUE

Written by Mr. DRYDEN.

HOW wretched is the Fate of those who write!
　　Brought muzzled to the Stage, for fear they bite.
Where, like Tom Dove, they stand the Common Foe;
Lugg'd by the Critique, Baited by the Beau.
Yet worse, their Brother Poets Damn the Play,
And Roar the loudest, tho' they never Pay.
The Fops are proud of Scandal, for they cry,
At every lewd, low Character,—That's I.
He who writes letters to himself, wou'd Swear
The World forgot him, if he was not there.
What shou'd a Poet do?　'Tis hard for One
To pleasure all the Fools that wou'd be shown:
And yet not Two in Ten will pass the Town.
Most Coxcombs are not of the Laughing kind;
More goes to make a Fop, than Fops can find.
　　Quack Maurus, tho' he never took degrees
In either of our Universities;
Yet to be shown by some kind Wit he looks,
Because he plaid the fool, and writ Three Books.
But if he wou'd be worth a Poet's Pen,
He must be more a Fool, and write again:
For all the former Fustian stuff he wrote,
Was Dead-born Doggrel, or is quite forgot;
His Man of Uz, stript of his Hebrew Robe
Is just the Proverb, and As poor as Job.
One wou'd have thought he cou'd no lower Jog;
But Arthur was a Level, Job's a Bog.
There, tho' he crept, yet still he kept in sight;
But here he flounders in, and sinks down right.
Had he prepar'd us, and been dull by Rule,
Tobit had first been turn'd to Ridicule:
But our bold Britton, without Fear or Awe,
O're-leaps at once, the whole Apocrypha;
Invades the Psalms with Rhymes, and leaves no room
For any Vandal Hopkins yet to come.

But what if, after all, this Godly Geer,
Is not so Senceless as it wou'd appear?
Our Mountebank has laid a deeper Train,
His Cant, like Merry Andrew's Noble Vein,
Cat-Calls the Sects, to draw 'em in again.
At leisure Hours, in Epique Song he deals,
Writes to the rumbling of his Coaches Wheels,
Prescribes in hast, and seldom kills by Rule,
But rides Triumphant between Stool and Stool.
    Well, let him go; 'tis yet too early day,
To get himself a Place in Farce or Play.
We know not by what means we should Arraign him,
For no one Category can contain him;
A Pedant, Canting Preacher, and a Quack,
Are Load enough to break one Asses Back:
At last, grown wanton, he presum'd to write,
Traduc'd Two Kings, their kindness to requite;
One made the Doctor, and one dubb'd the Knight.

Persons Represented

MEN.

Alphonso, an Old Angry Gentleman. Mr. *Johnson.*

Curio,
Seberto, } His two Friends.

Pedro, The Pilgrim, A Noble Gentleman, }
    Servant to *Alinda.*   Mr. *Wilks.*

Roderigo, Rival to *Pedro*, Captain of the }
    Outlaws.   M. *Powell.*

Lopez,
Jaques, } Two Outlaws under *Roderigo.*

An Old Pilgrim.

Governour of *Segovia.*   Mr. *Simson.*

Verdugo, A Captain under him.

A Gentleman of the Country.

Courtiers.   Porter.   Beggars.

Master and Keeper of the Mad folks.

A Scholar.   Mr. *Thomas.*

A Parson.   Mr. *Haynes.*

An Englishman. } Madmen.   Mr. *Cibber.*

A Welshman.   Mr. *Norris.*

A Taylor.   Mr. *Pinkethman.*

Servants.

Peasants.

WOMEN.

Alinda, Daughter to *Alphonso*, }
    in Love with *Pedro*.   Mrs. *Oldfield.*

Juletta, *Alinda's* Maid, a smart Lass. Mrs. *Moor.*

A Fool.

THE
PILGRIM

ACT I. SCENE I.

Enter Alphonso, Curio, *and* Seberto.

Cur. SEignior *Alphonso*, you are too rugged with her, too harsh; indeed you are.

Alph. Yes, it seems so.

Seb. A Father of so sweet a Child, so good, so beautiful; Fye, Sir, fye, so excellent a Creature.

Alph. She's a Fool; away.

Seb. Can you be angry? Can any wind blow rough upon a blossom so fair and tender? Can a Father's Nature, a Noble Father's too?

Alph. All this is but prating: Let her be rul'd; let her observe my Humour; with my Eyes let her see, with my Ears let her hear; I am her Father; I begot her, I bred her, and by *Jupiter* I will——

Seb. No doubt you may compel her, but think how wretched you by force may make her.

Alph. Wretched! wretched! Is't not a Man I force her to? A noble Man; A Rich Man; A Handsome Man; A Young Man; A Strong Man; none of your piec'd Companions, none of your washy Rogues, that fly to fitters upon every puff of Weather. I force her to a strong Dog, don't I? What wou'd the Flirt have?

Seb. I grant you, *Roderigo* is all these, and a brave Gentleman: But does it therefore follow, she must doat upon him? Will you allow no Liberty in chusing?

Cur. Alas! she's tender yet.

Alph. Tough, Tough, Tough as the Devil; you see I can't break her.

Seb. You put her to too hard a Tryal: You know, tho' he has Merit, he's a banish'd Man, an Out-law; you know the Life he leads; That he's the head of a rough Band of Robbers; Judge what Effect his bloody Rapines must needs e're this have workt upon his nature. A rugged Mate, I doubt, for such a Dove.

Cur. Rugged indeed; Such different Tempers, where can you ever hope to reconcile?

Alph. Abed, abed, D'ye hear? abed, Sir. She won't find him so rugged there, I'll warrant you: She'll find ways to soften him. And for the

(95)

Pranks he plays in's Banishment, it shews he's a mettled Fellow: He'll make e'm weary o' their Sentence; a small Composition will reſtore him. But I know the Secret of all this: My Minx has some other in View; some flickering Slave or other, some sweet-scented Coxcomb, that——a——Sings, I'll warrant you, and——a——Lutes it, Languishes, and has no Beard; ha! Is't not so?

Seb. So far from what you charge her with, I wou'd engage my Life, she has not yet a Glance to answer for.

Cur. I never yet beheld more Modeſty.

Seb. Nor I, in one so young; so much discretion.

Alph.——Hum——and yet there was a Fellow (Dead I hope) whom I have seen her glance at, till I thought the Hussy wou'd have ſtuck her Eyes into the Rascal.

Seb. Pray, who was that?

Alph. Pedro, Sir, only *Pedro*, old *Fernando's* hopeful Heir; my Mortal Foe, who's Family I wish consum'd; that's all, Sir.

Seb. If that be all, you have nothing left to fear; for *Pedro*, urg'd by secret discontent, has left his Father, Friends, and all; and, as 'tis said, is gone to range the World.

Alph. With all my heart: He was a Beggar, so ſtrolling is his Business.

Cur. He was a Beggar, but a noble Beggar; shame on the Court for suffering him to be so.

Alph. Shame on those who encourage Beggars, I say. Here's this young Slut, in the midſt of her Rebellion, is so very Religious, she undoes me with her Charity. Why, what a Crew of Vermin have I about my Door every day, to receive Meat, Drink, and Money, from her fair hands. Not a Rogue that can say his Prayers, groan, and turn his Pipe to Lamentation, but she thinks she's bound to dance to.

Enter Alinda, *and* Juletta.

Alph. O, are you there Miſtress? Well, how goes Disobedience to day?——That's a base down Look——Ah you ſturdy young Jade.

Cur. Pray be more gentle to her.

Alph. Pray be quiet; I know beſt how to deal with her: and I will make her obey, or I will make her——

Alin. Sir, you may make me any thing; you know I'm all Obedience, there's nothing but my Prayers and Tears oppose you.

Alph. Then will I oppose nothing but your Prayers and Tears. Now I hope you can't complain of me.

Cur. Poor Lady, how I pity her.

Alph. Pray, keep your Pity for a better occasion. Look you, Gentlewoman, you know my Will; and, in that, you know all; So I leave you to digeſt it; and I desire these Gentlemen will do so too.

Cur. Seb. A better hour attend you, Madam. { *Exit* Alphonso, *followed by* Curio *and* Seberto.

Alin. I thank ye Gentlemen: Alas! I want such Comforts. Wou'd I cou'd thank you too, Father; but your Cruelty won't give me leave. Grant, Heav'n, I mayn't forget my Duty to him.

Jul. If you do, Madam, Heav'n will forgive you for't, ne'er fear it. A perverse old Rogue.   *[Aside.*

Alin. What poor attend my Charity to day, *Juletta?*

Jul. Enow of all sorts, Madam; some that deserve your Pity, some that don't: But I wish you wou'd be merry with your Charity; a Chearful Look becomes it.

Alin. Alas! *Juletta,* what is there for me to be merry at? What Joy have I in View?

Jul. Joy; why what Joy, i'th name of *Venus,* wou'd you have, but a Husband? A handsome lusty young Fellow, that will make such a bustle about you, he'll send your Spleen to the *Devil,* Madam.

Alin. Away, light Fool; I doubt there's poor Contentments to be found in Marriage. Yet cou'd I find a Man——

Jul. You may, a thousand.

Alin. Meer Men, I know I may. But such a Man, from whose Example (as from a Compass) we may steer our Course, and safe arrive at such a Memory as shall become our Ashes; such Men are rare indeed. But no more of this, 'tis not Discourse that's suited to thy Giddy Temper: Let's in, and see what poor afflicted Wretches want my Charity.   *[Exeunt.*

SCENE II

Enter Porter, Beggars, Pedro, *and an old* Pilgrim.

Port. Stand off, and keep your Ranks. Twenty foot farther. There, louse your selves with Reason and Discretion—— The Sun shines warm. No nearer. The farther still the better: Your Beasts will bolt anon, and then 'tis dangerous.

1st. Beg. Hey ho! Heav'n bless our Mistress.

Port. Do's the Crack go that way, old Hunger, ha? 'Twill be o' my side anon.

2d. Beg. Pray, Friend, be kind to us.

Port. Friend! your Friend; and why your Friend, Sirrah, Meager Chaps? What do you see in me, Louse-trap, or without me, ha! that I shou'd be your Friend? Have I got the Itch, Scrub, or do I look like some of thy Acquaintance hung in Gibbets? Hast thou any Friends, Kindred, or Alliance, or any higher Ambition than an Alms-Basket? This young soft-hearted Mistress of mine do's make these Rogues so familiar.

2d. Beg. I'm sure I wou'd be your Worship's Friend.

Port. No doubt on't, Vermin; and so you shall, when I Quarter the same Louse with you.

3d. Beg. I'm sure it's Twelve a Clock.

Port. 'Tis ever so with thee, when thou hast done scratching; For that provokes thy stomach to ring Noon. O the infinite Seas of Porridge thou hast swallow'd! Alms do you call it, to relieve these Rascals?

Enter Alphonso, Curio, Seberto.

Alph. Look you there! Did not I tell you how she wou'd undo me? What Marts of Rogues and Beggars!

Seb. 'Tis Charity Methinks you are bound to love her for.

Alp. Yes, I'll warrant you. If Men cou'd Sail to Heav'n in Porridge-pots, with Masts of Beef and Mutton, what a Voyage shou'd I make? What are all these here?

1st. Beg. Poor People, an't like your Worship.

2d. Beg. Wretched poor People.

3d. Beg. Very hungry People.

Alph. And very Lousie. And what are you!   *[to the Pilg.*

Old Pilg. Strangers, that come to wonder at your Charity; yet People poor enough to beg a Blessing.

Cur. Use 'em gently, Sir, they have a reverend Mien. You are Holy Pilgrims, are you not?

Old Pil. We are, Sir, and bound far off, to offer our Devotions.

Alph. What do you do here then; We have no Reliques, no Holy Shrines.

Old Pil. The Holiest we ever heard of: You keep a living Monument of Goodness; a Daughter of that Pious Excellence, the very Shrines of Saints sink at her Virtue. We come to see this Lady, not with Prophane Eyes, or wanton Blood, to doat upon her Beauty; but through our tedious way, to beg her Blessing.

Alp. This is a new way of Begging; these Commendations cry Money for Reward, good store too: Ah! the Sainting of this young Harlot will Cost me Dear.

[To Pedro.] Well, Sir, have you got your Compliments ready too, and your empty Purse? Hah! what nothing but a bow; Modesty?

Cur. A handsome well look'd Man.   *[aside.*

Alph. What Country Craver are you? What! nothing but Motion? A Puppit Pilgrim.

Old Pil. He's a ſtranger, Sir, these four days I have travel'd in his Company; but little of his Business or his Language yet I have underſtood.

Seb. Both young and handsome; only the Sun has injur'd him.

Alph. Wou'd you have Mony, Sir, or Meat, or a Wench? What kind of Blessing doe's your Devotion point at? Still more Ducking? Are there any Saints that underſtand by sign only? Hah, more Motion yet? This is the prettyeſt Pilgrim; the Pink of Pilgrims.

Cur. Fye, Sir, Fye; rather beſtow your Charity then Jeſt upon him.

Alp. Say you so? Why then, look ye, Pilgrim; here's a poor *Viaticum*, very good Gold, Sir, I'm Sorry 'tis not heavier. But since the lighteſt Grain of earthly Dross wou'd be a Burthen to a Heav'nly mind—I'll put it up again.

Cur. O horrible! you are too Irreverent.

Alp. You are a——Muſt I give my Money to every Rogue that carries a grave Look in's Face? Muſt my good Angels wait upon him? I'll find 'em other business.

Seb. But consider, Sir, the Wrongs you do those Men may light on you: Strangers are entitul'd to a softer Usage.

Alph. Oon's, half the Kingdom will be ſtrangers shortly, if this young Slut's suffer'd to go on with her Prodigalities. But I muſt be an Ass: Here, Sirrah, see 'em reliev'd for once; do't effeĉtually too; d'ye hear? Burſt 'em, that I may never see 'em more. Were I young again, I'de sooner get Bear-whelps than She-Saints.   [*Exit.*

Cur. Such a Face as that, sure I have seen.

Seb. I thought so too; but we muſt be miſtaken.   [*Exit.*

Port. Come, will ye troop up, Porridge Regiment? Captain *Poor-Quarter*, will ye move?

Enter Alinda *and* Juletta.

Alin. Why are not these poor Wretches serv'd yet?

2 Beg. Bless our good Miſtress.

Port. They are too high fed, Madam; their Stomachs are not awake yet.

Alin. Do you make sport with their Miseries? Sir, learn more Humanity, or I shall find a way to teach it you.

3 Beg. Kind Heaven preserve her, and for ever bless her.

Alin. Bless the good end I mean it for.   [*Exit Beg.*

Jul. [*aside.*] Wou'd I knew what that were; if it be for a Man, I'de say *Amen* with all my heart.

You have a very pretty Band of Pensioners, Madam.

Alin. Vain Glory wou'd seek more and handsomer;

But I appeal to Virtue what my end is.

What men are these?

Julet. Holy Pilgrims they seem to be. What Pity 'tis that handsome young Fellow shou'd undergo so much Pennance: Wou'd I were the Saint he makes his Vow to; I'de soon grant his Request, let him ask what he wou'd.

Alin. You are Pilgrims, Sirs, Is't not so?

Old Pil. We are, fair Saint; may Heaven's Grace surround you;
May all good Thoughts and Prayers dwell about you;
Abundance be your Friend, and Holy Charity be ever at your hand to
Crown you Glorious.

Alin. I thank you, Sir; Peace guide your Travels too;
And what you wish for most, end all your troubles.
Remember me by this; [*Giving him Money*] and in
Your Prayers, when your strong Heart melts,
Meditate my poor Fortunes.

Old Pil. All my Devotions wait upon your Service.

Alin. Are you of this Country, Sir?

Old Pil. Yes, worthiest Lady, but far off bred: My
Fortune's farther from me.

Alin. I am no Inquisitor, whatever Vow or Pennace pulls you on, Sir, Conscience, or Love, or stubborn Disobedience; The Saint you Kneel to, hear and ease your Travels.

Old Pil. Yours ne'er begin; and thus I Seal my Prayers.   [*Exit.*

Alin. [*aside.*] How steadfastly this Man looks upon me? How he Sighs? Some great Affliction sure's the source of his Devotions.

To Ped. Right Holy Sir: He turns from us. Alas he weeps too: something presses him he wou'd reveal, but dares not. Sir, be Comforted: If you want, to me you appear so worthy of Relief, I'll be your Steward. Speak and take. He's dumb still. This Man stirs me strangely.

Jul. Wou'd he wou'd stir me a little; I like his shape well.   [*Aside.*

Alin. It may be he wou'd speak to me alone;   [*Aside.*
Retire a little, *Juletta*; but d'ye hear, don't be far off.

Jul. I shan't, Madam: Wou'd I were nearer him: A young smug handsome Holyness has no fellow.   [*Aside. Exit.*

Alin. Why do you grieve? Do you find your Penance sharp?
Are the Vows you have made, too mighty for you?
Or does the World allure you to look back, and make you mourn the softer Hours you have lost? You are young, and seem as you were form'd for Manly Resolution; Come, be Comforted:

Ped. I am, fair Angel: And such a Comfort from your words I feel, that tho' Calamities, like angry Waves, curl round, contending proudly, who shall first devour me, yet I will stem their Danger.

Alin. He speaks Nobly. [*Aside.*] What do you want, Sir?

Ped. All that can make me happy: I want my self.

Alind. Your self!   Who robb'd you, Pilgrim?
Why does he look so earnestly upon me?   I want my self.   [*Aside.*
Indeed you Holy wanderers are said to seek much,
     But to seek your selves——

Ped. *I seek my self, and am but my self's shadow,* have loſt my self, and
now am not so Noble.

Alin. [*Aside.*] I seek my self; sure, something I remember bears that
Motto?   It is not he; he's younger, has a smoother Face; yet for that
Self sake, Pilgrim, who so e're it be, take this.

Ped. Your hand I dare take; that be far from me: Your hand I hold,
and thus I kiss it; and thus I bless it too. *Be conſtant ſtill: Be good:* And
live to be a great Example.   [*Exit.*

Alin. One word more. He's gone: Heav'n! How I Tremble?
Be Conſtant ſtill; 'tis the very Poesie here; and here without, *Be Good.*
He wept too, as he left me. It muſt be *Pedro.* *Juletta.*

Enter Juletta.

Jul. Madam.

Alin. Take this Key, and quickly fetch me the Jewel that lies in my
little Cabinet.   That will determine all.   [*Exit* Julet.

It muſt be he: His Face was smoother when I saw him laſt; yet there's
a Manly Look, and Noble Shape, ſtill speak him *Pedro.*

Enter Juletta.

Alin. Let me see it: 'Tis so; it muſt be he. He spoke the words
juſt as they ſtand engraven here. *I seek my self, and am but my self's
shadow.*
Poor *Pedro!* But how shall I recover him?
Juletta, the Pilgrim, where is he? which way did he go?

Jul. Alas, Madam, I don't know; it's in vain to seek him now.

Alin. I tell thee, I muſt see him; I gave him nothing.

Jul. That was ill done, indeed; for he's the handsomeſt Fellow I have
seen this many a Day. What makes her look so thoughtful? Sure here's
something afoot more than ordinary.

Alin. [*Aside.*] 'Tis enough. He has done much for me: I'll try what
Recompence 'tis in my power to make him.   [*Exit.*

The End of the Firſt Aĉt.

ACT II.

Enter Alphonso, Curio, Seberto, Juletta *and Servants.*

Alph. CAn she slip through a Key-hole? Tell me that; resolve me; Can she fly i'th Air? Is she Invisible? Gone, and no body knew it!

Seb. Pray, be more moderate.

Alph. Some Goatish Rogue has watcht her hour of Itching, and has claw'd her, claw'd her; the Dog has claw'd her. 'Oons find her out, or I'll hang ye all; you, Wagtail, you know her Designs, you were of her Council [*to Julet*], her bawdy Adviser; where is she, Strumpet?

Jul. You wou'd know of me, Sir.

Alph. Of you Sir? Yes of you Sir; why, what are you Sir?

Jul. Her Servant, Sir, her faithful Servant.

Alph. Servant? Her Bawd; her Fiddle-ſtick; her Lady Fairy, to oil the Doors o'nights, that they mayn't creek. Where is she, Infamy?

Jul. 'Tis very well.

Alph. You Lie, 'tis ill, Damnable ill; and either confess, or——

Jul. Indeed I won't.

Seb. Why?

Jul. Because I can't; if I cou'd, I'd give another Reason.

Alph. Well said; but I shall deal with you, you Slut you. What say you, Thick-skull, which way did she get out? why were not my Doors shut?   *[To the Porter.*

Port. They were, a'nt Please you; nothing open but the Key-hole.

Alph. Where did she lye? Who lay with her?

Port. Not I, an't please you; I lay with *Frederick* in the Flea-Chamber.

Alph. Once more, of thee I demand her; tell me News of her, or expect——the Devil and all.   *[To Julet.*

Cur. Come *Juletta*, if you know any thing, tell him——

Jul. Look ye, Sir, if I knew all, and had been intruſted by her, not all the Devils you cou'd call upon, shou'd scare one single Hint from me. But, since I know nothing worth your knowing, I'll tell you what I do know. I know she's gone, because we can't find her. I know she's gone cunningly, because you can't find which way. I know she was weary of your Tyranny, because the Devil wou'd have been so too: And I know, if she's wise, she'll never come again——

Alph. Out of my Doors.

Jul. That's all my poor Petition. For were your house Gold, and she not in't, I shou'd think it but a Cage to whiſtle in.

Alph. Whore; if she be above ground, I'll have her——

Jul. I'd live in a Coalpit then, if I were she.

Cur. Indeed, Sir, I fancy she knows nothing of her Flight; you know her mad way of talking.

Alph. Hang her, hang her, she knows too much.

Enter Servant drunk.

Well Rascal, have you any News of her?

Serv. N.—N.——Not a Drop Sir. The Butler gave me the Key of the Cellar, to search the Cellar, Sir; so I have been searching the Cellar.

Alph. Here's a Dog for you.

Serv. I searcht every Hogshead, Sir, and open'd some Bottles, but cou'd not find a spoonfull of her.

Alph. You rascal, get you out of my reach, or I'll be thy Murderer.

Enter another Servant that ſtammers.

Serv. S, S, S, S, Sir.

Alph. Well, what News? Be quick:

Serv. My yo, yo, yo, yo, young La-Lady is gone——

Alph. I know she's gone, you Dog, but where?

Serv. Out at the P——

Alph. Out with't, you Son of a Whore——

Serv. The Po, ho, ho, ho, ho, hoſtern Gate of the Ga, ha, ha, ha, ha——

Alph. This Dog will make me mad; but one ſtammering Rogue in the Family, and it muſt fall to his share to give me an account of her. The Wind's in the *Eaſt* too ; The Dog won't get it out this Hour. Where was it, Sirrah, where was it?

Serv. The Ga-arden Sir, the Ga-arden.

Alph. The Garden, Sir, the Garden; was it so? And how do you know she got out at the Garden, ha?

Serv. I s—s— saw, an't p, p, p, p, p-lease you, the P—— Print of her fo, fo, fo, fo, Foot.

Alph. Right, a Foot, a little Foot, a young Whore's Foot ?

Serv. Ye, Yes Sir.

Alph. And from thence scrambled over the Wall into the Park, and so to the Devil?

Serv. So I sup,-p,-pose, Sir.

Alph. 'Tis very well, ye Stars, 'tis very well: This comes of Indulgence, I muſt needs allow her the Key of the Garden, to walk on Faſt-days, and Contemplate with a Pox: But I'll fetch her again, with a Fire-brand at her Tail. My horses there——

Seb. ⎱ You'll give us Leave to wait upon you?
Cur. ⎰

Alph. That you may if you please. My Horse there; dispatch. Are you so Hot, I Faith? I'll Cool you, Mistriss; Muſt you be jumping Joan? If I catch you again, I'll clap such a Clogg about your Neck, you shall leap no more Walls I'll warrant you; I'll hang *Roderigo* there, I'faith. My Horses, quick; and d'ye hear, keep me this young Lirry Poop within doors, faſt; I shall discover Dame——   [*Exit* Alph. *&c.*

Jul. Indeed you won't Sir.
[*Aside.*] Well, Love, if thou be'ſt with her; or whatever Power else arms her Resolution, conduct her carefully, and keep her from this Madman— Direct her to her Wishes; dwell about her; let no dishonourable End o'retake her, Danger or Want; and let me try my Fortune——

[SCENE II.]

Enter Roderigo *and four Out-Laws.*

1ſt Out. You are not merry Captain.
Rod. Why, we get nothing, we have no sport; Whoring and Drinking spoils us; we keep no Guard.
2d Out. I'm sure there's neither Merchant nor Gentleman passes, but we have Tribute.
Rod. Yes, and while we spend that idly, we let those pass that carry the beſt Booty: I'll have all searcht and brought in. Rogues and Beggars have found the Trick of late to become Bankers. In short, Gentlemen, I'll have none Escape but my Friends and Neighbours, who may be useful in laying my Innocence before the King: All others shall pay their Passport.
2d Out. You now speak like a Captain; if we spare any, flay us, and Coin our Cassocks.
Rod. You hear of no Preparations the King intends againſt us?
3d Out. Not a Word; Don't we see his Garrisons?
Rod. Who have we out now?
2d Out. Good fellows, that, if there be any Purchase ſtirring, won't slip it; *Jaques* and *Lopez*, Lads that know their Business.
Rod. Where's the Boy you brought in e'n now? he's a pretty Lad, and of a quick Capacity——
1 Out. He's within at Meat, Sir; the poor Knave's hungry; yet he seasons all he eats or drinks, with Tears.

2 *Out.* He's young; 'tis fear and want of Company.

Rod. Don't use him roughly, and he'll soon grow bolder. I intend to keep him to wait upon me; I like the Boy, there's something in his Face pleases me strangely: Be sure you all use him gently.

1 *Out.* Here's a little Box, Sir, we took about him, which almost broke his Heart to part with; I fancy there's something of Value in't; I can't open it.

Rod. Alas! some little Mony, I warrant you, the poor Knave carry'd to defray his Charge: I'll give it him again.

Enter Jaques, Lopez, *with* Pedro.

How now! Who's this? What have you brought me here, Soldiers?

Jaqu. Why Truly we don't well know; only he's a damn'd sullen fellow.

Rod. Where did you take him?

Lop. Upon the skirt of the Wood, sauntring and peeping about, as if he were looking for the best Access to our Quarters: Money he had enough, and when we threatned him, he smil'd and yielded, but wou'd not speak one word.

Rod. Pilgrim, come hither, are you a Pilgrim, Sir? A Piece of pretty Holiness; do you shrink my Master? A smug young Saint this. What Country were you born in, I pray? What, not a Word? had your Mother this excellent Virtue too? Sure, she was a Matchless Woman: What a blessed Family is this Fellow sprung from! sure he was begot in a Calm. Are your Lips Sealed, or do you scorn to Answer? Look you, Sir, you are in my Hands, and I shall be too hard for you: Put off his Bonnet, Soldiers. You have a speaking Face, Sir.

Lop. A Handsome one, I'm sure; this Pilgrim can't want She-Saints to pray to.

Rod. Stand nearer: Ha?

Ped. Come, do your worst; I am ready.

Rod. Have you found your Tongue then? Retire all, and let me talk with him alone; and keep your Guards strict. (*Ex. all but* Rod. *and* Ped. So, now, what art thou?

Ped. What am I? My habit shews me what I am.

Rod. A Desperate Fool; and so thy face shall tell thee. What Devil brought thee hither? For I know thee.

Ped. I know thou dost; and since it is my Fortune to light into thy hands, I must conclude, the most malicious of Devils brought me; yet some Men say thou art Noble——

Rod. Not to thee; that were a benefit to mock the giver. Thy Father hates my Friends and Family; and thou hast been the Heir of all his Malice; can two such Storms then meet, and part without Kissing?

Ped. You have the mightier hand.

Rod. And so I'll use it.

Ped. I cannot hinder you; less can I beg, submissive at his knees that knows no Honour, that bears the ſtamp of Man, and not his Nature. You may do what you please.

Rod. I will do all.

Ped. I do expeƈt thou wilt; for had'ſt thou been a Noble Enemy, thou wou'dſt have fought me whilſt I carried Arms, whilſt my good Sword was my Profession, and then have cri'd out, *Pedro*, I defy thee; then ſtuck *Alphanso's* Quarrel on thy point; the mercenary anger thou serv'ſt under, to get his Daughter. But now, thou poorly, basely, setteſt thy Toils to catch me, and like the trembling Peasant, that dares not meet the Lion in the face, dig'ſt crafty Pitfalls. Thou shame to Spanish Honour.

Rod. Thy bravery is to thy Habit due: That Holy dress thou think'ſt will be thy sanƈtuary; thou wilt not find it so.

Ped. I Look not for't; The more unhallow'd Wretch howe're art thou t'invade it.

Rod. When you were braveſt, Sir, and your Sword sharpeſt, I durſt affront you, you know I durſt; when the Court Sun guilded you, and every Cry was, The young hopeful *Pedro*, *Alonso's* sprightly Son, then I durſt meet you, when you were Maſter of this mighty Fame, and all your Glories in the full Meridian. Had we then come to Competition, which I often sought——

Ped. And I desir'd too.

Rod. You shoud have seen this Sword and felt it too, sharper than Sorrow felt it. Then like a Gentleman I wou'd have us'd thee, and given thee the fair Fortune of thy caſt: But since thou ſteal'ſt upon me like a Spye, and Thief-like think'ſt Holy Case shall save thee, base as thy Purposes thy end shall be. Soldiers, appear, and bring a halter with ye. I'll forgive your Holy Habit, Sir, but I'll hang you.

Enter Lopez, Jaques *and* Out Laws.

1. *Out.* Here's a Halter, noble Captain, what service have you for't?

Rod. That Traytor has Service for't. Truss him up.

1. *Out.* With all my heart; d'ye want a band, Sir? I'll fit it to your Collar immediately.

Lop. What's his fault, Captain?

Rod. Tis my will, he perish; that's his fault.

Ped. A Captain of good Government: Come, Soldiers, come, you are roughly bred, and Bloody; shew your Obedience, and the Joy you have, in executing Impious Commands. You have a Captain Seals you liberal Pardons: Be no more Chriſtians, 'tis not in your way, put Religion by, 'twill make you Cowards. Feel no Tenderness; nor let a thing call'd Conscience trouble you; alas! 'twill breed delay. Bear no Respect to what I seem; were I a Saint indeed, why shou'd that stagger ye? You know no Holiness; to be excellent in Evil is your Goodness; and be so, 'twill become you; have no Hearts for fear you shou'd repent, for Repentance will be dangerous.

Rod. Truss up the Preacher.

Ped. The Racks of Conscience are of dire Importance.
Be therefore steady in your Mischiefs; waver not.

Rod. Up with him, I say.

Ped. Why do you not obey your Chief? Come, this one daring stroak at Heav'n, will make ye hard'ned Soldiers of Iniquity.

Rod. What do the Villains gaze at? Why am I not obeyed?

Jaq. What would you have us do?

Rod. Dispatch the Babler——

Jaq. And have Religious Bloud hang o're our Heads?
We have sins enough already, to make our Graves loath us.

Rod. I shall not be obey'd then?

Lop. Obey'd? I don't know; tho' I am a Thief, I'm no Hangman: They are two Trades; I don't care to meddle with Holy Blood.

Rod. Holy, or Unholy, I'll have it done.

1 *Out.* If I do't, I'll be Damn'd.

2 *Out.* Or I.

3 *Out.* Or I. We'll do any thing that's reasonable; but the Devil wou'd flinch at such a Job.

Jaq. I have done as many Villanies as another; and tho' I say't with as few Qualms: But I don't like this, it goes against my Stomack.

Rod. Have ye then conspir'd, ye Slaves?

Ped. Why art thou so disturb'd at their Refusal; if 'tis my Life alone thou want'st, why with thy own curst hand dost thou not take it? Thine's the Revenge; Be thine the Glory: Engross it to thy self, take the whole sin upon thee, and be Mighty in Evil, as thou art in Anger. And let not those poor wretches howl for thy sake.

Rod. 'Tis enough; I'll make ye all repent this stubborness; nor will I yet be baffled, I'll find another means to have my Will obeyed. Let him not scape, I charge ye, on your Lives.   [*Exit* Rod.

Jaq. What the Devil have you done Pilgrim, to make him rave and rage thus? Have you kill'd his Father, or his Mother, or strangled any of his Kindred?

Lop. Or has he no Sisters? Han't you been Bouncing about them?

1 *Out.* O' my Conscience his Quarrel to thee is not for being Holier than he.

Lop. Nor for seeming an Honester Man; for we have no Trading here with such ſtuff. To be excellent Thieves is all we aim at. Hark thee, Pilgrim; wilt thou take a Spit and a Stride, and try if thou canſt out-run us?

Ped. No, I scorn to shift his Fury.

Jaq. Thou wilt be hang'd then.

Ped. I cannot dye with fewer faults about me.

1 *Out.* I fancy he'll shoot him; for the Devil's in't if he hang him himself.

Lop. No, he's too proud for that; he'll make some body do't: See, here he comes again, and as full of Rage as ever.

1 *Out.* He has got the Boy with him; sure he won't make him do't.

Lop. As like as not.

Enter Roderigo *and* Alinda.

Rod. Come, Sirrah, no wonders. Nay, don't Stare, nor hang back; do't, or I'll hang you, you young Dog———

Alin. Alas, Sir, What wou'd you have me do? Heaven's Goodness shield me.

Rod. Do? Why, hang a Rogue that wou'd hang me.

Alin. I'm a Boy, and weak, Sir; pray excuse me.

Rod. Thou art ſtrong enough to tye him to a Bough, and turn him off. Come, be quick.

Alin. For Heav'ns sake, Sir.

Rod. Do ye dispute, Sirrah?

Alin. O, no, Sir; I'll do the beſt I can. Which is the Man, Sir?

Rod. That in the Pilgrim's Coat there; that Devil in the Saint's Skin.

Alin. Guard me, ye Powers.

Rod. Come, Dispatch.

Ped. I wait thy worſt.

Jaq. to Lop. Will the Boy do it? Is the Rogue so bold? So young, so deep in Bloud!

Lop. He shakes and trembles.

Ped. Doſt thou seek more Coals ſtill to sear thy Conscience? Work Sacred Innocence to be a Devil? Do it thy self, for shame: Thou beſt becomeſt it.

Rod. Thou art not worthy on't. No, this Child shall ſtrangle thee. A Crying Girl, if she were here, should Maſter thee.

Alin. How shall I Save him? How my self from Violence? Are you prepar'd to dye, Sir?

Ped. Yes, Boy; Prithee to thy Business.

Jaq. The young Dog begins to look as if he wou'd do't in earneſt.

Alin. If y'are prepar'd, How can you be so angry, so perplext'd? Heaven's won by Patience, not by Heat and Passion.

Lop. The Baſtard will make a good Prieſt.

Ped. I thank thee, gentle Child, thou teacheſt rightly.

Alin. Methinks you seem to fear too.

Ped. Thou see'ſt more than I feel, Boy.

Alin. You tremble sure.

Ped. No, Boy, 'tis but thy tenderness; prithee make haſte.

Alin. Are ye so willing then to go?

Ped. Moſt willing. I wou'd not borrow from his Bounty, one poor hour of Life, to gain an Age of Glory.

Alin. And is your Reckoning ſtated right with Heav'n?

Pedro. As right as Truth, Boy; I cou'd not go more joyful to a Wedding.

Alin. Then to your Prayers! I'll dispatch you presently.

Rod. A good Boy; I'll reward thee well.

Alin. I thank you, Sir; but pray allow me a short word in private. Now guide my Tongue, ye blessed Saints above. [*Aside.*

Rod. What wou'dſt thou have, Child?

Alin. Muſt this Man Dye?

Rod. Why doſt thou ask that Queſtion?

Alin. Pray be not angry; if he muſt, I'll do it: But muſt he now?

Rod. What else; Who dares reprieve him?

Alin. Pray think again; and as the Injuries are great this Man has done you, so suit your Vengeance to 'em.

Rod. I do; 'tis therefore he muſt dye——

Alin. A Trifle.

Rod. What is a Trifle?

Alin. Death, if he dye now.

Rod. Why, my beſt Boy?

Alin. I love you, Sir, I wou'd not tell you else. Is it Revenge to Saint your Enemy; Clap the Dove's Wings of Downy Peace upon him, and let him soar to Heaven, is this Revenge?

Rod. Yet die he muſt.

Alin. Right. Let him die, but not prepar'd to die. That were the Blessing of a Father on him; and all who know and love Revenge would laugh at you. You see, thus fortified, he scorns your Threats, despises all your Tortures; smiles to behold your Rage; so blind your View, that while you aim his hated Soul to Hell, you shoot it up to Heav'n.

Shall he die now?

Lop. What has the Boy done to him?

Jaq. How thoughfully he looks?

Alin. Come, Sir, you are wise, and have the World's regard; you are valiant too, and see your Valour honour'd. 'Twill be a Stain to both, indeed it will, to have it said, you have given your Fury leave to prey on a poor passive wayward Pilgrim——

Rod. The Boy has shaken me: What wou'dst thou have me do?

Alin. Alas Sir, do you ask a Child? But since you do, I'll say the best I know. I'd have you then do bravely, scorn him, and let him go. You have made him tremble, now seal his Pardon; and when he appears a Subject fit for Anger, fit for you, his pious Armour off, his hopes no higher than your Sword may reach, then strike the noble Blow. *[Aside.* I hope I have turn'd him.

Rod. Here; Let the Fool go. I scorn his Life too much to take it from him. But if we meet again——

Ped. I thank ye, Sir.

Rod. No more: Be gone. *[Exit Pedro.*

Alin. Why this was greatly done, most noble. *[Aside.* But whither is he gone! Oh, shall we never meet happy?

Rod. Come, Boy, thou shalt retire with me; I love thy Company: Thou hast a pleasing Tongue; come with me, Child.

Alin. I'll wait upon ye, Sir. *[Aside.]* O! *Pedro* *[Ex. Rod. Alin.*

Lop. The Boy has don't; he has sav'd the Pilgrim. A cunning young Rogue, I shall love him for't heartily.

Jaq. And so shall I. But the Knave's so good, I'm afraid he'll ruine us, he'll make us all honest.

1 *Out.* Marry Heav'n forbid.

2 *Out.* He'll find that a harder Task, than to save the Pilgrim.

Lop. That I believe: But come, Gentlemen, let's to Supper; we'll Drink the Boy's Health, and so about our business. *[Exeunt.*

The End of the Second Act.

ACT III.

Enter Roderigo, Jaques, Lopez, *and three Out-Laws.*

Rod. 'Tis strange none of you should know her.

Jaq. Alas! we never saw her, nor heard of her, but from you.

Lop. I don't think 'twas she; Methinks a Woman shoud not dare——

Rod. Thou speak'st thou know'st not what: What dares not Woman, when she is provok'd? Or what seems dangerous to Love and Fury? That it is she, These Jewels here confirm me, for part of 'em I my self sent her, which (tho' against her Will) her Father forc'd her to accept and wear.

Lop. 'Tis very strange, a Wench and we not know it, I us'd to have a better Nose.

Jaq. But what could be her business here?

Rod. That's what distracts me. O! that canting Pilgrim, that Villain *Pedro;* there lies my Torture. How cunningly she pleaded for him? How artfully she sav'd him? Death and Torments, had ye been true to me, I nee'r had suffer'd this.

1 *Out.* Why, you might have hang'd him if you wou'd; and wou'd he had been hang'd, that's all we care for't, so we had not don't——

Rod. But where is she now? What care have ye had of that? Why have ye let her go, to despise and laugh at me?

Lop. The Devil that brought her hither, has carried her back again, I think; for none of us saw her go.

Jaq. No living thing came this Night through our Watches. You know she went with you.

Rod. And was by me, 'till I fell asleep. But when I wak'd and call'd was gone. Curse on my Dulness, why did I not open this? This wou'd have told me all.

Enter Alphonso *and two Out-Laws.*

Alph. Prithee bring me to thy Captain, where's thy Captain, Fellow? Oh, I am founder'd, I am melted; some Fairy has led me about all Night; the Devil has entic'd me with the voice of a Whore. Where's thy Captain, Fellow?

1 *Out.* Here Sir, there he stands.

Alp. O! Captain, how dost thou, Captain? I have been fool'd, bubbled, made an Ass on: My Daughter's run away; I have been haunted too; have lost my Horse, am starved for want of Meat, and out of my Wits.

Rod. I'm sorry, Sir; to see you engag'd in so many Misfortunes; But pray walk in, refresh your self, and I'll inform you what has hapned here; but I'll recover your Daughter, or lose my Life: In the mean time all these shall wait upon you.

Alph. My Daughter be damn'd. Order me Drink enough; I'm all-most Choak'd. [*Ex. Alp. Rod.*

Rod. You shall have any thing. What think you now Soldiers?

Jaq. I think, a Woman's a Woman; that's all.

Lop. And I think the next Boy we take, we shou'd search him a little nearer. [*Exeunt.*

(111)

Enter Juletta Sola, *in Boys Cloaths.*

Jul. This is *Roderigo's* Quarter; my old Master's gone in here, and I'll be with him soon; I'll startle him a little better than I have done. All this long Night have I led him out of the way, to try his Patience. I have made him Swear and Curse, and Pray, and Curse again: I have made him lose his Horse too, whistled him through thick and thin. Down in a Ditch I had him; there he lay blaspheming, till I called him out to guide his Nose pop into a Fuz bush. Ten thousand Tricks I have play'd him, and ten thousand will add to them before I have done with him. I'll teach him to plague poor Women. But all this while, I can't meet with my dear Mistress. I'm cruelly afraid she shou'd be in Distress; wou'd to kind Heav'n I cou'd come to comfort her: But, till I do, I'll haunt thy Ghost, *Alphonso*; I will, old Crab-Tree. He shan't sleep; I'll get a Drum for him, I'll frighten him out of his wits; I have such a Hurricane in my head. I have almost lost my own allready; and I'm resolv'd I won't be mad alone. When a Woman sets upon playing the Devil, 'twere a-shame she shou'd not do't to the purpose.   [*Exit.*

Enter Seberto *and* Curio.

Seb. 'Tis strange, in all the Tour we have made, we shou'd have no news at all of her.

Cur. I Can't think she's got so far.

Seb. She's certainly disguis'd; her Modesty wou'd never venture in her own shape.

Cur. Let her take any Shape, I'm sure I cou'd distinguish her.

Seb. So cou'd I, I think. Has not her Father found her?

Cur. Not he, he's so wild, he wou'd know not her if he met her.

Seb. I hope he wou'd not; for 'tis pity she shou'd fall into his hands. But where are we, *Curio?*

Cur. In a Wood, I think; hang me if I know else: And yet I have ridden all these Coasts, and at all hours.

Seb. I wish we had a Guide.

Cur. If I am not much mistaken, *Seberto*, we are not far from *Roderigo's* Quarters. I think 'tis in this Thicket he and his Out-Laws harbour.

Seb. Then we are where *Alphonso* appointed to meet us.

Curi. I believe we are, wou'd we cou'd meet some living thing to inform us.

Seb. What's that there?   [*Enter* Alinda.

Curi. A Boy, I think; stay, Why may not he direct us?

Alin. I am hungry, and I am weary, almost quite spent, yet cannot find him; keep me in my Wits, good Heav'n! I feel 'em wavering. O my Head.

Seb. Hey Boy, dost hear, thou stripling!

Alin. O my fears, some of *Roderigo's* wicked Crew. If I am carried back to him, I then indeed am wretched.

Curi. Doſt know what place this is, Child?

Alin. No indeed, Sir, not I. O my Bones!

Seb. What doſt thou complain for, Boy? A very pretty Lad this.

Curi. What's the matter with thee, Child?

Alin. Alas, Sir! I was going to *Segovia*, to see my sick Mother, and here I have been taken, robb'd, and beaten by drunken Thieves. O my back.

Seb. What Rogues are these to use a poor Boy thus! Look up Child, be of good cheer, hold up thy head,

Alin. O, I cannot, it hurts me if I do; they have given me a great blow on the Neck.

Curi. What Thieves are they, doſt know?

Alin. They call the Captain *Roderigo.* O Dear, O Dear.

Curi. Look you there; I knew we were thereabouts.

Seb. Doſt thou want any thing?

Alin. Nothing but ease, Sir.

Curi. There's some Mony for thee however, and get thee to thy Mother.

Alin. I thank ye Gentlemen, pray Heaven bless ye.

Seb. Come let's along, we can't lose our way now.   [*Exit.*

Alin. I'm glad you are gone, Gentlemen; I know you are honeſt men, but I don't know whether you are on my side upon this occasion; Lord how I tremble, send me but once into *Pedro's* Arms, Dear Fortune, and then come what will—Which way shall I go, or what shall I do? 'tis almoſt Night again, and I know not where to get either Meat or Lodging. These wild Woods, and the various fancies that possess my Brain will run me Mad. Hey ho.   [*Enter* Juletta *with a Drum.*

Jule. Boy, Boy.   *Alin.* More set to take me.

Jule. Doſt hear, Boy? a word with thee.

Alin. 'Tis a Boy too, and no bigger than I am, I can deal with him.

Jule. Hark ye young Man; Can you beat a Drum?

Alin. A Drum!

Jule. A Drum! Ay, a Drum; didſt never see a Drum, mun? Prithee try if thou canſt make it grumble.

Alin [*Aside.*] *Juletta's* Face and Tongue; is she run mad too? Or is there some design in this? I'm jealous of every thing.

Jule. I'll give thee a Royal, but to go along with me to Night, and hurry durry this a little.

Alin. I care not for your Royal nor you neither, I have other business, prithee Drum to thy self and Dance to't.

Jule. Why how now, you saucy young Dog you! I have a good mind to lay down my Drum, and take ye a slap o're the Face.

Enter Roderigo *and two Out-Laws.*

Alin. Hark; here comes more company, I shall be taken at laſt. Heaven shield me!   *[Exit.*

Jule. Baſto; who's there?   *[Aside.*

Lope. Do you need me any farther, Captain?

Rod. No, not a foot: Give me the Gown: so: the Sword.

Jule. This is the Devil Thief; and if he take me, woe be to my Gaskins.

Lope. Certainly Sir, she'll take her Patches off, and change her Habit.

Rod. Let her do what she will, she can't again deceive me. No, no, *Alinda,* 'tis not the Habit of a Boy can twice delude me.

Jule. A Boy, and Patches on, what a dull Jade have I been! *[Aside.*

Rod. If she be found i'th Woods, send me word presently, and I'll return; she can't be yet got far. If you don't find her, expeċt me—when you see me. No more, farewel.   *[Exit.*

Jule. I'm very glad thou art gone. This Boy in Patches was the Boy I talkt to; the very same, how hastily it shifted me! what a mop-ey'd Ass was I, I cou'd not know her. It must be she; 'tis she: now I remember her, how loath she was to talk: how shy she was of me. I'll follow her, but who shall plague her Father there? No, I muſt not quit him yet: I muſt have one flurt more at him, and then for the Voyage. Come, Drum, make ready. Thou muſt do me Service.   *[Exit.*

Enter Jaques, *and one Out-Law.*

Jaq. Are they all set?   *Out.* All, and each quarter's quiet.

Jaq. Is old *Alphonso* a-sleep?   *Out. An hour ago.*

Jaq. We muſt be very careful in our Captain's absence.

Out. It concerns us, he won't be long from us. Hark—*[Drum afar off.*

Jaq. What!   *Out.* A Drum.

Jaq. The Devil.   *Out.* 'Tis not the wind, sure.

Jaq. No: that's Still and Calm. Hark again.   *Out.* Tat. Tat.

Jaq. It comes nearer: we are surpriz'd; 'tis by the King's Command; we are all Dead men.

Out. Hark, hark, a Charge now. Our Captain has betray'd us all.

Jaq. This comes of Love: Poverty, a scolding Wife, and ten Daughters be his recompence.   *[Enter* Lopez.

Lop. D'ye hear the Drum?   *Jaq.* Yes, we do hear it.

1 *Out.* Hark, another on that side.   *[Enter two* Out-Laws.

1 *Out.* Fly, fly, fly, we are all taken, we are all taken.

2 *Out.* A Thousand Horse and Foot, a Thousand Prisoners, and every Man a Halter by his side.

Lop. A dismal Night, Companions! what's to be done?

Jaq. Every Man shift for himself.   *[Exeunt.*

Enter Alphonso.

Alph. Ay marry Sir, where's my Horse now? what a Plague did I do amongſt these Rogues? is there ne're a hole to creep into? I shall be taken for their Captain, and out of respeĉt to my Poſt, be hang'd up firſt. A Pox of all Ceremonies, cry I; what will become of me? I muſt be a Daughter-hunting, with a Pox to me: Lord! Lord! that a foolish young Whore shou'd lead a wise old Rogue into so much mischief. But hark: hark, I say: ay; here they come. That I had but the Strumpet here now, to find 'em a little Play while I made my escape——

Enter Seberto, Curio, *and* Out-Laws.

Seb. What do you fear? what do you run from? Here are no Souldiers, no Body from the King to Attack you, are you all mad?

1 *Out.* Ay, but the Drum, the Drum Sir, did you not hear the Drum?

Curi. I never saw such Pidgeon-hearted Rogues: what Drum, you Fools? What Danger? who's that ſtands shaking there behind, enough to infeĉt a whole Army with Cowardise. Mercy on me, Sir, is't you? what is't that frights you thus?

Alph. Is there any hopes; do ye think I cou'd buy my Pardon?

Seb. What is't that has frighted you thus out of your Senses? here's no danger near you. A Drum I heard indeed, and saw it, a Boy was beating it; Hunting Squirrils by Moon-Light.

Curi. Nothing else, upon my Word, Sir.

Alph. That Rogue, the very Boy, no doubt on't, that haunted me all laſt Night. I wish I had him, he has plagued my heart out. But come, let's go in, and let me get on my Cloaths; if I ſtay here any longer to be Martyr'd thus, I'll beget another Daughter. Where is that Jewel? Have you met her yet?

Seb. No; we have no news of her.

Alph. Then I can tell you some, she has been here in Boys Cloaths, she has truſt up her Modeſty in a Pair of Breeches. There has been a Pilgrim at her Tail too. I suppose the Game's almoſt up by this time.

Curi. A young Boy we met, Sir.

Alph. In a Gray-Hat.   *Curi.* In a Gray-Hat.

Alph. Patches on.   *Curi.* Patches on.

Alph. The Strumpet.   *Curi.* Impossible.

Alph. True—in the Litteral Sense.

Seb. 'Tis wonderful we shou'd not know her.

Alph. Dam her, that's all. Come get me some Wine, a great deal: This Halter makes me kekkle in the Throat ſtill.   [*Exit.*

Enter Juletta sola.

What a fright have I put 'em in! a brave hurly burly; I' faith, if this do but bolt him, I'll be with him again, with a new part. I'll ferk him; as he hunts her, I'll hunt him, no Fox with a kennel of Hounds at his Tail, ever had such a time on't.   *[Exit.*

SCENE [II] *Segovia.*

Enter Pedro *and a Gentleman.*

Gent. You need make no Apology Sir, I take a Pleasure in waiting upon Strangers, and shewing 'em what's worth their seeing in our City. Besides I observe you are sad, I wou'd divert your melancholy if I cou'd. Will ye view our Castle?

Ped. I thank ye, Sir, but I've already seen it; 'tis strong and well provided.

Gent. How do you like the Walks?

Ped. They are very pleasant; your Town stands cool and sweet.

Gent. But that I wou'd not add to your sadness—I cou'd shew you a place were worth your view.

Ped. Shews seldom alter me, Sir, pray what place is't?

Gen. 'Tis a House here, where People of all sorts, that have been visited with Lunacies, and Follies, wait their Cures. There's fancies of a thousand stamps and fashions: Some of Pity, that it wou'd make you melt to see their Passions: And some again as light that wou'd divert you. But I see your temper, Sir, too much inclin'd to Contemplation to have a taste of such diversions.

Ped. You mistake me, Sir, I shou'd be glad to see 'em; if you please, I'll wait upon you thither.

Gent. Since you are willing Sir, I shall be proud to be your guide.

Ped. I never yet had so much mind to take a view of misery.   *[Exeunt.*

[SCENE III.]

Enter two Keepers.

1 *Keep.* Carry mad *Bess* some meat, she roars like Thunder. And tye the Parson short; the Moon's i'th' full, he has a thousand pigs in's Brain. Who looks to the Prentice? Keep him from Women, he thinks he has lost his Mistress: And talk of no Silk Stuffs; 'twill run him Horn mad.

2 *Keep.* The Justice keeps such a stir yonder with his Charges, and such a coil with his Warrants.

1 *Keep.* Take away his Statutes; the Devil has possest him in the likeness of Penal Laws; keep him from *Aqua-vitæ*, for if that Spirit creep into his Quorum, he'll commit us all. How is't with the Scholar?

2 *Keep.* For any thing I see he is in's right Wits.

1 *Keep.* Thou art an Ass; his Head's too full of other Peoples Wits, to leave room for his own.   [*Enter English Madman.*

Engl. Give me some Drink.

1 *Keep.* O ho, here's the English Man.

Engl. Fill me a thousand Pots, and froth 'em, froth 'em; down o' your knees, you Rogues, and pledge me roundly; one, two, three—and four. To the great Turk, I'm his Friend, and will prefer him, he shall quit his Crown—and be a Tapster.

1 *Keep.* Peace, thou heathenish Drunkard, Peace for shame. These *English* are so Malt-mad, there's no medling with them; when they have a Fruitful Year of Barly there, the whole Island's thus.

Engl. Who talks of Barly? my Drink's small; down with the Malt-Tax. Huzza.

1 *Keep.* Hold your Tongue, you Bear you, or I shall so Chastise ye—

Eng. Who's that? An Excise man? The Devil.   [*Enter a she Fool.*

Fool. God give you good Even, Gaffer.

2 *Keep.* Who has let the Fool loose here?

1 *Keep.* If any of the Madmen get her, they'll Pepper her, they'll Bounce her, I'Faith.

Fool. Will you walk into the Coal-house, Gaffer?

2 *Keep.* She's as Leacherous as a she Ferret.

1 *Keep.* Who a Vengeance looks to her? Go in *Kate*, go in, and I'll give thee a fine Apple.

Fool. Will you buss me, and tickle me, and make me Laugh?

1 *Keep.* I'll whip you, Hussy.

Engl. Fool, fool, come up to me, fool.

Fool. Are ye peeping?   *Engl.* I'll get thee with five Fools.

Fool. O fine, O Dainty.

Engl. And thou shalt lie in a Horse-cloath like a Lady.

Fool. And shall I have a Coach?

Engl. Drawn with four Turkeys, and they shall tread thee too.

Fool. We shall have Eggs then; and shall I sit upon 'em?

Engl. Ay, Ay, and they shall be all Addle, and make a Tanzey for the Devil. Come, come away; I am taken with thy Love, Fool, and will mightily belabour thee.

1 *Keep.* How the Slut Bridles! How she twitters at him! These *English* men would stagger a wise Woman. If we should suffer her to

have her will now, we should have all the Women in *Spain* as mad as she here.

2 *Keep*. They'd strive who shou'd be most fool: Away with her.

Fool. Pray ye stay a little, let's hear him sing: He has a fine breast.

Enter Master, *three* Gentlemen, Pedro, *a mad* Scholar.

1 *Keep*. Here comes my Master: to the Spit, you whore; and stir no more abroad, but tend your business, you shall have no more sops i'th' pan else. Away with 'em both.   [*Exit* Keep. *with the Madman and fool.*

1 *Gen*. I'll assure you Sir, the Cardinal's angry with you for keeping this young Man.

Mast. I'm heartily sorry, Sir; if you allow him sound, pray take him with you.

2 *Gen*. We can find nothing in him Light nor Tainted; no starts, no rubs in all his Answers: His letters too are full of Discretion, Learning, and in a handsome stile.

Mast. Don't be deceiv'd Sir, mark but his Look.

1 *Gen*. His grief and his Imprisonment may stamp that there.

Mast. Pray talk with him agen then.

2 *Gen*. That will be needless, we have tryed him long enough, and if he had a taint, we should have met with't.

Ped. A sober Youth: 'Tis Pity so heavy a misfortune should attend him.

2 *Gen*. You find no sickness?

Scho. None Sir, I thank Heaven; nor nothing that disturbs my understanding.

1 *Gen*. Do you sleep a Nights?   *Scho*. Perfectly sound and sweet.

2 *Gen*. Have you no fearful Dreams?

Scho. Sometimes, as all have, who go to Bed with raw and windy stomach.

1 *Gen*. Is there no unkindness you have receiv'd from any Friend, or Parent? or Scorn from what you lov'd?

Scho. No truly Sir, I have not seen Villany enough, to make me doubt the truth of Friend or Kindred—and what Love is, unless it lie in Learning, I am ignorant.

1 *Gen*. This Man is perfect; I never met with one that talk'd more regularly.

Mast. You'll find it otherwise.

2 *Gen*. I must tell you plainly Sir, I think you keep him here to make him mad, but here's his Discharge from my Lord Cardinal. Come Sir, you are now at Liberty to go with us.

Scho. I thank ye, Gentlemen; Master farewel.

Mast. Farewel *Stephano*. Alas! Poor Man.

1 *Gen.* What flaws and gusts of Weather we have had these three days? How dark and hot it is. The Skie is full of mutiny.

Mast. It has been stubborn Weather.

2 *Gen.* Strange work at Sea, I doubt there's old Tumbling.

1 *Gen.* Bless my old Uncle's Bark, I have a Venture in't.

2 *Gen.* And so have I, more than I'd wish to lose, I'm in some fear.

Scho. Do you fear?   2 *Gen.* Ha! How he looks?

Mast. Nay, mark him better, Gentlemen.

2 *Gen.* Mercy on me, how he stares?

Mast. Now tell me how ye like him? What think ye of him for a sober Man now?

Scho. Does the Sea stagger ye?

Mast. Now you have hit the Nick.   *Scho.* Do ye fear the Billows?

1 *Gen.* What Ails him, who has stirr'd him?

Scho. Be not shaken: Let the storm rise; let it blow on, blow on: Let the Clouds wrastle, and let the Vapours of the Earth turn mutinous. The Sea in hideous Mountains rise, and tumble upon a Dolphin's back, I'll make all shake, for I am *Neptune.*

Mast. Now, what think you of him?   2 *Gen.* Alas! poor Man.

Scho. Your Bark shall Plough through all, and not a surge so sawcy to disturb her: I'll see her fate, my Pow'r shall fail before her——

> Down ye angry Waters all,
> Ye loud whistling Whirlwinds fall.
> Down ye proud Waves; ye Storms cease,
> I command ye, be at Peace;
> Fright not with your Churlish Notes,
> Nor bruise the Keel of Bark that floats.
> No devouring Fish come nigh,
> Nor Monster in my Empery
> Once shew his Head, or terrour bring,
> But let the weary Sailor sing,
> *Amphitrite*, with white Arms
> Strike my Lute, I'll sing Charms.

Mast. Now he must have Musick, his fit will grow worse else.

2 *Gen.* I pity him.   [*Musick.*

Mast. Now he'll go in quietly of himself,
And clean forget all.

Gen. We are sorry, Sir, and we have seen a wonder.
Pray Excuse our unbelief.   [*Exeunt Gent.*

Ped. This was a strange Fit.

Mast. Many have sworn him right, and I have thought so; yet on a sudden, from some word or other, when no Man could expect a fit, thus he has flown out. [*Enter* Alinda.

Alin. Must I come in too?

Mast. No, my pretty Lad, keep in thy Chamber, thou shalt have thy Supper.

Ped. Pray what is that, Sir?

Mast. A strange Boy that was found last Night wandring about the Town a little distracted, so was sent hither.

Ped. How the pretty Knave looks! and Plays, and Peeps upon me! Sure such Eyes I have seen.

Mast. Pray take care, Sir, if you seem to take notice of him, you'll make him worse.

Ped. I'll warrant you, I'll not hurt him: How he smiles! Let me look once again; but that the Cloaths are different——Sure 'tis not she—— How tenderly it presses me?

Mast. I must attend else where, pray take heed. [*Exit* Master.

Ped. Fear not: How my Heart beats and trembles! He holds me hard; thou hast a mind to speak to me, he Weeps: What would'st thou say, my Child? Dost know me?

Alin. O *Pedro, Pedro!*   *Ped.* O my Soul.

Gen. Hey, what fit's this; I think the Pilgrim's off the Hooks too.

Alin. Let me hold thee, and now come all the World, I fear not.

Ped. Be wise my Angel, you'll discover your self; oh, how I Love thee. How dost thou? tell me.

Alin. I have been Miserable. But your Eyes have blest me; pray think it not immodesty I kiss ye. Oh, my Head's wild still.

Ped. Be not so full of passion, nor hang so eagerly upon me, 'twill be observ'd.

Alin. Are ye then weary of me? but you shan't leave me: No, I'll hang here for ever. Kiss you eternally, O my dear Pilgrim.

Enter Master.

Mast. Look ye there now; I knew what you'd do. The Boy's in's Fit again: Are ye not asham'd to torment him thus? I told you, you'd bring it upon him. Either be gone, and presently, I'll force ye else: Who waits within! [*Enter two* Keepers.

Ped. Alas! good Sir, this is the way never to recover him.

Mast. Stay but one minute more, I'll complain to the Governour. Pull away the Boy; look ye there, d'ye see how he pulls, and tears himself. Be gone you had best, for if the Boy miscarry I'll make you rue it.

Ped. O Misery.   *Alin.* Farewel, for ever.   [*Exeunt different ways.*

The End of the Third Act.

ACT IV.

Enter Alphonso, *and a Gentleman.*

Juletta *follows 'em unseen.*

Gen. YOU are now within a Mile oth' Town, Sir; if my business would give me leave, I'd guide ye farther. But for such Gentlemen as you enquire for, I have seen none. The Boy you describe, or one much like it, was sent in t'other Night a little maddish, and now is in the House appointed for such Cures.

Alp. 'Tis very well, I thank ye Sir.

Jule [*aside.*] And so do I: for if there be such a place, I ask no more; you shall hear of me, I' faith, old Gentleman, I'll follow you there too as founder'd as I am. And make ye kick and roar afore I have done with you. I'll teach you to hunt Mad-Houses.

Alp. [*aside.*] It must be she. 'Tis very well, is your blood so hot, I'faith, my Minx? I'll have ye madded, I'll have ye worm'd.

Enter Alinda *as a Fool.*

Gen. Here's one belongs to the very House, Sir, 'tis a poor Ideot. But she'll shew you the way as well as a wiser Body. So, Sir, I leave you. [*Exit Gent.*

Alp. Your Servant. Here Fool, a word with thee, Fool.

Alin. O I am lost, 'tis my Father in all his rage.

Alp. Hark thee, Fool.

Alin. He does not know me, Heaven grant I may deceive him still! will ye give me two pence, Gaffer, and here's a Crow Flower, and a Dazie? I have some Pye in my Pocket too.

Alp. This is an errant Fool, a meer Changeling.

Alin. Think so, and I am happy. [*Aside.*

Alp. Dost thou dwell in *Segovia*, Fool?

Alin. No, no, I dwell in Heaven; and I have a fine little House made of Marmalad; and I am a lone Woman, and I spin for St. *Peter.* I have a hundred little Children, and they sing Psalms with me.

Alp. A very pretty Conversation I am falling into here, especially for a Man in a Passion. Canst thou tell me if this be the way to the Town?

Alin. Yes, yes, you must go over the top of that high Steeple, Gaffer.

Alp. A Plague of your Fools face.

Jul. (*aside.*] No; take her Counsel, do.

Alin. And then you shall come to a River, Gaffer, twenty Miles over,

(121)

and twenty Miles and ten; and then you muſt pray, Gaffer, and pray, and pray, and pray, and pray, and pray.

Alp. Pray Heav'n deliver me from such an Ass as thou art.

Alin. Amen, sweet Gaffer; and fling a Sop of Sugar-Cake into it, and then you muſt leap in naked.

Jul. [*aside.*] Wou'd he wou'd believe her.

Alin. And sink seven days together. Can ye sink, Gaffer?

Alp. Pox on thee, and a Pox o' that Fool that left me to thee. [*Exit. Alp.*

Alin. God be w'ye Nunkle.

Jul. How I rejoyce in any thing that vexes him! I shall love this Fool as long as I live, for putting her hand to the Plough. Cou'd I but see my Miſtress now, to tell her how I have labour'd for her, how I have worn my self away in her Service!—Well, sure I shall find her at laſt.

Alin. [*aside.*] 'Tis *Juletta.*—Sure she's honeſt; yet I dare not discover my self to her.

Jul. Here, fool, here's something for thee to buy Apples, for the sport thou haſt made in crossing thy Nunkle.

Alin. Thank ye, little Gentleman; Heaven bless ye. Pray keep this Nutmeg; 'twas sent me from the Lady of the Mountain, a Golden Lady.

Jul. How prettily it prattles!

Alin. 'Tis very good to rub your Underſtanding; and so good Night; the Moon's up.

Jul. Pretty Innocence!

Alin. [*aside.*] Now Fortune, if thou darſt do good, protect me. [*Exit. Al.*

Jul. I'll follow him to your Town; he shan't 'scape me.——Let me see.——I muſt counterfeit a Letter, a Letter of Authority for him.—— Yes, 'twill do; certainly do.——How I shall make his old Blood boil! Rare sport i'faith!——But what i'th' Name of Innocence has this Fool given me! She said 'twas good to rub my Underſtanding; is't Bread or Cheese?——Hah! a Ring! a right one! a Ring I know too!——The very same.——A Ring my Miſtress took from me, and wore it. I know it by the Posie. None could deliver this but she her self. 'Twas she. Curse o' my Sand-blind Eyes. Twice deceiv'd! Twice so near the Blessing I am seeking! What shall I do? Here are so many cross-ways, 'tis in vain to follow her. I hope however, for all her Dress, she's in her Senses ſtill, for sure she knew me.——Well, to divert my melancholy till I can meet with her again, I'll go and have th' other touch with her Father.
[*Exit. Jul.*

Enter Roderigo.

Rod. She's not to be recover'd; and, which doubles my Torment, he's got beyond my Vengeance. How they laugh at me! Death and Furies! But why shou'd I ſtill wander thus, and be a Coxcomb, tire out my Peace and Pleasure for a Girl? a Girl that scorns me too? a thing that hates me; and, consider at the beſt, is but a ſhort Breakfaſt for a hot Appetite? ——Well thought: That ſhort Repaſt I'll make on her, and so I'll reſt. ——Look to't, my young deceiver; we shall meet; which when we do, not all the Tears and Cries of trembling Chaſtity shall save you. You have fir'd my Dwelling, and shall quench my Flame. [*Enter* Alinda.

Alin. Is not that *Pedro?* 'Tis he; 'tis he.——Oh my——

Rod. What art thou? *Alin.* Hah!——Oh! I'm miserable. [*Aside.*

Rod. What the Devil art thou?

Alin. [*aside.*] No end of my misfortunes? Heav'ns! that Habit to betray me! ye holy Saints, can ye see that? Do your selves Juſtice, and protect me.

Rod. It dances! Hey-dey! The Devil in a Fool's Coat! Is he turn'd Changeling? What mops and mows it makes! How it frisks! Is't not a Fairy? It has a mortal Face, and I've a great mind to't. But if it shou'd prove the Devil!——

Alin. Come hither, Dear.

Rod. I think 'twill ravish me. It's a handsom thing, but basely Sunburnt. What's that it points at?

Alin. Doſt thou see that Star there? that juſt above the Sun? Prithee go thither and light me this Tobacco, and ſtop it with the Horns of the Moon.

Rod. The thing's mad, quite mad. Go sleep, fool, go sleep.

Alin. Thou canſt not sleep so quietly; for I can say my Prayers, and then slumber.

> I am not proud, nor full of Wine;
> This little Flow'r will make me fine:
> Cruel in heart, for I will cry
> If I see a Sparrow dye.

> I am not watchful to do ill,
> Nor glorious to pursue it ſtill;
> Nor pitiless to those that weep.
> Such as are, bid them go sleep.

Do, do, do; and see if they can.

Rod. It said true. Its words sink into me. Sure 'tis a kind of Sybil; some mad Prophet. I feel my Fury bound and fetter'd in me.

Alin. Give me your hand, and I'll tell you your Fortune.

Rod. Here, prithee do.

Alin. Fye! fye! fye! fye! fye! Wash your Hands and pare your Nails, and look finely, you shall never kiss the King's Daughter else.

Rod. I wash 'em daily. *Alin.* But foul 'em faſter.

Rod. [*aside.*] This goes nearer me. *Alin.* You shall have two Wives.

Rod. Two Wives!

Alin. Yes; two fine Gentlewomen. Make much of 'em, for they'll stick close to you, Sir. And these two in two days, Sir.

Rod. That's a fine Riddle!

Alin. To day you shall wed Sorrow, and Repentance will come to morrow.

Rod. Sure she's inspir'd.   *Alin.* I'll tell you more, Sir.   [*Sings.*

> *He call'd down his merry men all,*
> *By One, by Two, by Three.*
> William *wou'd fain have been the First,*
> *But now the Last is he.*

Rod. The very Chronicle of my misfortunes.

Alin. I'll bid you Good-Ev'n; for my Boat stays for me, and I must sup with the Moon to Night in the *Mediterranean.*   [*Exit. Alin.*

Rod. Can Fools and Mad-folks then be Tutors to me? Can they feel my Sores, yet I insensible? Sure this was sent by Providence to steer me right. I'm wondrous weary; my thoughts too, they are tir'd, which adds a weighty burden to me. I have done ill; I have pursu'd it too; nay, still run on. I must think better; be something else, or nothing. Still I grow heavier. A little rest wou'd help me; I'll try if I can take it; and Heaven's Goodness guard me.   [*Lies down.*

Enter four Peasants.

1 *Pea.* We have scap'd to day well. If the Out-Laws had known we had been stirring, we had pay'd for't, Neighbours.

2 *Pea.* A murrain take 'em, they have robb'd me thrice.

3 *Pea.* Me five times, my Daughter fifty; tho' to give 'em their due, they ne're take any thing from her, but what she can very well spare.

4 *Pea.* Ah! my poor Wife has been in their hands too: But, to say the truth, I don't find she has lost much neither.

1 *Pea.* For my part, I ought not to complain, for I have got three Children by 'em. Poor *Jone!* they have pepper'd her Jacket.

2 *Pea.* Wou'd we had some of 'em here, to thank 'em for their kindnesses.

3 *Pea.* So we were strong enough to Circumcise 'em, I don't care if we had.

4 *Pea.* What's that lies there?

1 *Pea.* An old Woman that keeps Sheep hereabouts.

2 *Pea.* Drunk, I suppose.

3 *Pea.* And a Sword by her side to keep the Wolves off?——Hah! Captain *Roderigo*, or the Devil.——Stand to your Arms, Gentlemen.

4 *Pea.* 'Tis he.   1 *Pea.* Speak softly.

2 *Pea.* Now's our time.

3 *Pea.* Stay, stay, let's be provident. Shall we wake him before we kill him, or after?

4 *Pea.* Let me kill my share of him before he wakes.

1 *Pea.* Let me have the first blow; he robb'd me last.

2 *Pea.* No, I ought to have the first; he Cuckolded me last.

3 *Pea.* Hold, hold; no Civil Wars, d'ye hear? Beat his Brains out between ye,——And then I'll pick his Pockets.   [*Aside.*

4 *Pea.* Draw your Knives, and every Man seize a Limb.

Omn. Huzzah!   *Rod.* Slaves! Villains! will ye murder me?

3 *Pea.* No, no; we'll only tickle you a little. D'ye remember *Joan*, Captain? I'll spoil ye for a Cuckold-maker.   [*Enter* Pedro.

Rod. For Heavens sake! as y'are Men; as y'are Christians.

3 *Pea.* Neither Man nor Christian upon this occasion, but a Cuckold with a Knife in my hand.

Rod. Oh help! Some help there!

Ped. Ye Villains! are ye at Murder? Off, ye inhuman Slaves!——Do ye not stir? Nay then have among ye.

Omn. Away, away, away.   [*Exeunt.*

Ped. Villains! use Violence to that Habit?

Rod. Pedro! Nay then I am more wretched than ever.   [*Aside.*

Ped. Hah! *Roderigo!* What makes him here thus clad? Is it Repentance, or a Disguise for Mischief?   [*Aside.*

Rod. To owe my Life to him, makes me all Confusion.   [*Aside.*

Ped. Ye are not much hurt, Sir?

Rod. No.——All I can call a Wound, is in my Conscience.   [*Aside.*

Ped. Have ye consider'd the Nature of these Men, and how they have us'd you? was it well?

Rod. [*aside.*] I dare not speak, for I have nought to answer.

Ped. Did it look noble to be o're-laid with odds? Did it seem manly in a multitude to oppress you? If it be base in Wretches low like these, what must it be in one that's born like you? Ah *Roderigo!* had I abandon'd Honesty, Religion, broke thro' the Bonds of Honour and Humanity, I had set as small a price upon thy Life, as thou didst lately upon mine: But I reserve thee to a nobler Vengeance.

Rod. I thank ye; you have the Nobler Soul, I must confess it; and of your Passions are a greater Master. Th' Example's glorious, and I wish to follow it. There is a stain of Infamy about me, and the Dye is deep; yet possibly occasion may present, that I may wash it off.

Ped. I'll give you one, a noble one, I think. We have a quarrel, we've a Mistress too. We are single, and our Arms alike. In one fair risque of Life let all determine, our Rancour past, and Happiness to come.

Rod. [*aside.*] His Virtue puzzles me.——I dare fight, *Pedro.*

Ped. I do believe you dare: Or if you wanted Courage, the beauteous Prize for which we now contend wou'd rouze you to't.

Rod. Hah!   *Ped.* If you deserve her, draw.

Rod. I do not, nor such a noble Enemy: I therefore will not draw.

Ped. I cou'd compel you to't, but wou'd not willingly.

Rod. You cannot, to increase my Guilt: The Load's already more than I can bear; I wo'not add to't.   *Ped.* Poor Evasion.

Rod. Thou wrong'st me, much thou wrong'st me; time will convince thee on't. I'll satisfie thee any way but this. I have been wicked, but cannot be a Monster. My Sword refuses to attempt the Man preserv'd me; its temper starts at thy Virtue. If thou wilt have me fight, give me an Enemy, for thou art none.

Ped. I'm more, for I'm thy Rival.

Rod. That is not in thy power, for I no more am thine. No, *Pedro;* the wrongs I've done my self and thee, let that fair Saint attone for: There's nothing more I or the World can give, and nothing less can expiate my Crimes, or recompence thy Virtue.

Ped. Is't possible thou canst be such a Penitent!

Rod. I am most truly such; and lest I should relapse again to Hell, forget the Debt I owe to thee and Heav'n, this sacred Habit I have so prophan'd, shall henceforth be my faithful Monitor.

Ped. Noble *Roderigo,* how glorious is this Change! Let me embrace thee.

Rod. Thou great Example of Humanity, dost thou forgive me?

Ped. I do; with joy I do.

Rod. Then I am happy——All I have more to ask, is, leave to attend you in your present difficulties; that by such service as I have power to render, I may confirm you I am what I seem.

Ped. There needs no further proof. However, in hopes I doubly may return those Services, I'll not refuse 'em.   [*Exeunt.*

[SCENE II.]

Enter Alphonso, *Master and Keepers.*

Mast. Yes, Sir, here are such People: But how pleasing they may be to you, I can't tell.

Alp. That's not your concern; I desire to see 'em, to see 'em all.

Mast. All? Why, they'll quite confound ye, Sir; like Bells rung backwards, they are nothing but confusion, meer Noise.

Alp. May be I love Noise?——But hark ye, Sir; have ye no Boys? handsom young Boys?

Maſt. One, Sir, we have, a very handsom Boy.   *Alp.* Long here?

Maſt. But two Days. A little craz'd, but may recover.

Alp. That Boy, I would see that Boy; perhaps I know him.——*[Aside.]* This is the Boy he told me of; it muſt be she——The Boy, Maſter, I beseech ye the Boy.

Maſt. You shall see him, Sir, or any else: But pray don't be so violent.

Alp. I know what to do, I warrant ye; I'm for all fancies; I can talk to 'em, and dispute if occasion be——Who lies here?

Keep. Pray don't disturb 'em, Sir; here lies such Youths will make you ſtart, if they begin to Dance their Trenchmores.

Maſt. Fetch out the Boy, Sirrah. *[Shaking of Irons within.]*——Hark!

Alp. Hey-boys!

Enter English Madman, Scholar and Prieſt.

Eng. Bounce. Clap her o'th' Starboard. Bounce. Top the Can.

Schol. Dead, ye Dog, dead! D'ye quarrel in my Kingdom? Give me my Trident.

Eng. Bounce!——'Twixt Wind and Water! Laden with Mackerel!— Oh brave Meat!

Scho. My Sea-Horses. I'll charge the Northern Wind, and break his Bladder.

Alp. Brave sport, i'faith!

Prieſt. I'll sell my Bells, before I'll be outbrav'd thus.

Alp. What's he.

Maſt. A Prieſt, Sir, that run mad for a Tythe-pig.

Alp. Curran-sawce cure him.

Prieſt. I'll curse ye all, I'll excommunicate ye. Thou English Heretick, give me the tenth Pot.

Eng. Sue me, I'll drink up all. Bounce I say once more—O-ho! have I split your Mizen? Blow, blow, thou Weſt-wind; blow till thou riſe, and make the Sea run roaring;——I'll hiss it down again, with a Bottle of Ale.

Scho. Triton! why, Triton!   *Eng.* Triton's drunk with Metheglin.

Scho. Strike, ſtrike the Surges, ſtrike.   *Prieſt.* I'll have my Pig.

Eng. Drink, drink; 'tis Day-light—Drink, diddle, diddle, diddle, Drink.

Priest. I'll damn thee.

Eng. Prieſt, proud Prieſt, a Pig's Tail in thy Teeth.

Prieſt. My Pig——or I'll marry thee.

Eng. Say no more. My Drink's out. Hush is the word—and to sleep.

Maſt. Their Fits are cool now; let 'em reſt.

Alp. Mad Gallants, mad Gallants, i'faith; I love their Faces; I never fell into better Company in my Life.   [*Enter mad Taylor.*

Tay. Who's that?—The King of *Spades?*
I'll make him a new Mantle?

Alp. Hey Day: A mad Taylor too! What
The Pox made thee Mad?

Tay. Cabbage——Snip goes the Sheers——
And the Coat's never the shorter.

Alp. Thou're a brave Fellow, and sha't make me
A new Doublet.

Tay. For thy Coronation——I'll do't;
But Mony down; dost hear? Mony down.
The King of *Spades* is a Courtier.

Priest. I'll have a new Gown.

Tay. So thou sha't, made of Shreds——and a
Tythe Louse——to prevent Damnation——

Alp. Wo't be my Chaplain?

Priest. And say Grace to boild Meat?——The Devil.

Alp. Can'st thou Preach?

Priest. Give me a Text.

Tay. Pudding.

Priest. Where is't?——I'll handle it——Divide it——
Subdivide it—and give my Parish—ne're a bit on't.

Tay. My Lady's Woman shall have a slice.

Priest. Mum.

Tay. I'll cut thee a pair of Britches, out of the tail of her Petticoat.

Priest. Warm ware——Dog Days——but Hush: Put out the Candle
Maiden-head's the Word. If the Cardinal hear's on't——he'll have a
Pair too.   [*Enter* Keepers, *and she* Fool *in* Alinda's *Cloaths.*

1 *Keep.* You stinking Whore, who did this for you? Who looks to
the Boy? Pox take him, he was asleep when I left him.

2 *Keep.* I suppose he made the Fool drunk.

Mast. What's this noise about? Where's the Boy?

1 *Keep.* Here's all the Boys we have found.

Mast. These are his Cloaths; but where's he?

1 *Keep.* Ay, that's all I want to know.

Mast. Where's the Boy, ye Slut you? Where's the Boy?

Fool. The Boy's gone a Maying; he'll bring me home a Cuckow's Nest.
Do you hear, Master? I put my Cloaths off, and I dizen'd him; I pinn'd
a Plume in his Forehead, and a Feather, and buss'd him twice, and bid him
go seek his fortune. He gave me this fine Mony, and he gave me fine Wine
too, and bid me sop; and gave me these trim Cloaths too, and put 'em
on, he did.   *Alp.* Is this the Boy you'd shew me?

Fool. I'll give you Two-pence, Master.

Alp. Am I Fool'd on all sides? I met a Fool in the Woods in a long py'd Coat; they said she dwelt here.

Mast. That was the very Boy, Sir.

Fool. Ay, ay, ay; I gave him leave to play forsooth? he'll come again to morrow, and bring Peascods.

Mast. I'll Peascods your Bones, you Whore.

Alp. Pox o' your Fools and Bedlams; Plague o' your Owls and Apes.

Mast. Pray, Sir, be moderate; such Accidents will happen sometimes, take what care we can.

Alp. Damn Accidents: You're a Juggler, and I'm abus'd.

Mast. Indeed, Sir, you are not.

Alp. It's false; I am abus'd, and I will be abus'd, whether you will or no, Sir.   [*Enter Welchman.*

Wel. Whaw, Mr. *Keeper.*   *Alp.* What a pox have we got here?

Wel. Give me some Cheese and Onyons; give me some Wash-prew; I have hunger in my pellies; give me apundance. *Pendragon* was a Shentleman, mark you, Sir? And the Organs at *Wrexham* were made by Revelations; there is a Spirit plows and plows the Pellows, and then they sing.

Alp. Why, this Moon Calf's madder than all the rest. Who the Devil is he?

Mast. He's a *Welch-man*, Sir: He ran mad, because a Rat eat up his Cheese.

Alp. The Devil he did. *Wel.* I will peat thy Faces as plack as a plue Clout.

Mast. He won't Hurt you, Sir, don't be afraid.

Wel. Give me a great deal of Cuns: Thou art the Devils, I know thee by thy Tails: I will peg thy Pums full of Pullets.

Alp. This is the rarest Rascal! He speaks as if h' had Buttermilk in's Mouth.

Wel. Basilus Manus is for an old Codpice, mark ye. I will porrow thy Ursip's Whore to Seal a Letter.

Alp. Ha, ha, ha.   *Mast.* Now he begins to grow Villanous.

Alp. Methinks he's best now.   *Mast.* Take him away.

Alp. He shan't go.   *Mast.* He must, Sir.

Wel. I will Sing, and dance, and do any thing.

Alp. Wilt thou declaim in *Greek?*

Scho. Do, and I'll confound thee.   *Wel.* I will eat some Puddings.

Eng. Pudding! where is't? Bak'd or Boil'd, Plums or Plain, 'tis mine by *Magna Charta.*——The King of *Spain* eats White-Pot.

Alp. Oh brave *English* Man? Wilt have any Beef, Boy?

Mast. Nay, now, Sir, y' have made him stark mad. Lay hold of him there quickly.

Eng. Beef! ye Gods! Beef!—I'le have that Ox for Supper—Knock him down—Chines, Surloins, Ribs, and Buttocks.—Lead me to the *French* Camp—They fly! they fly! they fly! they fly! they fly! they fly! Huzzah!

Mast. Away with him; he'll be so mad now, the Devil can't tame him. Take 'em all away.   [*Exit* Keeper and Madmen.]

Alp. He shan't go. What a Pox makes ye spoil company?

Mast. Away with him, I say.

Alp. I gad I'll see him in's Lodging then; I have a mind to sup with him. If he's such rare company now he's sober, what will he be over a Bottle?

Mast. What the Devil would this old Spark be at? I think he's as mad as any of 'em.   [*Enter* Juletta.

Jul. [*aside.*] He's in, and now have at him—Are you the Master, Sir?

Mast. Yes, What do you want?

Jul. I have a business from the Duke of *Medina*. Is there not an old Gentleman come lately here?

Mast. Yes; and a mad one too; but he's no Prisoner.

Jul. There's a Letter, pray read it——[*aside*] I shall be with you now, i'faith, my old Master; I'll rouze your Blood now to the purpose; I'll teach ye to plague Women, ye old put you.

Mast. This Letter says the Gentleman is Lunatick: I half suspected it.

Jul. 'Tis but too true, Sir; And such pranks he has plaid——

Mast. He's some Man of note, I suppose, the Duke Commands me with such care to look to him. He's in haste too, I find, for his Recovery; for he bids me spare no Correction.

Jul. He directed me to say the same thing to you. Pray, Sir, have no regard to his Age or Quality: But since 'tis for his Good, strap him soundly.

Mast. He shall have the sharpest Discipline, I promise you.——Pray how did you get him hither?

Jul. By a Train I laid for him; he's in Love with a Boy you must know; there lies his Crack.

Mast. He came hither to seek one.

Jul. Yes, I sent him. We should never have got him here by force.

Mast. Here was a Boy last Night.   *Jul.* He did not see him, did he?

Mast. No; he was slipt away first.

Jul. So much the better. Pray, Sir, look well to your Charge; I must see him lodg'd before I go; the Duke order'd me. I fancy you'll find him very rough.

Mast. Oh! that's nothing. We are us'd to that; we can be as rough as he, I'll warrant him.

Jul. See here he comes.——[*aside*] Oh! how it tickles me!

Enter Alphonso *and* 2d. Keeper.

Alp. What doſt talk to me of noises? I'll have more noise. I love noise! I'll have 'em all loose together. Your Maſter has let my Boy loose, and I'll do as much by his.

2 *Keep.* Will you go out, and not make diſturbances here?

Alp. I won't go out, you Rascal; I'll have 'em all out with me. There's no body mad here, but thee and thy Maſter.——[*Irons shake.*] Hey brave Boys! Mad Boys! Mad Boys!

Jul. Do you perceive him now?

Maſt. 'Tis too apparent.——D'ye hear, Sir? Pray will ye make less ſtir, and see your Chamber?   *Alp.* Ha!

2 *Keep.* Nay, I thought he was mad. I gad our Maſter has found him out. I'll have one long lash at your back, i' faith, old Spark.

Maſt. Come, Sir, will you retire quietly to your Chamber?

Alp. My Chamber! What doſt thou mean by my Chamber? Where's the Boy, you Blockhead you?

Maſt. Look ye, Sir, we are People of few words here; either go quietly to your Chamber, or we shall carry you there with a Witness.

Alp. A ſtrange fellow this!——And what Chamber is't thou would'ſt have me go quietly to?

Maſt. A Chamber the Duke has order'd to be prepar'd for you within? you shall be well lodg'd, don't fear.

Alp. The Duke! What, what, what haſt thou got in thy Head? what Duke, Monkey, ha?

Maſt. Hark ye, Sir, let me advise you, don't expose your self; you are an old Gentleman, and shou'd be Wise; you are a little mad, which you don't perceive; your Friends have found it out, and have deliver'd you over to me. [*Alph. Spits in his Face.*]——Say ye so, old Boy?—— A hey! Seize him here, and fifty slaps o' th' back presently.

Jul. [*aside.*] I'm afraid they'll make him mad indeed.——Rare sport!

Alp. Hold, hold, hold, hold, hold.——Hark ye, Gentlemen, Gentlemen, one word, but one word. Pray do me the favour to shew me my Chamber.

Maſt. O-ho! I'm glad to see you begin to come to your self, Sir. I don't doubt, by the blessing of Heaven, and proper methods, to bring you to your senses again.

Alp. Yes, Sir, I hope all will be well. Really I find my self at this time, as I think, very sensible——of some ſtroaks o'the back.   [*Aside.*

Maſt. I can see your madness very much abated.

Alp. Yes, truly, I hope it is; tho' I can't say but——a——I am ſtill ——a——little discompos'd.

Maſt. There muſt be some time to reſtore a Man. *Rome* was not built in a day. But since the Duke has so much kindness for you to be in haſte for your Cure, when your next fit comes, we'll double the Dose.——Here, lead the Gentleman to his Chamber. But he muſt have no Supper to night; take care of that.

Alp. Pray, Sir, may I sleep?

Maſt. A little you may. In the morning we'll take 30 or 40 Ounces of Blood away; which with a Watergrewel-Dyet for a Week or ten days, may moderate things mightily.——Go carry him in, I'll follow presently.

Alp. What a Wretched Dog am I!   [*Exit* Keepers *and* Alp.

Maſt. You see, Sir, the Duke's Orders are obey'd.   *Jul.* I'll not fail to acquaint him with it. Pray let the old Gentleman want nothing but his Wits.

Maſt. He shall be taken perfect care of.——My humble Duty to his Grace.   [*Exit Maſter.*

Jul. So, now I think I have fix'd thee. This has succeeded rarely!—— I cou'd burſt with laughing now, lye down and rowl about the Room, I'm so tickl'd with it: But I have other business to do; now's my time to serve my Miſtress. Good Stars guide me where she is, and I have nothing more to ask you, but a Husband.   [*Exit.*

ACT V.

Enter Seberto *and* Curio.

Seb. O'My Conscience we have quite loſt him: He's not gone home, we heard from thence this morning.

Cur. Faith, let's e'en turn back; this is but a Wildgoose-Chace.

Seb. No, hang't, let's see the end of these Adventures now we are out: They muſt end soon one way or other.

Cur. Which way shall we go? We have scowr'd the Champion-Country, and all the Villages, already.

Seb. We'll beat these Woods; and if nothing ſtart, we'll to *Segovia.*

Cur. I'm afraid he's sick, or fallen into some danger. He has no Guide nor Servant with him.

Seb. Hang him, he's tough and hardy; he'll bear a great deal.

Cur. Shall we part, and go several ways?

Seb. No, that will be melancholy; let's e'en keep on together. Come, we'll cross here firſt; and as we find the Paths, let them direct us. [*Exeunt.*

Enter Alinda *and* Juletta.

Jul. Indeed, Madam, 'tis very cruel in you to shew this ſtrange Miſtruſt of me. Have I not always serv'd you faithfully? Why do you shun me thus? What have I done to call my Truth in question? But I see you are ſtill doubtful; 'tis enough; I'll leave you; and may you light of one will serve you better. Farewel.

Al. Prithee forgive me. I know thou art faithful, and thou art welcome to me; a welcome Partner to my Miseries. Thou know'ſt I love thee too.

Jul. I have indeed thought so.

Al. Alas! my Fears have so diſtracted me, I durſt not truſt my self.

Jul. Pray throw 'em by then, and let 'em diſtract you so no more; at leaſt, consider how to prevent 'em. Pray put off this Fool's Coat; tho' it has kept you secret hitherto, 'tis known now, and will betray you. Your Arch Enemy *Roderigo* is abroad, and a thousand more are looking for you.

Al. I know it, and wou'd gladly change my Dress if I knew how: But, alas! I have no other.

Jul. I'll equip you. I lay laſt night at a poor Widow's house here in the Thicket, where I'll carry you, and disguise you anew; my self too to attend you.

Al. But haſt thou any Mony? for mine's all gone.

Jul. Enough for this occasion; I did not come out empty.

Al. Haſt thou seen *Roderigo* lately?

Jul. This very morning, in these Woods. Take heed, for he has got a new Shape.

Al. A Pilgrim's Habit, I know it. Was he alone?

Jul. No, Madam. And, which made me wonder, he was in Company with that very Pilgrim, that handsome Man you were concern'd you gave nothing to.

Al. Is't possible?

Jul. The very same.——See how one may be deceiv'd! I shou'd ne'er have thought him a Companion for such a Villain.

Al. Did they seem Friends?

Jul. The greateſt that cou'd be.

Al. Intimate?

Jul. Walk'd with their Arms about one another's Waſte.

Al. What can this mean?

Jul. Lord! how she trembles!

Al. Canſt thou shew 'em me?

Jul. Not for the World in this Dress: But come with me to my Old Woman's; and when we are new cas'd, I'll shew you any thing.

Al. Let's be speedy then, for I am full of Agitation. Come, as we go, I'll tell thee all my Secrets.

Jul. I'll keep 'em faithfully.—This is the way, Madam.   [*Exeunt.*

[SCENE II.]

Enter Governor, Verdugo, *and Citizens.*

Gov. Use all your Sports, good people, all your Solemnities; 'Tis the King's Birth-day, a Day we ought to honour.

1 *Cit.* We will, Noble Governor, and make *Segovia* ring with Joy.

2 *Cit.* We shou'd be a little more hearty in our Mirth tho', if your Honour wou'd take into your Consideration the Miseries we suffer by these Outlaws here. Our Trade's undone by 'em, Strangers dare not come near us; besides, our Wives and Daughters make woful Complaints of 'em.

Gov. I'm sorry for't, and have Orders from the King to help ye; You shan't be long perplex'd with 'em.

3 *Cit.* 'Tis time they were routed truly; for they grow fearful Confident. They'll come to Church sometimes, and carry off our Altar-Plate. Father *Dominic* has curs'd 'em all till he's grown hoarse again; so he says they are damn'd, which is some comfort.

1 *Cit.* If your Honour were not here to awe 'em a little, they'd come and make us a Visit at this good time.

3 *Cit.* Yes; they'd eat all our Meat, drink up our Drink, ring our Bells backwards, piss out our Bonfires; and when their Mettle was up, have at the Fairest i'faith.

2 *Cit.* Nay, have at All: They are none of your nice ones. My poor Mother's Fourscore and odd, and she made shift to get her self ravish'd amongst 'em.

Gov. Are they so fierce? D'ye hear, *Verdugo?* after this Solemnity is over, I'll send you with a Party to attack 'em. We'll try if we can tame 'em.

Ver. Their Captain *Roderigo* is to be piti'd; A Gentleman, and a brave Soldier too.

Gov. The Court has not rewarded him as his Services have deserv'd; their neglect of him has urg'd him to this Course.

Ver. They have a hungry Eye on his Estate; 'tis That, I doubt, keeps back his Pardon.

Gov. It had been pass'd e're this else: but he wants Temper to discern the Cause.

Ver. Have you ne'er heard, Sir, of the Noble *Pedro* yet?

Gov. Never. I fear he's dead. The Court bewails his loss; the King himself laments him.

Ver. He has reason; 'twas in his Service he undid himself: And if he had rewarded him as he deserv'd, h'had had him still to merit more.

Gov. If he be still alive, and e're returns, I know he is resolv'd to make him happy. But come, let's to the Church, and there begin the Celebration of our Royal Master's Birth-day.

[SCENE III.]

Enter Roderigo *and* Pedro.

Rod. How sweet these solitary Places are! how wantonly the Wind blows through the Leaves, and Courts and Plays with 'em! Will ye sit down and sleep? 'Tis wondrous Hot.

Ped. I cannot sleep, my Friend: My Heart's too watchful to admit of Slumbers.

Rod. The Murmurs of this Stream perhaps may lull you into Reſt: Hark! the Birds join too to Ease you. Pray sit down.

aside.] I fain wou'd wooe his Fancy into Peace; I see 'tis much disturb'd——Will you not try to take a moment's Reſt?

Ped. It is impossible: Have you seen no one yet?

Rod. No Creature.

Ped. What ſtrange Musick was that we heard far off?

Rod. I cannot guess; it was uncommon; sometimes it seem'd hard by, at leaſt I thought so.

Ped. It pleas'd me much: what cou'd it be? here's no Inhabitants.

Rod. They talk of Fairies, and such airy Beings: If there are such, methinks they cou'd not chuse a lovelier Dwelling.

Ped. Those Rocks there look like inchanted Cells, form'd for such Inhabitants. Hark! more Musick! [*Musick.*] 'Tis here again! Hark! gentle *Roderigo!* O Love! what fuel's this to feed thy Flame? O *Alinda!*

Rod. [*aside.*] By all his Woes, he weeps.   [*They lye down.*

Enter Alinda *and* Juletta *like Old Women.*

Rod. What are these?   *Ped.* What!

Rod. Those there; those things that come upon us: Did not I say these Woods had Wonder in 'em?

Jul. Now you may view 'em: There are the Men you wish'd for. There they are both; Now you may boldly talk with 'em, and ne're be guess'd at. Don't be afraid: See! they're surpris'd! they don't know what to make of us!

Alin. I tremble!——

Jul. Then you spoil all: Take Courage and attack 'em, I'll bring you off I'll warrant ye.

Alin. 'Tis he and *Roderigo;* What Peace dwells in their Faces? What a friendly Calm?

Rod. They seem Mortal: They come upon us ſtill.

Ped. Let's meet 'em; Fear won't become us. Hail Reverend Dames!

Alin. What, do you seek, good Men?

Ped. We wou'd seek happier Fortunes.

Alin. Seek 'em, and make 'em.

> Lie not ſtill, nor longer here;
> Here inhabits nought but Fear:
> Be Conſtant, Good, in Faith be clear,
> Fortune will wait ye everywhere.

Ped. Whither shou'd we go? For we believe thee, and will obey thee.
Alin. Go to *Segovia*; and there before the Altar pay thy Vows, thy Gifts and Prayers; unload thy Heaviness.

> There shed thy mournful Tears, and gain thy Suit;
> Such honeſt noble Showres ne'er wanted Fruit.

Jul. to *Rod.* And next for you.
> See how he Quakes!
> A secure Conscience never shakes.
> Thou haſt been ill, be so no more;
> A good Retreat, is a great Store:
> Thou haſt Commanded Men of Might;
> Command thy self, and then thou'rt right.

Alin. Command thy Will, thy foul Desires;
> Quench thy wild, unhallow'd Fires.
> Command thy Mind; let that be pure;
> A Blessing then thou may'ſt procure.

Jul. Take sage Advice: Go say thy Prayers;
> Thou haſt as many Sins as Hairs.
> Of Lawless Men, a Lawless Chief;
> A Rebel bloody, and a Thief.

Alin. Retire thou Trembling Guilt, retire;
> And purge thee perfeɕt in his Fire:
> His Life observe; be that thy Guide,
> And Heav'n may then on thy side.

Jul. At *Segovia*, both appear.
Alin. Be wise, and Happiness is near.
Both. Be wise, and Happiness is near.   [*Exeunt.*
Rod. Aſtonishment! what can this mean? They know my very Soul.
Ped. Mine they've Inspir'd:—Be wise, and Happiness is near. Those were their parting words. They had the awful Sound of sacred Truth, and I have faith to Comfort me. Come on my Friend. The Oracle enjoyns an easy Pilgrimage. Let's try what Fate intends us.   [*Exeunt.*

[SCENE IV.]

[Enter Master of the Mad-house, Seberto and Curio.]

Curi. We have told you what he is, what time we have sought him, his Nature and his Name. The seeming Boy too, we have given you I think a fair Account of.

Seb. That the Duke shou'd send that Letter, is Impossible; He knows him not. And for his madness, that we both can clear him of. A Humour-ist he is indeed a great one, violent too on every small occasion——but no more——

Curi. 'Twas some Trick that brought him hither; Th' Letter and the Page, both Counterfeits: If therefore you'd be well advis'd, don't keep him longer here.

Mas. Gentlemen you have satisfied me, and I'll release him: Tho' I must confess, whether you'll call it madness or not, I believe a little more of our Discipline wou'd do the old Gentleman a kindness. But I'll dispute no longer—you shall have him.

Seb. Sir, we thank you. *[Enter Lopez.*

Mas. Here, bring out the old Gentleman, I believe he may be some-thing weak, for we have Dieted him low, and taken a good deal of Blood from him.

Curi. Poor *Alphonso.*

[Enter Keeper with Alphonso.]

Seb. Poor *Alphonso* indeed! Was there ever such a Skeleton! Sir, I'm glad once more to meet with you, *[To Alphon.*

Curi. I'm overjoy'd to find you.

Alph. Soft, no flights: Passions are all forbid here. Let your Tongue go like a Pendulum, steddy: or that Gentleman there will regulate your Motion, with fifty Stroaks o' the back presently.

Seb. There's no danger: You are safe too; we have satisfied the Master, who, and what you are; And he has consented to release you.

Mas. Yes, Sir, these Gentlemen have assur'd me you are a sober Per-son, so I ask your excuse for what's past, and restore you to your Liberty.

Alp. Very concise indeed: Sir, I am much beholding to you truly, and do confess with great humility I have not deserv'd the Favours you have been pleas'd to bestow upon me. But if I have the Honour to see you at my House, I shall not forget to return your Bounty with some Strokes of Acknowledgement.

Mas. Sir, your very humble Servant.

Alp. Sir, Entirely yours.

Mas. Farewel Gentlemen. *[Exit Master.*

Alp. Come Friends, one under one Arm, and t'other under t'other. I muſt make a pair of Crutches of ye——

Seb. You are very weak indeed.

Curi. You look wretchedly.

Alp. A little in Love only, that's all. Ah *Seberto.* Ah *Curio*—such Discipline, the Lord have mercy on me. Had I been here till to morrow morning, this Dog wou'd not have left me Six Ounces of Blood in my whole Body.

Seb. Can you imagine who put this Trick upon you?

Alph. The Devil to be sure; but who gave him his Cue I can't tell—— Come, carry me off: Lead me to Church, I'm in a very Religious fit at this time, and will give some small Thanks for my Delivery: when that's over, I'll be reveng'd.   [*Exit.*

SCENE [V] an Altar.   [*Solemn Musick.*

Enter Governor, Verdugo, *Courtiers, Ladies, who make their several Offerings Kneeling.*

Gov. This——To Devotion sacred be.
   This——To the Kings Prosperity.
   This—To the Queen, and Chaſtity.

Cor. Sings. Long live the King;
   Prolong ye Powers, Prolong his Sway;
   Repeat, repeat this Joyful Day,
   Long live the King.

Ver.   These Oblations firſt we bring
   To Purge our selves: These to the King:
   To Love and Beauty these: Accept our Offering,

Cor.   Long live the King, &c.

               Enter Pedro *and* Roderigo.

Ped.   For our selves firſt Thus we bend;
Rod.   Forgive us Heaven, and be our Friend.
   With Glory bless, and Long preserve
   The Prince we do, or ought to serve;
   Accept our Offerings we Implore;
   The Peace which we have Loſt reſtore.

Ped.   Give me *Alinda,* and I ask no more.
Co.   Long Live the King, &c.

               Enter Alphonso, Curio, Seberto.

(138)

Alp. For my Loſt Wits (Let me see)
First I pray; and Secondly,
To be at home again and Free;
And if I Travel more,——hang me.
Next for the King, and for the Queen,
That they be wise, and never seen
Where I was, in the Madman's Inn.
For my Daughter I should pray;
But since the Strumpet's run away,
In Heaven's presence I forsake her
And give the Devil leave to take her.

[*Co.*] Long live the King, *&c.*

Enter Alinda *and* Juletta *like Shepherdesses.*

Jule. Here they all are, Madam, but fear nothing: The Place proteꞔts you. My old *Bilboa* Maſter, o' my Conscience. How in the name of mischief got he out? but they have pepper'd him I see. That's some Comfort.

Alin. Hail to the sacred Place.   [*Going to the Altar.*

Seb. 'Tis She, sure.

Cur. 'Tis, certainly.

Ped. Is it a Vision? or is it She?

Rod. 'Tis she, and what you were fortold is now at hand. Rejoice, my Friend, for happiness attends you.

Gov. [*aside.*] What is't these Strangers seem so much surpriz'd at?

Alph. I had a Daughter once with juſt such a young whorish Leer as that: A Filly too, that waited on her; much such a Slut as t'other. Are they come to keeping of Goats: 'tis very well.

Alind. Thus we kneel, and thus we pray,
Happiness attend this Day.
Our sacrifice we hither bring,
And sue for Blessings on the King.

Julet. These of Purple, Damask, Green,
Sacred to the Virtuous Queen,
Here we hang; As these are now,
May her Glories spring and flow.

Alind. These for our selves, our Hopes and Loves,
Full of Pinks and Ladies Gloves.
Of hearts-ease too, which we wou'd fain,
As we labour for, Attain.
Hear me Heav'n, and as I bend
With faith and hope, some comfort send;

Julett. Hear her, hear her, if there be
A spotless Sweetness, this is She.

Co. Long live the King, &c.

Ped. Now *Roderigo* I may ſtand in need of your Assiſtance.

Rod. My Life is yours.

Ped. Then with a Joy that Lovers know, but none can else conceive, Let me approach this beauteous Wanderer.

Alin. O *Pedro.*

Ped. My Life, my Heav'n.

Alp. *Pedro*: The Devil it is?

Gov. *Pedro*, Noble *Pedro*, are we so happy to have you ſtill among us! This is an Unexpected Blessing.

Alph. [*aside.*] A very Great Blessing indeed.

Ped. In spite of all my Griefs, Life ſtill prevails: Fate seems to have some farther business for me; if 'tis to wander on with fruitless Care, and buffet ſtill with Disappointments, let Manhood be my Aid. But if the sullen cloud that long has lowring hung about my head, be deſtin'd to withdraw, 'tis the warm Influence of your blessing Sir, that muſt disperse it.   [*Kneels to* Alphonso.

Alp. I bless thee!——ha, ha:——Damn thee.

Gov. Sir, tho' I am a Stranger both to you, and the Requeſt the Noble *Pedro* makes you, his merit's so well known to me, that I muſt be his second in his suit, and tell you nothing can er'e be in your Power to grant, but his desert may claim.——

Alp. I don't know what his desert may claim, Governor: But if he claims any thing but a Gallows, he's a very impudent Fellow.

Rod. Perhaps I being a Mediator, Sir, may change your thoughts of him——

Alp. *Roderigo?*

Rod. *Roderigo*, Sir, becomes a supplicant for *Pedro*, that you wou'd bless your self in blessing him, and bless him with the Fair *Alinda.*

Alp. [*aside.*] Here's a Dog for you: He finds the Jade's a Scamperer, so he has a mind to be off of the Lay.

to Rod. Are you serious in this requeſt, Sir?

Rod. Moſt serious, Sir,

Alp. [*aside.*] I believe you may. Let me see: he has a mind to be rid of her, why should not I? *Pedro's* a Dog, and if I cou'd hang him, I wou'd. But since I can't, I'll be reveng'd another way: He shall marry the Whore.

[*to Ped.*] Look ye Sir; and Madam, [*Bowing to* Alinda.] I have made some short Reflections upon the present Poſture of Affairs, and am come to a short Conclusion. As to my Blessing, I can't Conveniently spare it you; but if you can contrive to bless one another, you may e'en be as Blessed as you please.

Ped. Moſt Generous *Alphonso.*——

Alp. Moſt Courtly *Pedro:* you may spare your Compliment; for if you take my word for it, the Present I have made you do's not deserve it.

Jule. But I that know her better than he that got her, say she deserves the world.——

Alp. Hark you, Madam, you had a Gillian once; nimble Chaps I think we call'd her: Pray is this the Lady?

Jule. No, Sir, She's at home as you order'd her; I'm a little Footboy that walk a Nights, and Frighten old Gentlemen, make 'em lose Hats and Cloaks.

Alp. And Horses too, ha?

Jule. Sometimes I do Sir, when the Case requires it. I teach 'em the way too through Hedges and Ditches: And how to break their Shins againſt a Stile.

Alp. A very pretty Art truly.

Jule. Sometimes I'm a Drum, Sir; a Drum at midnight, Ran tan dan, dra dan tan, Sir; a Page too upon occasion to carry Letters for the securing of old Strolers.

Alph. Thou art the Devil.

Jule. I'm worse, Sir, I'm an old Woman sometimes that tells Fortunes.

Rod. Ha!

Jule. And fright Pilgrims, and send 'em to *Segovia* for their Fortunes. I am Musick too, any thing to do her good. And now she has got her Lover, I am *Juletta* again, and at your service Sir, if you please to forgive me.

Alp. I dare do no otherwise, leſt thou shou'dſt follow me ſtill: so I desire we may be Friends with all my heart; and Gentlemen, if any of you have a mind to marry her——

Jule. Sir, I am oblig'd to you; but I'm marry'd to my Miſtriss; with her I hope to pass some three or fourscore Years; so when you have any more Pranks to Play, Sir, you know where to have me——

Alp. 'Tis very well, I ſhall be sure to send to thee.

Ped. One reconciliation more lies on my hands: In which I muſt engage th' generous Governor. *Roderigo,* Sir, is not unknown to you; nor is he a Stranger to your intereſt with the King. I hope you will employ it to reſtore him.

Gov. The King indeed is much incens'd; but when his merit shall be laid before him, I hope he'll find it easy to forget his Crimes. Be it my Care to set him right at Court.

Alp. And mine to get home to my house again; and if I leave it for such another Expedition.

To Jule. May'ſt thou be my Fellow-Traveller.

Gov. I hope before you go, Sir, you'll share with us, an Entertainment the late great Poet of our Age prepar'd to Celebrate this Day. Let the Masque begin.

SONG of a *Scholar* and his *Mistress*, who being Cross'd by their Friends, fell mad for one another; and now first meet in *Bedlam*.

Written by Mr. DRYDEN.

[*Musick within.*]

  [*The Lovers enter at Opposite Doors, each held by a Keeper.*]

Phillis. LOok, look, I see——I see my Love appear:
    'Tis he——'Tis he alone;
    For, like him, there is none:
   'Tis the dear, dear Man, 'tis thee, Dear.

Amyntas. Hark! the Winds War
   The foamy Waves roar;
   I see a Ship afar,
   Tossing and Tossing, and making to the Shoar:
    But what's that I view,
    So Radiant of Hue,
   St *Hermo*, St *Hermo*, that sits upon the Sails?
    Ah! No, no no.
   St *Hermo*, Never, never shone so bright;
   'Tis *Phillis*, only *Phillis*, can shoot so fair a Light:
   'Tis *Phillis*, 'tis *Phillis*, that saves the Ship alone,
   For all the Winds are hush'd, and the Storm is overblown.

Phillis. Let me go, let me run, let me fly to his Arms.

Amyntas. If all the Fates combine,
   And all the Furies join,
   I'll force my way to *Phillis*, and break through the Charm.
   [*Here they break from their Keepers; run to each
       other, and embrace.*]

Phillis. Shall I Marry the Man I love?
    And shall I conclude my Pains?
   Now blest be the Powers above,
   I feel the Blood bound in my Veins;
   With a lively Leap it began to move,
    And the Vapours leave my Brains.

Amyntas. Body join'd to Body, and Heart join'd to Heart,
    To make sure of the Cure;
   Go call the Man in Black, to mumble o're his part.

Phillis. But suppose he should stay——

Amyntas. At worst if he delay;
    'Tis a Work must be done;
   We'll borrow but a Day,
    And the better the sooner begun.   [*Chorus of Both.*

[*At worst if he delay, etc.*:   [*They run out together hand in hand.*

THE SECULAR MASQUE.

Written by Mr. DRYDEN.

Enter Janus.

Janus. CHronos, Chronos, *mend thy Pace,*
    An hundred times the rowling Sun
Around the Radiant Belt has run
In his revolving Race.
Behold, behold, the Goal in sight,
Spread thy Fans, and wing thy flight.

Enter Chronos, *with a Scythe in his hand, and a great Globe on his Back,*
which he sets down at his entrance.

Chronos. Weary, weary of my weight,
    Let me, let me drop my Freight,
      And leave the World behind.
I could not bear
Another Year
The Load of Human-kind.

Enter Momus Laughing.

Momus. Ha! ha! ha! Ha! ha! ha! well hast thou done
    To lay down thy Pack,
    And lighten thy Back,
The World was a Fool, e'er since it begun,
And since neither *Janus,* nor *Chronos,* nor I,
    Can hinder the Crimes,
    Or mend the Bad Times,
'Tis better to Laugh than to Cry.
Cho. of all 3. *T'is better to Laugh than to Cry.*

Janus. Since *Momus* comes to laugh below,
    Old Time begin the Show.
That he may see, in every Scene,
What changes in this Age have been.
Chronos. Then Goddess of the Silver Bar begin.

Horns, or Hunting-Music within.

Enter Diana.

(143)

Diana.　With Horns and with Hounds I waken the Day,
　　　　And hye to my Woodland walks away;
　　　　I tuck up my Robe, and am buskin'd soon,
　　　　And tye to my Forehead a wexing moon.
　　　　I course the fleet Stagg, unkennel the Fox,
　　　　And chase the wild Goats or'e summets of Rocks,
　　　　With shouting and hooting we pierce thro' the Sky;
　　　　And Eccho turns Hunter, and doubles the Cry.

Cho. of all. *With shouting and hooting, we pierce through the Sky*
　　　　And Eccho turns Hunter, and doubles the Cry.

Janus.　Then our Age was in it's Prime,
Chronos.　Free from Rage.
Diana.　——— ——— And free from Crime.
Momus.　A very Merry, Dancing, Drinking,
　　　　Laughing, Quaffing, and unthinking Time.

Cho. of all. *Then our Age was in it's Prime*
　　　　Free from Rage, and free from Crime,
　　　　A very Merry, Dancing, Drinking,
　　　　Laughing, Quaffing, and unthinking Time.

　　　　Dance of Diana's *Attendants.*

　　　　Enter Mars.

Mars.　Inspire the Vocal Brass, Inspire;
　　　　The World is past its Infant Age:
　　　　　　Arms and Honour,
　　　　　　Arms and Honour,
　　　　Set the Martial Mind on Fire,
　　　　And kindle Manly Rage.
　　　　Mars has lookt the Sky to Red;
　　　　And Peace, the Lazy Good, is fled.
　　　　Plenty, Peace, and Pleasure fly;
　　　　　　The Sprightly Green
　　　　In *Woodland*-Walks, no more is seen;
　　　　The Sprightly Green, has drunk the *Tyrian* Dye.

Cho. of all. *Plenty, Peace, &c.*

Mars.　Sound the Trumpet, Beat the Drum,
　　　　Through all the World around;
　　　　Sound a Reveille, Sound, Sound,
　　　　　　The Warrior God is come.

Cho. of all. *Sound the Trumpet, &c.*

(144)

Momus.   Thy Sword within the Scabbard keep,
          And let Mankind agree;
        Better the World were fast asleep,
          Than kept awake by Thee.
        The Fools are only thinner,
          With all our cost and care;
        But neither side a winner,
          For things are as they were.

Cho. of all. The Fools are only, &c.

Enter Venus.

Venus.   Calms appear, when Storms are past;
        Love will have his Hour at last:
        Nature is my kindly Care;
        Mars destroys, and I repair;
        Take me, take me, while you may,
        Venus comes not ev'ry Day.

Cho. of all. Take her, take her, &c.

Chronos.   The World was then so light,
        I scarcely felt the Weight;
        Joy rul'd the Day, and Love the Night.
        But since the Queen of Pleasure left the Ground,
          I faint, I lag,
          And feebly drag
        The pond'rous Orb around.

Momus.   All, all, of a piece throughout;

Pointing to Diana.   Thy Chase had a Beast in View;

to *Mars.*   Thy Wars brought nothing about;

to *Venus.*   Thy Lovers were all untrue.

Janus.   'Tis well an Old Age is out,

Chro.   And time to begin a New.

Cho. of all. All, all, of a piece throughout;
        Thy Chase had a Beast in View;
        Thy Wars brought nothing about;
        Thy Lovers were all untrue.
        'Tis well an Old Age is out,
        And time to begin a New.

Dance of Huntsmen, Nymphs, Warriours and Lovers.

FINIS.

EPILOGUE

By Mr. *Dryden*.

Perhaps the Parson stretch'd a point too far,
⠀⠀⠀When with our Theatres he wag'd a War.
He tells you, That this very Moral Age
Receiv'd the first Infection from the Stage.
But sure, a banisht Court, with Lewdness fraught,
The Seeds of open Vice returning brought.
Thus Lodg'd, (as Vice by great Example thrives,)
It first debauch'd the Daughters and the Wives.
London, a fruitful Soil, yet never bore
So plentiful a Crop of Horns before.
The Poets, who must live by Courts or starve,
Were proud, so good a Government to serve;
And mixing with Buffoons and Pimps profain,
Tainted the Stage, for some small Snip of Gain.
For they, like Harlots under Bawds profest,
Took all th' ungodly pains, and got the least.
Thus did the thriving Malady prevail,
The Court, its Head, the Poets but the Tail.
The Sin was of our Native growth, 'tis true;
The Scandal of the Sin was wholly new.
Misses there were, but modestly conceal'd;
White-Hall the naked Venus first reveal'd.
Who standing, as at Cyprus, in her Shrine,
The Strumpet was ador'd with Rites Divine.
E're this, if Saints had any secret Motion,
'Twas Chamber Practice all, and Close Devotion.
I pass the Peccadillo's of their time;
Nothing but open Lewdness was a Crime.
A Monarch's Blood was venial to the Nation,
Compar'd with one foul Act of Fornication.
Now, they would silence us, and shut the Door
That let in all the barefac'd Vice before.
As to reforming us, which some pretend,
That work in England is without an end;
Well we may change, but we shall never mend.

EPILOGUE

Yet, if you can but bear the present Stage,
We hope much better of the coming Age.
What wou'd you say, if we shou'd first begin
To stop the Trade of Love, behind the Scene:
Where Actresses *make bold with married Men?*
For while abroad so prodigal the Dolt *is,*
Poor Spouse at home as ragged as a Colt is.
In short, we'll grow as Moral as we can,
Save here and there a Woman *or a* Man:
But neither you, nor we, with all our pains,
Can make clean work; there will be some Remains,
While you have still your Oats, *and we our* Hains.

THE

FALSE

FRIEND

A COMEDY

As it is ACTED

AT THE

Theatre Royal

IN

Drury Lane,

By

His Majesty's Servants.

Source

IN 1700 there was printed at The Hague, and issued by Meindert Untwerf, a duodecimo collection, " Le / Theatre / Espagnol / Ou les meilleurs / Comedies / Des plus fameux Auteurs / Espagnols. / Traduites en François." The first of these was " Le Traître Puni," of which this is the usual free Vanburghian adaptation. The French translation was a *ballon d'essai* on the part of Le Sage, in whose finished works it appears with some inconsiderable alterations which are merely in the nature of polishing. The verbal differences are considerable, and some portions are very much cut, thus bringing the play nearer the very rigid form Le Sage came to prefer. Dancourt put Le Sage's version into verse as " La Trahison Punie."

The text of 1700, with which we are concerned, since it is the one Vanbrugh evidently worked on (perhaps Tonson, who published the English version, brought it back from one of his visits to Amsterdam), differs considerably from the original, " La Traicion busca el castigo," by Francisco de Rojas Zorilla. The Spanish is in verse, and in three acts. Le Sage, making the whole less rough and more symmetrical, expands the last act into three, and certainly de Rojas's third act is confusingly complicated.

Vanbrugh's translation is fairly faithful, especially in the first three acts. In the fourth act he interpolates a scene, of which the Spanish also is innocent, namely, that between Don Guzman and Jacinta. The names are slightly changed, for some reason, and sometimes the speeches are given to different persons. The Don John of the original is the Don Pedro of Vanbrugh's play, Vanbrugh giving the first name to the more Juanesque character. But instead of allowing Don John to describe his erotic technique himself (Act I), he gives the speech to the valet. Where necessary for the English stage, Vanbrugh thickens a little, as was always his custom when translating. We may take the opening scenes of the play as illustration. A few verses of the Spanish are given, for the benefit of the curious, though there is no need to suppose that Vanbrugh ever looked at it, nor is there any evidence that he knew a word of the language.[1]

> *Don André.* O me teneis por menguado,
> ò os parezco muy sufrido,
> hermano os he recibido
> por confejero ò criado?
> *Mogicon.* Que agradezcas es razon,
> que te he aconsejado bien. (1640 Ed.)

Le Sage opens as follows:

Mogicon. Ahi! ahi! ahi!

D. André. Je te rouërai de coups, maraud, si tu t'avises jamais. . . .

---

[1] Ward supposed it from knowing only Le Sage's later version: he quotes a passage which he says Vanbrugh restored from the Spanish, whereas it comes from 1700

Mogicon. Doucement, Seigneur Don André, doucement, quel mal vous ai-je fait?
D. André. Ou tu me prends pour un grand sot, ou tu me crois bien endurant.
Mogicon. Oh! pour endurant, non, vous me donnés tous les jours trop de marques du contraire.
D. André. Je te donne ton congé. Etc.

Vanbrugh sometimes weakens the original a little. Compare the parting remarks of Don John and Don Felix in Act I: " I won't Marry." " 'Tis enough." with:

D. Felix. Tenez-vous sur vos gardes.
——Et vous sur vos bequilles.

Vanbrugh was always inclined to rely more on humour than on wit, but perhaps he thought that particular piece too cheap or too ill-natured (it is at any rate difficult to translate); but often he improved the wit. Where he has:

D. Pedro. Just as he was, I find, Galliard still.
Lopez. I find it very unwholesome to be otherwise, Sir.

Le Sage merely makes Mogicon reply sententiously, " la joye est la mère nourrice de la santé."

But where Vanbrugh most improves for the English stage he introduces that touch of burlesque repugnant to the French taste, but by no means so to the Spanish. Compare:

Galindo. Voilà une porte qui est bien étroite aujourd'hui.
Galindo. The Devil's in this door; I think 'tis grown too little for me. Shrunk this wet weather, I presume.

which is a touch Quevedo might not have been ashamed of.

Text

THE text is from the first quarto of 1702, and is collated with its next appearance, namely, the first collected edition of 1719. The text, however, is faithfully that of 1702, except where otherwise noted, down to the curious punctuation. The edition of 1719 has, however, been followed as regards the names of the characters before speaking; e.g. *Don John* instead of *D. Jo*, italicising the whole, however, instead of printing Don *John*.

Theatrical History

THERE is no record of the first performance of *The False Friend*, which, to judge from the date of publication (*Post Man*, 10 February), must have taken place some time in late January or early February, 1702. Whincop says that it was acted "with good success," but his is a lonely voice; and indeed, seeing that it was not revived for eight years, as far as the evidence goes, it looks as though it failed. The cast was not an over-strong one, lacking the names of Betterton, since it was a Drury Lane production, Booth, Doggett, Barry and Bracegirdle, while Mrs. Oldfield was not yet an acknowledged star. However, it must have run to four performances, for "on the fourth day Cibber was hurt and could not act his part." At any rate, Bullock and Pinkethman were there, and Griffin, an obscure but fairly popular actor, who had left the stage for the army and returned.

Wilks, who had four years before come to London for the second time, where he was ever becoming more fixed in the popular favour, played Don Pedro. Originally from Smock Alley, he was to become one of the important managers with Cibber and Booth. "He was young, erect, and of a pleasing aspect," a good learner both of parts and "business," and though raw when he first came over, had improved himself by sheer hard work. He was, however, a very jealous actor. He founded his style on that of the unfortunately murdered Mountfort, and though the judicious withheld their highest praises, the majority gave him an exalted place. His fault was being a little too vivacious and vehement with his words, and he "would too frequently break into the time and measure of the harmony by too many spirited accents in one line." Though successful in tragedy, his voice was not full enough, a fact he himself regretted. But he was well-companioned in this play, for "Mrs. Oldfield and Mr. Wilks, by their frequently playing against one another, in our best comedies, very happily supported that humour and vivacity which is so peculiar to our English stage."

The play was revived at the Haymarket in 1710, was played three times at Drury Lane in 1715, and then was billed for Lincoln's Inn Fields on 14 October, 1724, "not acted 10 years." That excellent actor Quin took Don John, Ryan took Pedro, Mrs. Bullock played Leonora, a part she was still playing in the same theatre in 1732. It was acted four times. These long intervals betray the unpopularity of the play up to this date, but then it had a short run of favour, being acted yearly at Lincoln's Inn Fields until 1733, that is for ten years. Then Covent Garden took it over, producing it once in 1734, once in 1735, and three times in 1736.

It reappeared at that theatre on 18 March, 1738, with Delane playing Don John; Bridgewater Don Felix; Walker Don Guzman; and Hippisley Galindo. Mrs. Stevens played Jacinta. Hippisley was "a Comedian of a lively humour and droll pleasantry, which he often pushed to their full extent, but he would generally stop short when he was on the brink of excess or offence—at his first appearance he was always received with a loud laugh and a burst of applause . . . his own performance on the stage was much heightened by a distortion of his face, occasioned by an accidental burn in his youth." It was acted three times that season and three times the next.

For a performance at Covent Garden on 28 January, 1752, it was advertised as "not acted 8 years," so some revival must have taken place, presumably somewhere in the neighbourhood of 1742, as though these statements are apt to lengthen the time, they do not usually shorten them; but no record of this performance has come to hand. In the 1752 revival, when it was twice acted, Sparks played Don John; Ryan Pedro, as in 1724; Bridgewater playing Don Felix, as in 1738; and Mrs. Vincent Isabella. The part of Lopez was taken by Macklin. "His voice was strong, clear and resonant, and he had no vices of delivery and no stage tricks. He was robust in frame [he lived to be over a hundred], and his features were rugged and corrugated." "He anticipated Garrick in the reformation of the stage" (D.N.B.). At this time he was some sixty years of age. The performance was repeated on 6 February, 1753.

On 31 March, 1767, it was played at Drury Lane with Holland, Powell (not the old one), Yates, Mrs. Yates, and Baddeley in the cast, though it is not known what part each took. It may have been for the benefit of Yates. Its last appearance seems to have been in a version hacked about by Kemble, who played Don John, in which the catastrophe is altered, Don John not being killed as in the original. It was acted twice, the first time being 24 October, 1789, at Drury Lane, with Bannister junior playing Lopez; Wroughton Don Pedro; Barrymore Don Guzman; R. Palmer Galindo; Miss Farren Leonora; and Miss Pope Jacinta: a fairly strong cast. An ephemeral theatrical journal called *The Prompter* said that Bannister was everything that could be wished, and that Kemble excelled in action, though he did not always look the part. Once a play has got to the stage of being adapted it usually dies, and this *The False Friend* seems now to have done. This account is apart from the Irish adaptation *Friendship à la Mode* printed in 1766.

PROLOGUE

Spoken by Capt. GRIFFIN.

YOU Dread Reformers of an Impious Age,
 You awful Catta-nine-Tailes to the Stage,
 This once be Just, and in our Cause engage.

To gain your Favour, we your Rules Obey,
And Treat you with a Moral Piece to Day;
So Moral, we're afraid 'twill Damn the Play.

 For tho' y'ave long been Leagu'd (as People tell)
T'reduce the Power Exorbitant of Hell;
No Troops you send, t'abate it in this Field,
But leave us still expos'd, to starve, or yield.
Your Scouts indeed, sometimes come stealing in,
T'observe this Formidable Camp of Sin,
And whisper, If we'll Piously declare,
What Aids you then will send, to help us through the War.

 To this we Answer, we're a feeble State,
And cannot well afford to Love or Hate,
So shou'd not meddle much in your Debate.
But since your Cause is good, thus far we'll go,
When Portugal declares, we'll do so too.
Our Cases, as we think, are much alike,
And on the same Conditions, we should strike;
Send to their Aid a hundred Men of War,
To Ours, a hundred Squadrons of the Fair;
Rig out your Wives and Daughters all around,
(I mean, wh' are fit for Service, Tight and Sound)
And for a Proof our meaning is Sincere,
See but the Ships are good, and if you fear
A Want of Equipage, we'll Man 'em here.

 These are the Terms on which you may Engage
The Poet's Fire, to Batter from the Stage.
Useful Ally; whose Friendship lets you in
Upon the weak, and naked Side of Sin;

Against your old Attack, the Foe's prepar'd,
Well fortifi'd, and always on his Guard;
The Sacred Shot you send, are flung in vain,
By Impious Hands, with insolent Disdain,
They're gather'd up, and fir'd at you again.
Thro' baffled Toyles, and unsuccessful Cares,
In Slaughter, Blood, and Wounds, and Pious Snares,
Y' ave made a Flanders *War, these fifteen hundred Years.*
Change then your Scheme, if you'll your Foe annoy,
And the infernal Bajazet *destroy:*
Our Aid accept,
W'ave gentler Stratagems, which may succeed;
We'll tickle 'em where you wou'd make 'em Bleed;
In Sounds less harsh, we'll teach 'em to Obey;
In softer Strains, the Evil Spirit lay,
And steal their Immorality away.

Dramatis Personæ

MEN.

Don *Felix*, a Gentleman of *Valencia*,	Capt. *Griffin*.
Don *Pedro*,	Mr. *Wilks*.
Don *Guzman*, } Lovers of *Leonora*,	Mr. *Mills*.
Don *John*,	Mr. *Cibber*.
Lopez, Servant to Don *John*,	Mr. *Pinkethman*.
Galindo, Servant to Don *Guzman*,	Mr. *Bullock*.

WOMEN.

Leonora, Daughter to *Don Felix*,	Mrs. *Rogers*.
Isabella, her Friend & Sister to *Guzman*,	Mrs. *Kent*.
Jacinta, Woman to *Leonora*,	Mrs. *Oldfield*.

SCENE at *VALENCIA*.

THE

FALSE FRIEND

ACT I. SCENE *Don John's* Lodgings.

Enter Don John *beating* Lopez.

Lop. HOLD Sir, hold; there's enough in all Conscience; I'm reasonable, I ask no more; I'm content.

Don John. Then there's double Content, you Dog, and a Brace of Contents more into the Bargain. Now is't well?   [*Striking again and again.*

Lop. O, mighty well, Sir; you'll never mend it; pray leave it as 'tis.

Don John. Look you, you Jackanapes, if ever I hear an offer at your impertinent Advice again——

Lop. And why, Sir, will you stifle the most useful of my Qualifications?

Don John. Either, Sirrah, I pass for a very great Blockhead with you, or you are pleas'd to reckon much upon my patience.

Lop. Your patience, Sir, indeed is great: I feel at this time forty proofs on't upon my Shoulders: But really, Sir, I wou'd advise you to——

Don John. Again? I can bear thee no longer. Here, Pen and Ink, I'll give thee thy Discharge. Did I take you for a Vallet, or a Privy-Counsellor, Sir?

Lop. 'Tis confesst, Sir, you took me but for humble Employment; but my intention was agreeably to surprize you with some superiour Gifts of Nature, to your faithful Slave.

I profess, my noble Master, a most perfect Knowledge of Men and Manners. Yours, gracious Sir, (with all Respect I speak it) are not irreprehensible. And I'm afraid, in time, Sir, I am indeed, they'l riggle you into some ill-favour'd Affair, whence with all my Understanding, I shall be puzzled to bring you off.

Don John. Very well, Sir.

Lop. And therefore, Sir, it is, that I (poor *Lopez* as I am) sometimes take leave to Moralize.

Don John. Go, go, moralize in the Market-Place: I'm quite worn out. Once more, march.

Lop. Is the Sentence definitive?

Don John. Positive.

Lop. Then pray let us come to Account, and see what Wages are due?

Don John. Wages? Refund what you have had, you Rascal, you, for the plague you have given me.

Lop. Nay, if I muſt lose my Money, then let me claim another Right; Losers have leave to speak. Therefore advance, my Tongue, and say thy pleasure; tell this Maſter of mine, he shou'd die with shame at the Life he leads; so much unworthy of a Man of Honour: Tell him————

Don John. I'll hear no more.

Lop. You shall indeed, Sir.

Don John. Here, take thy Money and be gone.

Lop. Counters all; adieu, you glittering Spangles of the World; farewel, ye Tempters of the Great; not me. Tell him————

Don John. Stay.

Lop. Go on; tell him he's worse among the Women, than a Ferret among the Rabbets; at one and all, from the Princess to the Tripe Woman; handsom, ugly, old Women and Children, all go down.

Don John. Very well.

Lop. It is indeed, Sir, and so are the Stories you tell 'em to bring 'em to your matters. The Handsome, she's all Divinity to be sure; the Ugly, she's so agreeable, were it not for her Virtue, she'd be overrun with Lovers; the light, Airy Flipflap, she kills him with her Motions; the dull, heavytail'd Maulkin melts him down with her Modeſty; the scragged lean pale Face, has a shape for Deſtruction; the fat over-grown Sow, has an Air of Importance; the tall aukward Trapes, with her Majeſty wounds; the little short Trundle-tail, shoots a *je ne scay quoy.* In a word, they have all something for him————and he has something for 'em all.

Don John. And thus, you Fool, by a general Attack, I keep my Heart my own; lie with them that like me, and care not sixpence for them that don't.

Lop. Well said, well said, a very pretty Amuzement truly: But pray, Sir, by your leave (Ceremony aside) since you are pleas'd to clear up into Conversation, what mighty Matters do you expeÉt from Boarding a Woman you know is already Heart and Soul engag'd to another?

Don John. Why I expeÉt her Heart and Soul shou'd disingage in a Week. If you live a little longer with me, Sirrah, you'l know how to inſtruÉt your next Maſter to the purpose: and therefore that I may charitably equip you for a new Service, now I'm turning you out of my own, I'll let you know, that when a Woman loves a Man beſt, she's in the moſt hopeful way of betraying him; for Love like Fortune turns upon a Wheel, and is very much given to rising and falling.

Lop. Like enough: But as much upon the Weather-cock as the Ladies are, there are some the Wind muſt blow hard to fetch 'em about: When such a ſturdy Hussy falls in your Honour's way, what account may Things turn to then, an't please ye?

Don John. They turn to a Bottle, you Puppy.

Lop. I find they'l always turn to something; but when you pursue a poor Woman only to make her Lover Jealous, what pleasure can you take in that?

Don John. That pleasure.

Lop. Look you there again.

Don John. Why, Sirrah, d'you think there's no pleasure in spoiling their sport, when I can't make my own.

Lop. O! to a good-natur'd Man, besure there muſt; but suppose; inſtead of fending and proving with his Miſtress, he shou'd come to—a— parrying and thruſting with you? What becomes of your Joy then, my noble Maſter?

Don John. Why do you think I'm afraid to fight, you Rascal?

Lop. I thought we were talking of what we lov'd, not what we fear'd, Sir.

Don John. Sir, I love every thing that leads to what I love moſt.

Lop. I know, Sir, you have often fought upon these occasions.

Don John. Therefore that has been no ſtop to my Pleasures.

Lop. But you have never been kill'd once, Sir, and when that happens, you will for ever lose the pleasure of——

Don John. [*ſtriking him.*] Breaking your Head, you Rascal, which will afflict me heartily. See who knocks so hard. [*Knocking.*

Lop. Somebody that thinks I can hear no better, than you think I can feel.

Enter Don Guzman.

Don Guz. *Don John de Alvarada*, is he here?

Lop. There's the Man. Shew me such another, if you can find him. [*Aside.*

Don Guz. *Don John*, I desire to speak with you alone.

Don John. You may speak before this Fellow, Sir, he's truſty.

Don Guz. 'Tis an affair of Honour, Sir.

Don John. Withdraw, *Lopez.*

Lop. Behind the door I will, and no farther. [*Aside.* This Fellow looks as if he came to save me a broken Head. [*Lopez retires.*

Don Guz. I call my self *Don Guzman de Torrellas*, you know what Blood I spring from; I am a Cadet, and, by consequence, not Rich; but I am eſteem'd by Men of Honour: I have been forward to expose my self in Battles abroad, and I have met with Applause in our Feaſts at home.

Lop. So much by way of Introduction. [*Aside.*

Don John. I underſtand your Merit, Sir, and shou'd be glad to do as much by your business.

Don Guz. Give Attention, and you'll be inſtructed. I love *Leonora,* and from my Youth have done so. Long she rejected my Sighs, and despised my Tears, but my Conſtancy at laſt has vanquiſht. I have found the way to her Heart, and nothing is wanting to compleat my Joy, but the Consent of her Father, whom I cannot yet convince, that the wants in my Fortune, are recompens'd, by the Merits of my Person.

Lop. He's a very dull Fellow indeed. [*Aside.*

Don Guz. In the mean while, the objeƈt of my Vows, is a sharer in my Grief, and the only Cordial we have, is the Pleasure of a secret Conversation, through a small Breach I have made in a thin Partition that divides our Lodgings. I truſt you, *Don John*, with this important Secret; Friend or Enemy, you are Noble, therefore keep it, I charge your Honour with it.

Lop. You cou'd not put it in better hands. [*Aside.*

Don Guz. But more; my Passion for this Lady is not hid; all *Valencia* is acquainted with my Wishes, and approves my Choice. You alone, *Don John de Alvarada*, seeming ignorant of my Vows, dare traverse my Amour.

Don John. Go on.

Lop. These words import War; lie close, *Lopez*. [*Aside.*

Don Guz. You are the *Argus* of our Street, and the Spy of *Leonora*; whether *Diana*, by her borrow'd Light supplies the Absence of the *Aſtre* of Day, or that the shades of Night cover the Earth with impenetrable Darkness; you ſtill attend till *Aurora*'s return, under the Balcony of that adorable Beauty.

Don John. So.

Don Guz. Wherever she moves, you ſtill follow as her Shadow, at Church, at Plays; be her business with Heaven or Earth, your Importunity is such, you'l share it.

Lop. He is a forward Fellow, that's the truth on't. [*Aside.*

Don Guz. But what's ſtill farther, you take the Liberty to Copy me; my Words, my Aƈtions, every motion is no sooner mine, but your's. In short, you ape me, *Don*, and to that point, I once design'd to ſtab my self, and try if you wou'd follow me in that too.

Lop. No, there the Monkey wou'd have left you. [*Aside.*

Don Guz. But to conclude.

Don John. 'Tis time.

Don Guz. My Patience, *Don*, is now no more; and I pronounce, that if henceforth I find you under *Leonora*'s Window, who never wish'd fond Man, to see you there, I by the ways of Honour, shall fix you in another ſtation; I leave you to consider on't. Farewel. [*Exit* Don Guz.

Don John. Hold, Sir, we had e'en as good do this Honourable Deed now.

Re-enter Lopez.

Lop. No, pray Sir, let him go, and may be you mayn't have occasion to do it at all.

Don John. I thought at first the Coxcomb came upon an other Subject, which wou'd have embarrast me much more.

Lop. Now this was a Subject wou'd have embarrast me enough in all conscience.

Don John. I was afraid he came to forbid me seeing his Sister *Isabella*, with whom I'm upon very good Terms.

Lop. Why now that's a hard Case, when you have got a Man's Sister, you can't leave him his Mistress.

Don John. No Changeling, I hate him enough, to love every Woman that belongs to him; and the Fool has so provok'd me by his threat'ning, that I believe I shall have a Stroke at his Mother, before I think my self even with him.

Lop. A most admirable way to make up Accounts truly.

Don John. A Son of a Whore! s'death, I did not care sixpence for the Slut before, but now I'll have her Maidenhead in a Week; for fear the Rogue shou'd Marry her in Ten Days.

Lop. Mum; here's her Father: I'll warrant this old Spark comes to correct our way of living too.

Enter Don Felix.

Don Fel. Don *John*——

Don John. Don *Felix*, do I see you in my poor Dwelling? Pray to what lucky accident do I owe this Honour?

Don Fel. That I may speak to you without constraint, pray send away your Servant.

Lop. What the Pox have I done to 'em, they are all so uneasie at my Company?   [*Aside.*

Don John. Give us Chairs, and leave the Room.

Lop. If this old Fellow comes to quarrel with us too, he'll at least do us less harm.   [*Aside.*

Don Fel. Won't you retire Friend?   [*Looking behind.*

Don John. Be gone, Sirrah.

Lop. [*aside.*] Pox take ye——you old Prig you: But I shall be even with you.   [*Lopez hides himself.*

Don Fel. You know me, Sir?

Don John. I do, Sir.

Don Fel. That I call myself——

Don John. Don *Felix*.

Don Fel. That I am of the House of——

Don John. *Cabrera*, one of the first of *Valencia*.

Don Fel. That my Estate is——

Don John. Great.

Don Fel. You know that I have some Reputation in the World.

Don John. I know your Reputation equals your Birth.

Don Fel. And you are not ignorant, that Heav'n, for the Consolation of my Gray Hairs has given me an only Daughter, who is not deform'd.

Don John. Beauteous as Light.

Don Fel. Well shap'd, witty, and endow'd with——

Don John. All the good Qualities of Mind and Body.

Don Fel. Since you are satisfy'd with all this, hearken, I pray, with attention, to the Business that brings me hither.

Don John. I shall.

Don Fel. We all know *Don John*, some by their own experience, some by that of others, how nice a Gentleman's Honour is, and how easily tarnish'd; an Eclaircissement manag'd with prudence, often prevents Misfortunes that perhaps might be upon the point of attending us. I have thought it my Duty to acquaint you, that I have seen your Designs upon my Daughter: You pass Nights entire under her Window, as if you were searching an opportunity to get into my House; there is no body in the Town but has taken notice of your Proceedings; you give the Publick a Subject for disadvantagious Discourse; and tho' in reality *Leonora's* Virtue receives no prejudice by it, her Reputation daily runs some risque. My years have taught me to judge right of Things: and yet I have not been able to decide what your end can be; you can't regard my Daughter on a foot of Gallantry, you know her Virtue, and my Birth too well; and for a Wife you seem to have no thought, since you have yet made no Demand to me; what then is your Intention? You have heard perhaps, I have hearken'd to a Gentleman of *Toledo*, a Man of merit. I own I have, and I expect him daily here; but, *Don John*, if 'tis that which hinders you from declaring in Form, I'll ease you of a great deal of trouble, which the Customs of the World impose upon these Occasions, and, in a Word, I'll break with him, and give you *Leonora*.

Lop. Good.   [*Aside.*

Don Fel. You don't answer me! What is't that troubles you?

Don John. That I have been such a Sot, old Gentleman, to hear you with so much Patience.   [*Rising.*

Don Fel. How *Don?* I'm more astonish'd at your Answer, than I was with your Silence.

Don John. Astonish'd! Why han't you talk'd to me of Marriage? He asks me to Marry, and wonders what I complain of!

Don Fel. 'Tis well——'tis well, *Don John*, the outrage is Violent! You insult me in your own House. But know, Sir——   [*Rising.*

Don John. But know, Sir, there needs no Quarrel, if you please, Sir; I like your Daughter very well; but for Marrying her——*Serviteur.*

Don Fel. Don Guzman de Torrellas has not less Merit than you, *Don.*

Don John. Agreed; what then?

Don Fel. And yet I have refus'd him my Daughter.

Don John. Why then, you have us'd him better than you have done me, which I take very unkindly.

Don Fel. I have us'd you, Sir——

Don John. Us'd me, Sir, you have us'd me very Ill, to come into my own House to seduce me.

Don Fel. What Extravagance!

Don John. What Persecution!

Don Fel. Am I then to have no other Answer?

Don John. Methinks you have enough in all Conscience.

Don Fel. Promise me at least, you'l cease to love my Daughter.

Don John. I won't affront your Family so far neither.

Lop. I'gad my Master shines to day.   [*Aside.*

Don Fel. Know *Don*, that I can bear no more.

Lop. If he cou'd, I think there's no more to lay upon him.   [*Aside.*

Don Fel. If I find you continue to importune *Leonora*, I shall find a way to satisfie my offended Honour, and punish your Presumption.

Don John. You shall do what you please to me, provided you don't Marry me.

Don Fel. Know, *Alvarada*, there are ways to Revenge such Outrageous Affronts as these.

Don John. I won't marry.

Don Fel. 'Tis enough.   [*Exit* Don Felix.

                     Re-enter Lopez.

Lop. So; the old Fellow's gone at last, and has carry'd great content along with him.   [*Aside.*

Don John. *Lopez.*

Lop. Sir——

Don John. What dos't think? he wou'd have Marry'd me!

Lop. Yes, he had found his Man. But you have been even with him.

Don John. What, thou hast heard us then?

Lop. Or I were no Vallet: But pray what do's your Honour intend to do now? Will you continue the Siege of a Place, where, 'tis probable they will daily augment the Fortifications, when there are so many open Towns you may march into without the trouble of opening the Trenches.

Don John. I am going, *Lopez*, to double my Attacks: I'll beat up her Quarters six times a Night, I am now down-right in Love; the Difficulties pique me to the Attempt, and I'll conquer or I'll die.

Lop. Why, to confess the Truth, Sir, I find you much upon my taste in this matter; Difficulties are the Rocombolle of Love, I never valu'd an easy Conquest in my life. To rouze my Fire, the Lady must cry out (as softly as ever she can) have a care, my Dear, my Mother has seen us; My

Brothers suspect me; my Husband may surprise us: O, dear Heart, have a care, I pray! Then I play the Devil: But when I come to a fair one, where I may hang up my Cloak upon a Peg, get into my Gown and Slippers——

Don John. Impudent Rogue. *[Aside.*

Lop. See her stretch'd upon the Couch in great security, with——my dear, come kiss me, we have nothing to fear; I droop, I yawn, I sleep.

Don John. Well, Sir, whatever you do with your fair one, I am going to be very busie with mine; I was e'en almost weary of her, but *Guzman* and this old Fellow have reviv'd my dying Fire, and so, have at her.

Lop. 'Tis all mighty well, Sir, mighty well, Sir, as can be in the World. But, if you wou'd have the Goodness to consider *en passant*, or so, a little now and then, about Swords and Daggers, and Rivals, and old Fellows, and Pistols and great Guns, and such like Baubles, only now and then at leisure, Sir, not to interrupt things of more consequence.

Don John. Thou art a Cowardly Rascal, I have often consider'd that.

Lop. Ay, that's true, Sir, and yet a Blunderbuss is presently discharg'd out of a Garret Window.

Don John. Come, no more words; but follow me. How now! what Impertinence have we here now to stop me?

Enter Don Pedro.

Lop. 'Tis *Don Pedro*, or I'm a Dog.

Don John. Impossible! *Don Pedro* return'd!

Don Ped. 'Tis I, my dearest Friend; I'm come to forget all the Miseries of a long Absence in one happy Embrace. *[They embrace.*

Don John. I'm over-joy'd to see you.

Don Ped. Mine's not to be exprest. What, Friend *Lopez* here still! How dos't do, *Lopez?* What, dos't not know me?

Lop. As well as my Father's Seal, Sir, when he sends me a Bill of Exchange.

Don Ped. Just as he was, I find, Galliard still.

Lop. I find it very unwholesome to be otherwise, Sir.

Don John. You have then quitted the Service in *Flanders*, I suppose.

Don Ped. I have so, Friend; I have left the Ensigns of *Mars*, and am lifting myself in a softer Militia.

Don John. Explain, pray.

Don Ped. Why, when your Father's Death oblig'd you to leave *Brussels*, and return hither to the plentiful Fortune he left you; I stay'd in *Flanders* very trist for your loss, and past three years in the Trade of War. About two Months since, my Father writ to me from *Toledo*, that he was going to Marry me very Advantageously at *Valencia*: He sent me the Picture of the Lady, and I was so well pleased with it, that I immediately got my

Conge and Embark'd at *Dunkirk;* I had a quick Passage to the *Groyn,* from whence, by the way of *Madrid,* I am come hither with all the speed I cou'd.

I have you muſt know, been two days in Town, but I have lain *Incognito,* that I might inform my self of the Lady's Conduct I'm to Marry; and I have discover'd, that she's serv'd by two Cavalliers of Birth and Merit. But tho' they have both given many proofs of a moſt violent Passion, I have found for the quiet of my Honour that this virtuous Lady, out of modeſty or prudence, has shewn a perfect Indifference to them and their Gallantries; her Fortune is considerable, her Birth is high, her Manners Irreproachable, and her Beauty so great, that nothing but my Love can equal it.

Don John. I have hearken'd to you, *Don Pedro,* with a great deal of Attention, and Heaven's my Witness, I have a mighty Joy in seeing you; but the Devil fetch me, it makes my Heart bleed to hear you are going to be Married.

Don Ped. Say no more of that, I desire you; we have always been Friends, and I earneſtly beg we ever may be so; but I am not come to ask Council about my Marriage, my Party is taken, and my inquiries have so much heightned my Desire, that nothing can henceforth abate it. I muſt therefore expect from you, dear Friend, that you won't oppose it, but that you'l aid me in haſtening the moment of my Happiness.

Don John. Since 'tis so impossible for you to resolve for your own good, I muſt submit to what you'l have me: But are not we to know the Name of this Piece of Rarity, that is to do you this good Turn?

Don Ped. You'l know it presently; for I'm going to carry you to her House.

Don John. You shall tell me at leaſt who are her two Gallants.

Don Ped. One, they cou'd not tell me his Name; t' other is——But before we talk any more of these affairs, can you let me dispose of *Lopez,* till the Return of a Servant, I sent three days ago to——

Don John. Carry News of you to *Papa* I suppose.

Don Ped. You are right; the good Man is thirty Leagues off, and I have not seen him these six years.

Don John. Lopez, do you wait upon *Don Pedro.*

Lop. With all my Heart. It's at leaſt a suspension of Boxes oth' Ear, and Kicks o' the Backside. [*Aside.*

Don Ped. Then, honeſt *Lopez,* with your Maſter's leave, go to the New Inn, the King of *France* on Horseback, and see if my Servant's return'd; I'll be there immediately, to charge thee with a Commission of more Importance.

Lop. I shall perform your Orders, Sir, both to your Satisfaction, and my own Reputation. [*Exit* Lopez.

Don John. Very quaint. Well, old Acquaintance, you are going to be Married then? 'Tis resolv'd: Ha!

Don Ped. So says my Star.

Don John. The foolishest Star that has said any thing a great while.

Don Ped. Still the same I see! Or, more than ever, resolv'd to love nothing.

Don John. Love nothing! Why, I'm in Love at this very time.

Don Ped. With what?

Don John. A Woman.

Don Ped. Impossible!

Don John. True.

Don Ped. And how came you in Love with her?

Don John. Why I was order'd not to be in Love with her.

Don Ped. Then, there's more Humour than Love in't.

Don John. There shall be what you please in't. But I shan't quit the Gentlewoman, till I have convinc'd her there's something in't.

Don Ped. Mayn't I know her Name?

Don John. When you have let me into your conjugal Affection.

Don Ped. Pray stay here, but till I have sent *Lopez* to my Father-in-law: I'll come back and carry you with me in a moment.

Don John. I'll expect you.

Don Ped. Adieu, dear Friend; may I in earnest see you quickly in Love.   [*Exit* Don Pedro.

Don John. May I, without a Jest, see you quickly a Widower.
Solus.

He comes, he says, to Marry a Woman of Quality that has two Lovers ——If it should be *Leonora.*——But why she? There are many, I hope, in that condition in *Valencia*——I'm a little Embarrass'd about it, however.———

Friendship take heed, if Woman interfere ;
Besure the hour of thy Destruction's near.   [*Exit.*

ACT II.

SCENE *Leonora's* Appartment.

Enter *Leonora, Isabella,* and *Jacinta.*

Leon. DEAR *Isabella,* come in: How I am plagu'd with this troublesome Wretch. *Jacinta,* have you shut the outer Gates?

Jacin. I have, Madam.

(168)

Leo. Shut the Window too; we shall have him get in there, by and by.

Isab. What's this you are in such Apprehensions of, pray?

Leo. Nothing worth naming.

Isab. You dissemble: something of Love in the case, I'll warrant you.

Leo. The Reverse on't; 'tis aversion. My impertinent Star has furnish'd me with a Lover for my Guard, who is never from my Window; he persecutes me to Distraction; I affront him fifty Times a day; which he receives with a Bow down to the Ground: In short, all I can do, is doing nothing at all, he still persists in loving me, as much as I hate him.

Isab. Have a Care he don't get the better on't, for all that; for when a Man loves a Woman well enough to persevere, 'tis odds but she at last loves him well enough to make him give it over. But I think I had as good take off my Scarf; for, since my Brother *Don Guzman* knows I'm with you, he won't quarrel at my return for the length of my Visit.

Leo. If he shou'd, I shou'd quarrel with him, which few things else wou'd make me do. But methinks, *Isabella,* you are a little Melancholly.

Isab. And you a little Thoughtful.

Leo. Pray tell me your Affliction.

Isab. Pray don't conceal yours.

Leo. Why truly, my Heart is not at ease.

Isab. Mine, I fear, never will.

Leo. My Father's Marrying me against my Inclination.

Isab. My Brother is hindring me from Marrying with mine.

Leo. You know I love your Brother, *Don Guzman.*

Isab. And you shall know, I'm uneasie for *Don John de Alvarada.*

Leo. Don John!

Isab. The same.

Leo. Have you any Reason to hope for a return?

Isab. I think so.

Leo. I'm afraid, my Dear, you abuse your self.

Isab. Why?

Leo. Because he is already in Love with——

Isab. Who?

Leo. Me.

Isab. I wou'd not have you too positive in that, Madam, for I am very sure that——

Leo. Madam, I am very sure that he's the troublesome Guest I just now complain'd of: And you may believe——

Isab. Madam, I can never believe he's troublesome to any Body.

Leo. O dear Madam: But I'm sure I'm forc'd to keep my Windows shut, till I'm almost dead with Heat, and that I think is troublesome.

Isab. This Mistake is easily set right, *Leonora;* our Houses join, and when he looks at my Window, you fancy 'tis at yours.

Leo. But when he attacks my Door, Madam, and almost breaks it down, I don't know how in the World to fancy 'tis yours.

Isab. A Man may do that to disguise his real Inclination.

Leo. Nay, if you please, believe he's dying for you. I wish he were; then I shou'd be troubled no more with him. Be sure *Jacinta* you don't open a Window to night.

Isab. Not while I'm here, at least; for if he knows that he may chance to press in.

Leo. Look you, *Isabella,* 'tis entirely alike to me, who he's fond of; but I'm so much your Friend, I can't endure to see you deceiv'd.

Isab. And since I have the same Kindness for you, *Leonora,* Know in short, that my Brother is so allarm'd at his Passion for me, that he has forbid him the Street.

Leo. Bless my Soul! and don't you plainly see by that he's Jealous of him upon my account?

Isa. smiling.] He's jealous of his Honour, Madam, lest he shou'd debauch his Sister.

Leo. I say, he's jealous of his Love, least he shou'd corrupt his Mistress.

Isab. But why all this Heat? If you love my Brother, why are you concern'd *Don John* shou'd love me?

Leo. I'm not concern'd: I have no Designs upon him, I care not who he loves.

Isab. Why then are you angry?

Leo. Why do you say he does not care for me?

Isab. Well, to content you then: I know nothing certain, but that I love him.

Leo. And to content you; I know nothing so certain, as that I neither Love him, nor never can Love him: And so I hope we are Friends again.

Isab. Kiss me, then, and let us never be otherwise.

Leo. Agreed: [*They kiss.*] And now my Dear, as my Misfortune's nearest, I am first to be pity'd. I am the most wretched Woman living. My Father every moment expects a Gentleman from *Flanders,* to whom he has resolv'd to marry me. But neither Duty, nor Prudence, nor Danger, nor Resolution, nor all I can summon to my Aid, can drive your Brother from my Heart; but there he's fixt to ruin me.

Jacin. Madam, here's *Don Guzman* at the Chamber door; he begs so passionately to come in, sure you can't refuse him.

Leo. Heav'ns; but does he consider to what he exposes me?

Jacin. Madam, he considers nothing; if he did, I'd say he were an impudent Fellow to pretend to be in Love with you.

Leo. Shall I venture, *Isabella?*

Isab. You know best.

Enter Don Guzman.

(170)

Jacin. Marry, methinks he knows best of us all, for here he comes.

Don Guz. Forgive me, lovely *Leonora*; 'tis the last time perhaps that I may beg your Pity. My Rival is not far; excess of Modesty is now our Ruin. Break through it, for this moment you have left, and own to your old Father how you Love. He once did so himself; our Scene of Sorrow may perhaps recal some small remembrance of his tender Years, and melt him into Mercy.

Leo. Alas, *Don Guzman*——

Jacin. O Heav'ns, Madam——

Leo. What's the matter?

Jacin. Y' are undone, here's your Father.

Isab. What an unlucky Accident.

Leo. Has he seen *Don Guzman?*

Jacin. Nay, the Deuce knows.

Isab. Where shall he hide himself?

Jacin. In the Moon, if he can get thither.

Enter Don Felix.

Don Guz. I must e'en stand it now.

Don Fel. Good News, my Daughter, good News; I come to acquaint you, that——How now? What's the Meaning of this? *Don Guzman* in my Daughters Chamber!

Don Guz. I see your surprize, Sir, but you need not be disturb'd; 'twas some suddain Business with my Sister, brought me here.

Don Fel. 'Tis enough, Sir. I'm glad to find you here; you shall be a Witness, that I know how to preserve the Honour of my Family.

Don Guz. What mean you, Sir?

Don Fel. To Marry *Leonora* this Moment.

Don Guz. How say you?

Don Fel. I say you shall have nothing left to ask of me.

Don Guz. Is't possible? O Heavens! what Joy I feel!

Don Fel. Leonora, prepare your Hand and Heart.

Leo. They both are ready, Sir; and in giving me the Man I Love, you charge me with a Debt of Gratitude can never be repay'd.

Don Guz. [*Kneeling.*] Upon my Knees, I thank the best of Men, for blessing me with all that's blest in Woman.

Isab. How well that kind, that gentle Look becomes him!

Jacin. Now, methinks, he looks like an old Rogue. I don't like his Looks. [*Aside.*

Enter Lopez.

Lop. To all whom it may concern, greeting, *Don Pedro Osorio*, acknowledging himself most unworthy of the Honour intended him, in the Person of the fair *Leonora*, Addresses himself (by me his small Ambassador) to the Generosity of *Don Felix*, for leave to walk in and take Possession.

Don Fel. I had already given order for his entrance.

Don Guz. What is't I hear?

Leo. Support me.

Isab. She faints.

Don Guz. Look Tyrant here, and, if thou can'st be Cruel!

[Holding her.

Don Fel. Bring in *Don Pedro*.

Don Guz. Barbarian.

Jacin. Look up, Madam, for Heaven's sake; since you must Marry the Fellow, e'en make the most on't.

Leo. Hoh——

Enter Don Pedro *and* Don John.

Jacin. So——How d'ye do now? Come, chear up. See, here he comes. By my Troth, and a pretty Turn'd Fellow. [*Aside.*] He'll set all to rights by to morrow morning, I'll answer for him.

Don Fel. Don Pedro, you are Welcome; let me Embrace you.

Don Ped. In what Terms, Sir, shall I express, what I owe you for the Honour you do me. And with what prospect of Return can I receive this inestimable Present. Your Picture, Madam, made what Impression Art cou'd stamp, but Nature has done more. What Wounds your Sex can give, or ours receive, I feel.

Don Fel. Come Son, (for I'm in hast to call you so)——But what's this I see? *Alvarada* here! Whence, Sir, this Insolence; to come within my Doors after you know what has past? Who brought you here?

Don Ped. 'Twas I, Sir.

Don Fel. But do you know that he——

Don Ped. Sir, he's the best of my Friends.

Don Fel. But do you know, I say, that he wou'd——

Don Ped. Hinder this Marriage, 'tis true.

Don Fel. Yes, because he design'd——

Don Ped. I know his Design, Sir, 'tis to hinder all his Friends from Marrying. Pray forgive him.

Don Fel. Then to prevent for ever, his Designs here, come hither, *Leonora*, and give *Don Pedro* your hand.

Don John. Keep down, my kindling Jealousie: I've something tortures me I never felt till now. [*Aside.*

Don Ped. [*to* Leo.] Why this backwardness, Madam, where a Father chuses, a Daughter may with modesty approve? Pray give me your Hand.

Don Guz. I cannot see it. [*Turning from 'em.*

Don Fel. [to Leo. *aside.*] Are you Distracted? Will you let him know your Folly? Give him your Hand, for shame.

Leo. Hoh! *Don Guzman*, I am yours.

                       [*Sighing, and giving carelesly her Hand.*

Don Guz. Madam!   [*Turning.*

Don Fel. What a fatal Slip!   [*Aside.*

Leo. 'Twas not to you I spoke, Sir.

Don Ped. But him it was she nam'd, and thought on too, I fear. I'm much Alarm'd.

Don Fel. [*to* Leo.] Repair what you have done, and look more chearful on him.

Leo. Repair what you have done, and kill me.

Don Fel. Fool.

Leo. Tyrant.

Jacin. A very hum-drum Marriage this.   [*Aside.*

Don Guz. Pray Sister let's retire; for I can bear the sight no longer.

Isab. My Dear, farewel, I pity you indeed.

Leo. I am indeed, an Object of your pity.

                      [*Exit* Don. Guz. *and* Isab.

Don Fel. Come Daughter, come my Son, let's to the Church and tie this happy Knot.

Don Ped. I'll wait upon you, Sir.   [*Exit* Don Fel. *leading* Leo.

Don John. I love her, and I'll love her still. Fate, do thy worst, I'll on.

                              [*Aside.*

Don Ped. To name another Man in giving me her Hand.

Don John. [*aside.*] How am I wrackt and torn with Jealousie!

Don Ped. 'Tis doubtless so, *Don Guzman* has her Heart.   [*Aside.*

Don John. [*aside.*] The Bridegroom's Thoughtful. The Lady's Trip has furnish'd him with some Matrimonial Reflections: They'l agree with him at this time perhaps, better than my Company. I'll leave him. *Don Pedro*, adieu, we shall meet again at Night.

Don Ped. Pray stay; I have need of a Friend's Council.

Don John. What already?

Don Ped. Already.

Don John. That's to say, you have already enough of Matrimony.

Don Ped. I scarce know what I have, nor am I sure of what I am.

                  Enter Lopez.

Lop. An't please your Honour, yonder's your Man *Bertrand* just arriv'd; his Horse and he so tired of one another, that they both came down upon the Pavement at the Stable Door.

Don Ped. [*to* Don John.] He brings News from my Father.

Lop. I believe he do's, and hasty News too; but if you stay till he brings it hither, I believe it will come but slowly. But here's his Packet; I suppose that will do as well as his Company.   [*Gives a Letter.*

Don Ped. [*Reads to himself.*] My dear Friend, here's ill News.

Don John. What's the Matter?

Don Ped. My poor old Father's Dying.

Don John. I'm mighty sorry for't; 'tis a weighty Stroke I must confess; the burthen of his Estate will almost bear you down. But we must submit to Heavens good will.

Don Ped. You talk, *Alvarada*, like a perfect Stranger, to that tenderness methinks every Son shou'd feel for a good Father: For my part, I've receiv'd such repeated Proofs of an uncommon Affection from mine, that the Loss of a Mistress cou'd scarce touch me nearer. You'l believe me, when you see me leave *Leonora* a Virgin, till I have seen the good old Man.

Don John. That will be a Proof indeed; Heavens Blessing must needs fall upon so Dutiful a Son; but I don't know how its Judgments may deal with so indifferent a Lover.

Don Ped. O! I shall have time enough to repair this seeming small neglect: But before I go, pray a word or two with you alone. *Lopez*, wait without.   [*Exit* Lop.

You see, my dearest Friend, I am engag'd with *Leonora*; perhaps I have done wrong; but 'tis gone too far, to talk or think of a Retreat; I shall go directly from this place to the Altar, and there Seal the Eternal Contract. That done, I'll take Post to see my Father, if I can, before he dies. I leave then here a Young and Beauteous Bride; but that which touches every string of Thought, I fear, I leave her wishing I were *Guzman*. If it be so, no doubt he knows it well; and he that knows he's lov'd by *Leonora*, can let no fair Occasion pass to gain her; my absence, is his Friend, but you are mine, and so the danger's balanc'd.

Into your Hands, my dear, my faithful *Alvarada*, [*Embracing him.*] I put my Honour, I put my Life; for both depend on *Leonora*'s Truth. Observe her Lover, and——neglect not her. You are Wise, you are Active, you are Brave and True. You have all the Qualities that Man shou'd have for such a Trust; and I by consequence have all the Assurance Man can have, you'll, as you ought, discharge it.

Don John. A very hopeful Business you wou'd have me undertake, keep a Woman honest; Uds death, I'd as soon undertake to keep *Portocarero* honest. Look you, we are Friends, intimate Friends; you must not be angry if I talk freely. Women are naturally bent to Mischief, and their Actions run in one continued Torrent, till they die. But the less a Torrent's checkt, the less Mischief it does; let it alone, perhaps 'twill only kiss the Banks and pass, but stop it 'tis insatiable.

Don Ped. I wou'd not stop it; but cou'd I gently turn its Course where it might run, and vent itself with Innocence, I wou'd. *Leonora* of her self is Virtuous, her Birth, Religion, Modesty and Sense, will guide her Wishes where they ought to point. But yet, let Guards be what they will, that Place is safest that is ne'er attackt.

Don John. As far as I can serve you, in hindring *Guzman*'s Approaches, you may command me.

Don Ped. That's all I ask.

Don John. Then all you ask is granted.

Don Ped. I am at ease, farewel.

Don John. Heaven bring you safe to us again.   [*Exit* Don Ped.

Don John *solus.*

Yes, I shall observe her, doubt it not. I wish no Body may observe me, for I find I'm no more Master of my self. *Don Guzman*'s Passion for her, adds to mine; but when I think on what *Don Pedro* 'll reap, I'm Fire and Flame. Something must be done: What, let Love direct, for I have nothing else to guide me.

Enter Lopez.

Lop. [*aside.*] *Don Pedro* is mounting for his Journey, and leaves a young, warm, liquorish Hussy with a watry Mouth, behind him——Hum—— If she falls handsomly in my Master's way, let her look to her——'st— there he is. Doing what? Thinking? That's new: And if any Good comes on't, that will be newer still.

Don John. [*aside.*] How? Abuse the Trust a Friend reposes in me? And while he thinks me waking for his Peace, employ the stretch of Thought, to make him wretched?

Lop. Not to interrupt your pious Meditations, Sir, pray have you seen? Seen what, Fool? Why he can't see thee. I'gad, I believe the little blind Bastard has whipt him through the Heart in earnest.

Don John. [*aside.*] *Pedro* wou'd never have done this by me——How do I know that?——Why——he Swore; he was my Friend——Well; and I swore I was his——Why then if I find I can break my Oath, why should not I conclude he will do as much by his?

Lop. [*aside.*] His Countenance begins to clear up: I suppose Things may be drawing to a Conclusion.

Don John. [*aside.*] Ay, 'tis just so: And I don't believe he wou'd have debated the Matter half so long as I have done: I'gad I think I have put my self to a great Expence of Morality about it. I'm sure at least, my Stock's out. But I have a Fund of Love, I hope may last a little longer.

O, are you there, Sir?   [*Seeing* Lop.

Lop. I think so, Sir; I won't be positive in any thing.

Don John. Follow me: I have some Business to employ you in, you'll like. [*Exit* Don John.

Lop. I won't be positive in that neither. I guess what you are going about——There's Roguery a-foot: This is at *Leonora*, who I know hates him; nothing under a Rape will do't——He'll be hang'd——And then, what becomes of thee, my little *Lopez?* Why, the Honour to a——dingle dangle by him. Which he'll have the good Nature to be mighty sorry for. But I may chance to be before-hand with him: If we are not taken in the Fact, they'll perhaps do him the Honour to set a Reward upon his Head. Which if they do Don, I shall go near to follow your Moral Example, secure my Pardon, make my Fortune, and hang you up for the Good of your Country.

ACT III

SCENE, Don Felix's *House.*

Enter Don Felix, Don Pedro, Leonora, *and* Jacinta.

Don Fel. HOW Son! oblig'd to leave us Immediately say you?
    Don Ped. My ill Fortune Sir, will have it so.
Leo. [*Aside.*] What can this be?
Don Fel. Pray what's the Matter? You Surprize me.
Don Ped. This Letter Sir will inform you.
Don Fel. [*Reads.*] *My dear Son,* Bertrand *has brought me the Wellcome News of your Return, and has given me your Letter; which has in some sort Reviv'd my Spirits in the Extremity I am in. I daily expect my Exit from this World; 'Tis now Six years since I have seen you; I shou'd be glad to do it once again before I die; If you will give me that Satisfaction, you must be Speedy. Heaven preserve you.*

[To *Don Ped.*] 'Tis enough: The Occasion I'm sorry for, but since the Ties of Blood and Gratitude Oblige you, far be it from me to hinder you. Farewel, my Son, may you have a Happy Journey, and if it be Heaven's Will, may the Sight of so good a Son, revive so kind a Father. I leave you to bid your Wife adieu. [*Exit* Don Fel.

Don Ped. I must leave you my lovely Bride; but 'tis with bitter pangs of Separation. Had I your Heart to Chear me on my way, I might with such a Cordial run my Course; But that Support you want the Power to give me.

Leo. Who tells you so?

Don Ped. My Eyes and Ears, and all the Pains I bear.

Leo. When Eyes and Ears are much Indulg'd, like Favourite Servants they are apt to abuse the too much Trust, their Master places in 'em.

Don Ped. If I'm abus'd, assist me with some fair Interpretation of all that present Trouble and Disquiet, which is not in my power to overlook, nor yours to hide.

Leo. You might methinks have spar'd my Modesty; and without forcing me to Name your Absence have laid my trouble there.

Don Ped. No no, my fair Deluder, that's a Veil too thin to cover what's so hard to hide, my Presence not my Absence is the Cause; Your cold Reception at my first Approach, prepar'd me for the Stroke; and 'twas not long before your Mouth confirm'd my Doom; *Don Guzman, I am yours.*

Leo. Is't then Impossible the Mouth shou'd utter one Name for another?

Don Ped. Not at all; when it follows the Dictates of the Heart.

Leo. Were it even so, what wrong is from that Heart receiv'd, where Duty and where Virtue are its Rulers?

Don Ped. Where they preside, our Honour may be safe, yet our Minds be on the Wrack.

Leo. This discourse will scarce produce a Remedy, we'll end it therefore if you please, and leave the rest to time. Besides the Occasion of your Journey presses you.

Don Ped. The Occasion of my Delay, presses you I fear much more; you count the tedious Minutes I am with you, and are reduc't to mind me of my Duty, to free your self from my Sight.

Leo. You urge this thing too far, and do me Wrong. The Sentiments I have for you, are much more favourable than your Jealousy suffers 'em to Appear. But if my Heart has seem'd to lean another way, before you had a Title to it, you ought not to conclude, I shall suffer it to do so long.

Don Ped. I know you have Virtue, Gratitude and Truth, and therefore 'tis, I love you to my Ruin. Cou'd I believe you False, Contempt wou'd soon release me from my Chains, which yet I can't but wish to wear for ever: Therefore Indulge at least your pitty to your Slave, 'tis the Soft Path in which we tread to Love. I leave behind a Tortur'd heart to move you.

> *Weigh well it's Pains, think on it's Passion too,*
> *Remember all it's Torments, Spring from you,*
> *And if you cannot Love at least be true.*

[Exit Don Pedro.

Jacin. Now by my troth Madam, I'm ready to Cry. He's a Pretty Fellow, and deserves better Luck.

Leo. I own he do's: And his Behaviour wou'd engage any thing that were unengag'd. But alas! I want his Pitty, more than he do's mine.

Jacin. You do? Now I'm of another mind. The Moment he sees your Picture, he's in Love with you: The Moment he's in Love with you, he Embarques, and like lightning, in a Moment more he's here; where you are pleas'd to receive him with a *Don Guzman, I am yours.* Ah——poor Man.

Leo. I own *Jacinta*, he's Unfortunate, but still I say my Fate is harder yet. The Irresistable Passion I have for *Guzman*, renders *Don Pedro* with all his Merit Odious to me; yet I must in his favour, make eternal War against the Strength of Inclination and the Man I Love.

Jac. [aside.] Um——If I were in her Case, I cou'd find an Expedient for all this Matter. But she makes such a bussle with her Virtue, I dare not propose it to her.

Leo. Besides *Don Pedro* possesses what he Loves, but I must never think on poor *Don Guzman* more.   [*Weeping.*

Jac. Poor *Don Guzman*, indeed. We han't said a word of the Pickle he's in yet. Hark! Somebody knocks———at the Old Rendezvous. It's he on my Conscience.

Leo. Let's be gone; I must think of him no more.

Jac. Yes, let's be gone; but let's know whether 'tis he or not first.

Leo. No *Jacinta*, I must not speak with him any more. [*Sighing.*] I'm marry'd to another.

Jac. Marry'd to another? well, marry'd to another, why if one were Marry'd to Twenty Others, one may give a Civil Gentleman an Answer.

Leo. Alas! what would'st thou have me to say to him?

Jac. Say to him? Why one may find Twenty things to say to a Man: Say that 'tis true you are Marry'd to Another, and that a——'twould be a Sin to think of any Body but your Husband, and that——you are of a Timorous Nature, and afraid of being Damn'd, and that a——You wou'd not have him Die neither, That a——Folks are Mortal, and things sometimes come strangely about, and a Widdow's a Widdow, and——

Leo. Peace Levity. [*Sighing.*] But see who 'tis knocks.

Jac. Who's there?

Isa. [Behind the Scenes.] 'Tis I, *Isabella*.

Leo. Isabella? What do you want my Dear?

Isa. Your Succour for Heaven's sake *Leonora*. My Brother will destroy himself.

Leo. Alas! it is not in my power to save him.

Isa. Permit him but to speak to you, that possibly may do.

Leo. Why have not I the Force to refuse him?

Don Guz. [Behind the Scenes.] Is it you I hear, my poor lost Mistress. Am I so happy, once more to meet you, where I so often have been blest?

Jac. Courage Madam, say a little something to him.

Don Guz. Not one kind Word, to a diſtracted Lover? No pitty for a Wretch, you have made so Miserable?

Leo. The only way to end that Misery, is to forget we ever thought of Happiness.

Don Guz. And is that in your Power? Ah *Leonora,* you ne'er lov'd like me.

Leo. How I have lov'd, to Heaven I Appeal; but Heaven do's now permit that Love no more.

Don Guz. Why do's it then permit us Life and Thought? Are we deceiv'd in it's Omnipotence? is it reduc't to find it's Pleasures in it's Creatures pain?

Leo. In what or where, the Joys of Heaven consiſt, lies deeper than a Woman's Line can fathom; But this we know, a Wife muſt in her Husband seek for hers, and therefore I muſt think of you no more.——Farewell.

[*Exit* Leo.

Don Guz. Yet hear me Cruel *Leonora.*

Jac. It muſt be an other time then, for she's whipt off now. All the Comfort I can give you is, that I see she durſt not truſt herself any longer in your Company. But hush, I hear a noise, get you gone, we shall be catcht.

Leo. [*within.*] *Jacinta.*

Jac. I come, I come Madam. [*Exit* Jac.

Enter Lopez.

Lop. If I miſtake not, there are a Brace of Lovers, intend to take some Pains about Madam, in her Husband's Absence. Poor *Don Pedro:* Well; my thinks a Man's in a very merry Mood that Marries a handsome Wife: When I dispose of my Person, it shall be to an Ugly one. They take it so kindly, and are so full of Acknowledgment: Watch you, wait upon you, Nurse you, Humour you, are so Fond, and so Chaſt. Or if the Hussy has Presumption enough to think of being otherwise, Away with her into the Mountains Fifty Leagues off; no body opposes. If she's Mutinous, give her Discipline; every body approves on't. Hang her says one, he's kinder than she deserves; Damn her says another, why do's not he Starve her, But if she's Handsome, Ah, the Brute crys one, Ah the Turk crys t'other; Why don't she cuckold him says this Fellow; why do's not she Poison him says that, and away comes a Pacquet of Epiſtles to advise her to't. Ah poor *Don Pedro!* But enough: 'Tis now Night all's hush and ſtill; every Bodies a Bed, and what am I to do? Why as other truſty Domeſtiques, sit up to let the Thief in. But I suppose he won't be here yet, with the help of a small Nap before hand, I shall be in a better Condition to perform the duty of a Centinel, when I go to my Poſt. This Corner will juſt fit me; come *Lopez,* lie thee down, short Prayers and to sleep. [*He lies down.*

Enter Jacinta *with a Candle in her Hand.*

Jac. So, I have put my poor Lady to Bed with nothing but Sobs, Tears, Sighs, Wishes and a poor Pillow to mumble; instead of a Bridegroom Poor Heart. I pitty her but every body has their Afflictions, and by the Beads of my Grandmother, I have mine.

Tell me kind Gentlemen, if I have not something to excite you? Methinks I have a Roguish Eye, I'm sure I have a Mettled Heart. I'm soft and Warm, and sound may it please ye.

Whence comes it then, this Rascal *Lopez,* who now has been two Hours in the Family, has not yet thought it Worth his while to make one Motion towards me. Not that the Blockheads Charms have mov'd me, but I'm angry mine han't been able to move him. I doubt, I must begin with the Lubber; my Reputation's at Stake upon't, and I must Rouze the Drone, some how.

Lopez *rubbing his Eyes, and coming on.*

Lop. What a damn'd Condition is that of a Vallet, no sooner do I in comfortable Slumber, close my Eyes; but methinks my Master's upon me, with Fifty slaps o' th' Back, for making him wait in the Street. I have his Orders to let him in here to Night, and so I had e'en———Who's that?———*Jacinta?*———Yes———a Caterwauling?———like enough.

Jac. The Fellow's there: I had best not lose the Occasion.

Lop. The Slut's handsome. I begin to kindle. But if my Master shou'd be at the Door?———Why there let him be till the matter's over.   *[Aside.*

Jac. Shall I advance?   *[Aside.*

Lop. Shall I Venture?   *[Aside.*

Jac. How severe a Look he has.   *[Aside.*

Lop. She seems very Reserv'd.   *[Aside.*

Jac. If he shou'd put the Negative upon me?   *[Aside.*

Lop. She seems a Woman of great Discretion. I Tremble.   *[Aside.*

Jac. Hang it I must venture.   *[Aside.*

Lop. Faint Heart never won Fair Lady.   *[Aside.*

Jac. Lopez!

Lop. Jacinta!

Jac. O dear Heart, is't you?

Lop. Charming *Jacinta,* fear me not.

Jac. O ho! he begins to talk soft———then let us take upon us again.   *[Aside.*

Lop. Cruel *Jacinta,* whose Mouth (small as it is) has made but one Morsel of my Heart.

Jac. It's well he prevents me, I was going to Leap about the Rascall's Neck.   *[Aside.*

Lop. Barbare *Jacinta*, cast your Eyes
On your poor *Lopez*, e're he dies.

Jac. Poetry too? Nay then I have done his Business.   [*Aside.*

Lop. Feel how I Burn, with hot Desire,
Ah! Pitty me, and quench my Fire.
Deaf my fair Tyrant? Deaf to my Woes?
Nay then, Barbarian, in it go's.   [*Drawing a Knife.*

Jac. Why how now Jack Sauce, why how now Presumption, what Encouragement have I given you, Jack-alent, to Attaque me with your Tenders? I cou'd tear your Eyes out Sirrah, for thinking I'm such a one. What indecency have you seen in my Behaviour, Impudence, that you shou'd think me for your Beastly turn; you Goat you.

Lop. Patience, my much offended Goddess, 'tis Honourably I wou'd share your Bed.

Jac. Peace I say—Mr. Liquorish. I, for whom the most Successful Cavaliers employ their Sighs in Vain, shall I look down upon a Crawling Worm Pha—See that Crop Ear there, that Vermin that wants to Eat at a Table, wou'd set his Master's mouth a Watering.

Lop. May I presume to make an humble Meal, upon what Savory Remnants he may leave?

Jac. No.

Lop. 'Tis hard, 'tis wondrous hard!

Jac. Leave me.

Lop. 'Tis Pittiful, 'tis wondrous Pittiful!

Jac. Begon I say.
Thus, Ladies 'tis, perhaps sometimes with you;
With Scorn you fly, the thing which you persue.   [*Exit* Jac.

Lop. [*Solus.*] 'Tis very well, Mrs. Flipflap, 'tis very well, but do you hear——Tawdery, you are not so Alluring as you think you are—— Comb-brush, nor I so much in Love——your Maidenhead may chance to grow Mouldy with your Airs,—the Pox be your Bed-fellow, there's that for you. Come let's think no more on't. Saylors must meet with Storms; my Master's going to Sea too. He may Chance to fare no better with the Lady, than I have done with her *Abigail:* There may be foul Weather there too. I reckon at present he may be lying by, under a Mizen at the Street Door, I think it Rains too, for his Comfort. What if I shou'd leave him there an hour or two in fresco, and try to work off the Amour that way. No; People will be Physick't their own way. But perhaps I might save his Life by't——Yes, and have my Bones broke for being so Officious; Therefore, if you are at the Door *Don John*, walk in, and take your Fortune.   [*Opens the Door.*

        Enter Don John.

Don John. Hist, hist.

Lop. Hiſt, hiſt.

Don John. *Lopez*.

Lop. [*Aside*.] The Devil——Tread softly.

Don John. Are they all a Sleep?

Lop. Dead.

Don John. Enough, shut the Door.

Lop. 'Tis done.

Don John. Now be gone.

Lop. What? Shut the Door firſt, and then be gone? Now, my thinks I might as well have gone firſt, and then shut the Door.

Don John. I bid you be gone you Dog, do you find the way.

Lop. [*Aside*.] Stark mad; and always so, when a Woman's in chace. But Sir, will you keep your Chief Miniſter out of the Secrets of your State? Pray let me know what this Night's Work is to be?

Don John. No Queſtions but march.   [*Lop. go's to the Door and returns*.

Lop. Very well——— But Sir, shall I ſtay for you in the Street?

Don John. No, nor Stir out of the House.

Lop. So: Well Sir, I'll do juſt as you have Order'd me, I'll be gone, and I'll ſtay, and I'll March, and I won't Stir, and—juſt as you say Sir.

Don John. I see you are afraid you Rascal you.

Lop. Passably.

Don John. Well, be it so; but you shan't leave the House Sir, therefore begon to your Hogſtie, and wait farther Orders.

Lop. [*Aside*.] But firſt I'll know how you intend to dispose of your self.

[*Lop. hides behind the Door*.

Don John *solus*.

Don John. All's hush and ſtill; and I am at the Point of being a Happy ——Villain. That Thought comes uninvited——Then like an uninvited Gueſt let it be treated: Begone Intruder. *Leonora*'s Charms, turn Vice to Virtue, Treason into Truth, Nature who has made her the Supream Objeƈt of our Desires, muſt needs have design'd her the Regulator of our Morrals. Whatever points at her; is pointed right. We are all her due, Mankind's the Dower, which Heaven has settled on her; and he's the Villain that wou'd rob her of her Tribute. I therefore as in Duty bound, will In, and pay her mine.

Lop. [*Aside*.] There he goes I'faith; he seem'd as if he had a Qualm juſt now; but he never go's without a Dram of Conscience Water about him, to set Matters right again.

Don John. [*Aside*.] This is her Door. 'Tis Lock't. But I have a Smith about me, will make her Staple Fly.

[*Pulls out some Irons, and forces the Lock*.

Lop. [*Aside.*] Hark, hark, if he is not equip't for a Housebreaker too. Very well; he has provided Two Strings to his Bow, if he scapes the Rape, he may be hang'd upon the Burglary.

Don John. [*Aside.*] There 'tis done. So: No Watch Light burning. [*Peeping into her Chamber.*] All in Darkness? So much the better. 'Twill save a Great deal of Blushing on both sides. Methinks I feel myself mighty Modeſt, I tremble too. That's not proper at this time. Be firm my Courage, I have business for thee——So——How am I now?——pretty well. Then by your leave *Don Pedro.* I muſt supply your Negleſt. You shou'd not have Married till you were ready for Consummation, a Maidenhead ought no more to lie upon a handsom Bride, than an Impeachment upon an Innocent Miniſter. [Don John *enters the Chamber.*

Lop. [*Coming forwards.*] Well done; Well done; Gad a marcy my little *Judas.* Unfortunate *Don Pedro,* thou haſt left thy Purse in the Hands of a Robber: And while thou art Galloping to pay thy laſt Duty to thy Father, he's at leaſt upon the Trot, to pay the firſt to thy Wife. Ah the Traytor! What a Capilotade of Damnation will there be Cook't up for him. But softly: Let's lay our Ear to the Door, and pick up some Curiosities.——I hear no noise——There's no Light. We shall have him Blunder where he shou'd not do by and by——Commit a Rape upon her Tea Table perhaps; break all her China, and then she'll be sure to hang him. But hark—now I hear——nothing. She do's not say a Word: She sleeps curiously:——How if she shou'd take it all for a Dream now? Or her Virtue shou'd be fallen into an Appoplex? Where the Pox will all this end?

Leo. [*Within.*] *Jacinta, Beatrix, Fernandes,* Murder, Murder help, help, help.

Lop. Now the Play begins it opens finely.

Leo. [*Within.*] Father, *Alphonso,* Save me, O save me.

Lop. Comedy or Tragedy, for a Ducat? for fear of the latter, Decamp *Lopez.* [*Exit* Lopez.

Scene changes to Leonora's *Bed-Chamber, discovers* Leonora *in a Gown, holding* Don John *by the Sleeve.*

Leo. Whoever you are Villain you shan't escape me, and tho' your efforts have been in vain, you shan't fail to receive the Recompence of your Attempt, help ho, help there, help.

[Don John *breaks from her, but can't find the Door.*

Don John. [*Aside.*] S'death I shall be undone, where is this damn'd Door?

Leo. He'll get away; a Light there, quickly.

Enter Don Guzman *with his Sword drawn.*

Don Guz. Where are you fair Angel? I come to lose my Life in your Defence.

Don John. [*Aside.*] That's *Guzman's* Voice: The Devil has sent him. But we are still in the Dark; I have one tour yet Impudence be my Aid. Lights there ho; Where is the Villain that durst Attempt the Virtuous *Leonora?*

Don Guz. His Life shall make her Satisfaction.

Don John. Or mine shall fall in his pursuit.

Don Guz. 'Tis by my hands, that she shall see him die.

Don John. My Sword shall lay him bleeding at her Feet.

Leo. [*Aside.*] What can this mean? But here's Lights at last thank the Just bounteous Heaven.

Don John. Enter with the Light there; but Secure the Door, lest the Traytor Scape my Vengeance.

> *Enter* Don Pedro, *with a Light, he finds* Leonora *between 'em.*
> *Both their Swords drawn.*

Leo. O Heaven's what is't I see?

Don John. Don Pedro here?

Don Ped. What Monstrous Scene is this?   [*Aside.*

Don Guz. What Accident has brought him here?   [*Aside.*

Don John. Now I'm Intrigu'd, indeed.   [*Aside.*

                    [*Don Pedro* steps back and shuts the Door.

Don Ped. [*Aside.*] This Mystery must unfold before we part. What Torments has my Fate provided me? Is this the Comfort I'm to reap, to dry my Tears for my poor Father's Death? [*To Leo.*] Ah *Leonora.*

Leo. [*Aside.*] Alas! where will this end?   [*Falling into a Chair.*

Don Ped. [*Aside.*] Naked; and thus attended at the dead of Night, my Soul is froze at what I see. Confusion sits in all their Faces, and in large Characters I read, the Ruin of my Honour and my Love.

[*To the Men.*] Speak Statues; if you yet have power to speak, Why at this time of Night, you are found with *Leonora?*——None speak? *Don John*, it is from you I ought to know.

Don John. My Silence may inform you.

Don Ped. Your Silence do's inform me of my Shame, but I must have some Information more; Explain the whole.

Don John. I shall. You remember, *Don Pedro*——

Don Ped. Be quick.

Don John. You remember you charg'd me before you went.

Don Ped. I remember well, go on.

Don John. With the care of your Honour.

Don Ped. I did, dispatch.

Don John. Very well; you see *Don Guzman*, in this Appartment:

You see your Wife Naked, and you see me, my Sword in my Hand. That's all.

Don Ped. [*Drawing upon* Don Guz.] 'Tis here then I am to revenge my Wrongs.

Don Guz. Hold.

Don Ped. Villain, defend thy self.

Leo. O Heaven.

Don Guz. Yet hear me.

Don Ped. What canst thou say?

Don Guz. The Truth, as holy Heaven itself is Truth. I heard the Shrieks and Crys of *Leonora;* what the occasion was I knew not, but she repeated 'em with so much Vehemence, I found whatever her Distress might be, her Succour must be suddain; So leapt the Wall that parts our Houses, and flew to her Assistance. *Don John* can if he please, inform you more.

Don Ped. [*Aside.*] Mankind's a Villain, and this may be true. Yet 'tis too Monstrous for a quick Conception. I shou'd be cautious how I wrong *Don John.* Sure 'tis not right to Ballance. I yet have but their Words against their Words; I know *Don John* for my Friend, and *Guzman* for my Rival. What can be Clearer? Yet hold: If *Leonora's* Innocent, she may Untangle all.

Madam, I shou'd be glad to know (if I have so much Interest left) which way your Evidence will point my Sword.

Leo. My Lord I'm in the same perplexity with you; All I can say, is this; One of 'em came to Force me; T'other to save me; but the Night confounding the Villainy of the Guilty, with the Generosity of the Innocent; I still am ignorant to which I owe, my Gratitude, or my Resentment.

Don Guz. But Madam, did you not hear me cry I came to help you?

Leo. I own it.

Don John. And did you not hear me threaten to destroy the Author of your Fears?

Leo. I can't deny it.

Don Guz. What can there be more to clear me?

Don John. Or me?

Don Ped. Yet One's a Villain still.

[*Aside.*] My Confusion but encreases; yet why confus'd? It is, it must be *Guzman.* But how came *Don John* here? Right. *Guzman* has said, how he came to her Aid, but *Alvarada* cou'd not enter but by Treason. Then Perish———

Don Guz. Who?

Don John. Who?

Don Ped. Just Gods Instruct me who?

Don Felix knocks.

Don Fel. [*Within.*] Let me in, open the Door.

Leo. 'Tis my Father.

Don Ped. No matter, keep the Door faſt.
[*Aside.*] I'll have this matter go no farther, 'till I can reach the depth on't.
Don Guzman, leave the House: I muſt suspend my Vengeance for a time.

Don Guz. I obey you; but I'll lose my Life, or shew my Innocence.
[*Exit Don Guz.*

Don Fel. [*Within.*] Open the Door, Why am I kep't out?

Don Ped. *Don John,* follow me by this back Way. And you *Leonora,*
retire. [*Exit* Leonora.

Don John. [*Aside, following* Don Ped.] If *Don Guzman's* Throat were
cut, wou'd not this Bussle end?—Yes——Why then if his Throat be not
cut, may this Bussle end me.

The End of the Third Aƈt.

ACT IV

Scene, Don Guzman's *House.*

Enter Don Guzman, *and* Galindo.

Don Guz. **G** *Alindo!*

[*Musing.* **G** *Gal.* Sir.

Don Guz. Try if you can see *Jacinta,* let her privately know I wou'd
fain speak with her.

Gal. It shall be done, Sir. [*Exit* Gal.

Don Guzman *solus.*

Sure Villainy and Impudence were never on the Stretch before: This
Traytor, has wrackt them till they Crack. To what a Plunge the Villain's
Tour has brought me. *Pedro's* Resentment, muſt at laſt be pointed here:
But that's a Trifle, had he not ruin'd me with *Leonora,* I easily had pass'd
him by the reſt.——What's to be done? Which way shall I convince her
of my Innocence? The Blood of him, who has dar'd declare me Guilty
may satisfie my Vengenace, but not Aid my Love. No, I am loſt with
her for ever.——

Enter Jacinta.

Speak; is't not so *Jacinta?* Am I not ruin'd with the Virtuous *Leonora?*

Jacin. One of you I suppose is.

Don Guz. Which doſt thou think.

Jacin. Why he that came to spoil all, who shou'd it be?

Don Guz. Prithee be Serious with me if thou can'ſt for one small Moment, and Advise me, which way I shall take to convince her of my Innocence, That it was I that came to do her Service.

Jacin. Why you both came to do her Service did not you?

Don Guz. Still trifling?

Jacin. No by my Troth not I.

Don Guz. Then turn thy Thoughts to ease me in my Torment, and be my faithful Witness to her, That Heaven and Hell and all their Wrath I Impricate, if ever Once I knew One Fleeting Thought, that durſt propose to me, so Impious an attempt. No *Jacinta;* I love her well; but Love with that Humility, whatever Misery I feel, my Torture ne'er shall urge me on to Seize, more than her Bounty gives me leave to take.

Jacin. And the Murrain take such a Lover, and his Humility both say I. Why sure Sir, you are not in earneſt in this Story, are you?

Don Guz. Why do'ſt thou queſtion it?

Jacin. Because I really and seriously thought you Innocent.

Don Guz. Innocent? What doſt thou mean?

Jacin. Mean? Why what shou'd I mean? I mean that I concluded you Lov'd my Lady to that degree, you cou'd not Live without her: And that the Thought of her being given up to another, made your Passion Flame out like Mount *Etna*. That upon this, your Love got the Bridle in his Teeth and ran away with you into her Chamber, where that Impertinent Spy, upon her and you, *Don John*, follow'd and prevented farther Proofs of your Affeſtion.

Don Guz. Why sure——

Jacin. Why sure; Thus I thought it was, and thus she thinks it is. If you have a mind in the depth of your Discretion to convince her of your Innocence—May your Innocence be your Reward. I'm sure were I in her place, you shou'd never have any other from me.

Don Guz. Was there then no Merit, in flying to her Assiſtance when I heard her Cries?

Jacin. As much as the Conſtable and the Watch might have pretended to something to Drink.

Don Guz. This is all Raillery, 'tis impossible she can be pleas'd with such an Attempt.

Jacin. 'Tis impossible she can be pleas'd with being reduc'd to make the Attempt upon you.

Don Guz. But was this a proper way to save her Blushes?

Jacin. 'Twas in the dark, that's one way.

Don Guz. But it must look like down right Violation.

Jacin. If it did not feel like it, what did that signify? Come Sir, Waggery apart. You know I'm your Servant, I have given you proofs on't. Therefore don't distrust me now if I tell you; this Quarrel may be made up with the Wife, tho' perhaps not with the Husband; In short, she thinks you were first in her Chamber, and has not the worse Opinion of you for it; she makes allowance for your Sufferings, and has still Love enough for you, not to be displeas'd with the utmost Proofs you can give, that you have still a warm remain for her.

Don Guz. If this be true, and that she thought 'twas me, why did she Cry out to expose me?

Jacin. Because at that time she did not think 'twas you. Will that content you? And now she do's think 'twas you, your Business is to let her think so on; for in a word, I can see she's concern'd at the Danger she has brought you into, and I believe wou'd be heartily glad to see you well out on't.

Don Guz. ——'Tis impossible she can forgive me.

Jacin. Oons—Now Heaven forgive me, for I had a great Oath upon the Very tip of my Tongue; You'd make one mad with your Impossibles and your Innocence, and your Humilities. 'Sdeath Sir d'you think a Woman makes no distinction between the Assaults of a Man she likes and one she don't? My Lady hates *Don John*, and if she Thought 'twas he had done this Job, she'd hang him for't in her own Garters; She likes you, and if you shou'd do such an other, you might still die in your Bed like a Bishop, for her.

Don Guz. Well, I'll dispute no farther. I put myself into thy hands. What am I to do next?

Jacin. Why, do as she bids you; be in the way at the old Rendezvous, she'll take the first Occasion she can to Speak to you; and when you meet, do as I bid you, and instead of your Innocent and Humble, be Guilty and Resolute. Your Mistriss is now Marry'd, Sir, consider that. She has chang'd her Situation, and so must you your Battery. Attack a Maid Gently, a Wife Warmly, and be as rugged with a Widdow as you can. Good buy t' ye Sir.   [*Exeunt several Ways.*

Scene [II], Don Felix's *House.*

Enter Don Pedro *Solus.*

In what Distraction have I past this Night! Sure I shall never close my Eyes again! No Wrack can equal what I feel. Wounded in both my Honour and my Love; They have pierc'd me in two Tender parts. Yet cou'd I take my just Revenge, it wou'd in some degree asswage my smart. O guide me Heaven to that Cordial drop——Hold! A glance of Light I think begins to—— Yes——Right. When Yesterday I brought *Don John* hither, was not *Don Felix* much disturb'd?——He was; and why? ——That may be worth enquiring. But something more occurs. At my Arrival in this City, was I not told two Cavaliers were warm in the Pursuit of *Leonora?* One I remember well they Nam'd, 'twas *Guzman:* The other, I am yet a stranger to. I fear I shall not be so long——'Tis *Alvarada;* O the Traytor; yet I may wrong him much. I have *Guzman*'s own Confession that he past the Wall to come to *Leonora*——O, but 'twas to her Assistance——And so it might, and he a Villain still. There are Assistances of various sorts——What were her Wants?—That's dark— But whatso'ere they were, he came to her Assistance. Death be his Portion for his ready Service.

Enter Don Felix.

Don Fel. You avoid me *Don Pedro;* 'tis not Well. Am I not your Father, have you not Reason to believe I am your Friend?

Don Ped. I have.

Don Fel. Why do you not then treat me like a Father and a Friend? The Mystery you make to me of last Nights disturbance, I take unkindly from you. Come tell me your Grief, that if I can I may asswage it..

Don Ped. Nothing but Vengeance, can give me ease.

Don Fel. If I desire to know your wrongs, tis to Assist you in Revenging 'em.

Don Ped. Know then, that last Night in this Apartment I found *Don Guzman* and *Don John.*

Don Fel. Guzman and *Alvarada?*

Don Ped. Yes; and *Leonora* almost Naked between them, crying out for Aid.

Don Fel. Were they both guilty?

Don Ped. One was come to force her, t'other to rescue her.

Don Fel. Which was the Criminal?

Don Ped. Of that I yet am Ignorant. They accuse each other.

Don Fel. Can't your Wife determine it?

Don Ped. The Darkness of the Night, put it out of her Power.

Don Fel. But I perhaps may bring some Light to Aid you. I have part in the Affront: And tho' my Arm's too Old and Weak to serve you; my Council may be useful to your Vengeance. Know then, that *Don Guzman* has a long time pursu'd my Daughter; and I as resolutely, refus'd his Suit: which however has not hindred him from searching all Occasions to see and speak to her.

Don John, on his Side——

Don Ped. Don John's my Friend, and I am confident——

Don Fel. That Confidence deſtroys you. Hear my Charge, and be your self his Judge. He too has been, a pressing Suitor to my Daughter.

Don Ped. Impossible.

Don Fel. To me my self, he has own'd his Love to her.

Don Ped. Good Gods. Yet ſtill this leaves the Myſtery where it was; this Charge is equal.

Don Fel. 'Tis true; but yonder's One (if you can make her speak) I have reason to believe can tell us more. Ho, *Jacinta.*

Enter Jacinta.

Jacin. Do you call me Sir?

Don Fel. Yes; *Don Pedro* wou'd Speak with you. [*To* Don Pedro *aside.*] I'll leave you with her; press her both by Threats and Promises; and if you find your Wife in fault; Old as I am, her Father too, I'll raise my arm to plunge this Dagger in her Breaſt; and by that fermety convince the World, my Honours dearer to me than my Child.   [*Exit* Don Fel.

Don Ped. [*Aside.*] Heaven grant me power to ſtifle my Rage, till 'tis time to let my Vengeance fly. *Jacinta* come near. I have some Business with you.

Jacin. [*Aside.*] His Business with me at this time, can be good for nothing I doubt.

Jacin. [*to* Don Ped.] What Commands have you Sir for me? for I'm not very well.

Don Ped. What's your disorder?

Jacin. A little Sort of a something towards an Ague, I think.

Don Ped. You don't seem so ill, but you may tell me——

Jacin. O, I can tell you nothing Sir, I assure you.

Don Ped. You Answer me before you hear my Queſtion. That looks as if you knew——

Jacin. I know that what you are going to ask me, is a Secret I'm out at.

Don Ped. [*offering her a Purse.*] Then this shall let thee into it.

Jacin. I know nothing of the Matter.

Don Ped. Come, tell me all, and take thy Reward.

Jacin. I know nothing of the matter, I say.

Don Ped. [*drawing his Sword.*] Speak; or by all the Flame and Fire of Hell Eternal——

Jacin. O Lard, O Lard, O Lard.

Don Ped. Speak; or th'art dead.

Jacin. But if I do Speak, shan't I be Dead for all that?

Don Ped. Speak, and thou art safe.

Jacin. Well—O Lard——I'm so Frighted——But if I must Speak then——O dear Heart——give me the Purse.

Don Ped. There.

Jacin. Why truly, between a Purse in one's hand—and—a Sword in one's Guts, I think there's little room left for debate.

Don Ped. Come, begin, I'm Impatient.

Jacin. Begin? let me see; where shall I begin? At *Don Guzman*, I think.

Don Ped. What of him?

Jacin. Why he has been in love with my Lady these Six Years.

Don Ped. I know it; but how has she receiv'd him?

Jacin. Receiv'd him? Why—as young Maids use to receive Handsome Fellows; at first Ill; afterwards better.

Don Ped. [*Aside.*] Furies!
Did they ever meet?

Jacin. A little.

Don Ped. By Day or Night?

Jacin. Both.

Don Ped. Distraction. Where was their Rendezvous?

Jacin. Where they cou'd not do one another much good.

Don Ped. As how?

Jacin. As through a Hole in a Wall.

Don Ped. The Strumpet Banters me: Be Serious Insolence, or I shall spoil your Gayety: I'm not dispos'd to Mirth.

Jacin. Why I am serious. If you like my Story the better for't.

Don Ped. [*Aside.*] How miserable a Wretch am I!

Jacin. I tell you there's a Wall parts their two Houses, and in that Wall there's a Hole. How the Wall came by the Hole, I can't tell; may hap by chance, may hap by no chance; but there 'tis, and there they use to Prattle.

Don Ped. And this is Truth?

Jacin. I can't bate you a Word on't, Sir.

Don Ped. When did they meet there last?

Jacin. Yesterday. I suppose 'twas only to bid one another Adieu.

Don Ped. Ah, *Jacinta*, thou hast pierced my Soul!

Jacin. [*Aside.*] And yet I han't told you half I cou'd tell you my *Don*.

Don Ped. Where is this Place you speak of?

Jacin. There 'tis, if you are Curious.

Don Ped. When they wou'd speak with one another, what's the Call?

Jacin. Tinkle Tinkle.

Don Ped. A Bell?

Jacin. It is.

Don Ped. Ring.

Jacin. What do you mean Sir?

Don Ped. [*hastily.*] Ring.

Jacin. 'Tis done.

Don Ped. [*Aside.*] I'll make use of her to Examin him. Do's he come?

Jacin. Not yet.

Don Ped. Pull again.

Jacin. You must give him time, Sir: My Lady always do's so.

Don Ped. I hear something.

Jacin. 'Tis he.

Don Guz. [*within.*] Who's there?

Don Ped. [*softly.*] Say you are *Leonora.*

                 [*Dumb show of, her unwillingness, and his threatning.*

Jacin. [*softly.*] 'Tis *Leonora.*

Don Guz. What are your Commands Madam? Is it possible so Unfortunate a Wretch as I, can be capable of serving you?

           [*Don Ped. whispers* Jacinta, *who seems backward to speak.*

Jacin. I come to ask you, how cou'd you so far forget that Infinite regard you have profest, as to make an attempt so dangerous both to your self and me; and which, with all the Esteem and Love I have ever born you, you scarce cou'd hope I ever shou'd forgive you.

Don Guz. Alas! my hopes and fears were Vanish't too. My Council was my Love and my dispair. If they advis'd me wrong, of them complain, for it was you who made 'em my Directors.

Don Ped. [*Aside.*] The Villain owns the Fact. It seems he thinks he has not so much to fear, from her Resentment. O Torture!

               Enter Leonora.

Jacin. [*Aside.*] So; she's here; that's as I expected; now we are blown up.

Leo. [*Aside, not seeing them.*] If I don't mistake, I heard *Don Guzman's* call. I can't refuse to Answer it. Forgive me Gods, and let my Woman's weakness, plead my Cause.—How? my Husband here? Nay then——

Don Ped. You seem disorder'd Madam; pray what may be the Cause?

Leo. [*confus'd.*] I don't know really; I'm not——I don't know that—

Don Ped. You did not know that I was here I guess?

Leo. Yes I did, and——came to speak with you.

Don Ped. I'm not at present, in a talking Humour, but if your Tongue is set to Conversation, there's one behind the Wall, will entertain you.

Don Guz. But is it possible fair *Leonora*, that you can pardon my Attempt?

Don Ped. [*to Leo.*] You hear him Madam, he dares Own it to you.

Leo. [*Aside.*] *Jacinta* winks; I guess what Scene they have been Acting here. My part is now to play.

[*To* Don Ped.] I see Sir he dares Own it; Nor is he the first Lover has presum'd beyond the Countenance he ever has receiv'd. Pray draw near, and hear what he has more to say: It is my Interest you shou'd know the Depth of all has ever passed between us.

Leo. [*to* Don Guz.] I fain wou'd know *Don Guzman*, whether in the whole Conduct of my Life, you have known one step, that cou'd encourage you to hope I ever cou'd be yours, but on the terms of Honour which you sought me?

Don Guz. Not one.

Leo. Why then shou'd you believe I cou'd forgive, the taking that by force, which you already were convinc'd I valu'd more the keeping, than my Life?

Don Guz. Had my Love been as temperate as yours, I with your Reason, had perhaps debated. But not in Reason, but in Flames, I flew to *Leonora*.

Leo. If strong Temptation be allow'd a Plea, Vice, in the worst of shapes, has much to Urge: No, cou'd any thing have shaken me in Virtue, it must have been the strength of it in you. Had you shone bright enough to dazzle me, I blindly might have mist the Path I meant to tread: But now you have clear'd my Sight for ever. If, therefore, from this moment more you dare to let me know one Thought of Love, tho' in the humblest Stile, expect to be a Sacrifice to him you attempt to wrong. Farewel.

[*She retires from him.*

Don Guz. O stay and hear me, I have wrong'd my self; I'm Innocent, by all that's Sacred, Just and Good, I'm Innocent!

Don Ped. [*Aside.*] What do's he mean?

Don Guz. I have own'd a Fact I am not Guilty of; *Jacinta* can inform you, she knows I never——

Jacin. I know? The Man's mad; Pray begone, Sir, my Lady will hear no more. I'll shut him out Madam, shan't I? [*She shuts the Hole.*

Leo. I have no farther Business with him.

Enter Isabella *hastily.*

Isab. O Heavens *Leonora*, where are you? *Don Pedro*, you can assist me better.

Leo. What's the Matter?

Don Ped. What is it Madam I can serve you in?

Isab. In what the Peace of my whole Life consists, the Safety of my

Brother; *Don John*'s Servant has this moment left me a Letter for him, which I have Open'd, knowing there is an Animosity of some time between 'em.

Don Ped. Well Madam?

Isab. O dear it is a Challenge, and what to do I know not; if I shew it my Brother, he'll immediately fly to the place Appointed; and if I don't, he'll be Accus'd of Cowardise. One way I Risque his Life, T'other I ruin his Honour.

Don Ped. What wou'd you have me do Madam?

Isab. I'll tell you, Sir: I only beg you'll go to the place where *Don John* expects him; tell him I have Intercepted his Letter, and make him promise you he'll send no more: By this generous Charity you may hinder two Men (whose Piques are on a frivolous occasion) from Murdering one another; and by this good office, you'll repay the small Debt you owe my Brother, for flying laſt Night to *Leonora*'s Succour; and doubly pay the Obligation you have to me upon the same occasion.

Don Ped. What Obligation Madam? I am Ignorant, pray inform me.

Isab. 'Twas I Sir that firſt heard *Leonora*'s Cries, and rais'd my Brother to her Aid. Pray let me receive the same assiſtance from your Prudence, which you have had from my Care, and my Brother's Generosity. But pray lose no time, *Don John* is perhaps already on the Spot, and not meeting my Brother, may send a second Message, which may be Fatal.

Don Ped. Madam be at reſt; you shall be satisfy'd, I'll go this moment. I'll only ask you firſt whether you are sure you heard my Wife call out for Succour, before your Brother paſt the Wall?

Isab. I did; why do you ask that Queſtion?

Don Ped. I have a reason you may be sure.
[*Aside.*] Juſt Heaven I adore thee, the Truth at laſt shines clear, and by that Villain *Alvarada* I'm betray'd. But enough, I'll make use of this Occasion for my Vengeance. [*To* Isab.] Where Madam is it, *Don John* is waiting?

Isab. But here, in a small Feild behind the Garden.

Don Ped. [*Aside.*] His blood shall do me Reason for his Treachery.

Isab. Will you go there directly?

Don Ped. I will. Be Satisfy'd. [*Exit* Don Ped.

Leo. You weep *Isabella?*

Isab. You see my trouble for a Brother, for whom I wou'd Die, and a Lover for whom I wou'd live. They both are Authors of my Grief.

Leo. They both are Inſtruments of my Misfortune.

The End of the Fourth Act.

ACT V

Enter Lopez.

OHO! my good Seignior *Don John*, you are mistaken in your Man; I am your humble Vallet, 'tis true, and I am to Obey you; but when you have got the Devil in your Body, and are upon your Rantipole Adventures; you shall Quixot it by your self for *Lopez*. Yonder he is, waiting for poor *Guzman*, with a Sword of a Fathom and a half; a Dagger for close Engagement; and (if I don't mistake) a Pocket Pistol for extraordinary Occasions. I think I am not in the wrong to keep a little out of the way; These Matters will end in a Court of Justice, or I'm wrong in my foresight: Now that being a place where I am pretty well known, and not over-much reputed, I believe 'tis best, neither to come in for Prisoner nor Evidence. But hold; Yonder comes another *Toledo*. *Don Guzman* I presume, but I presume wrong, 'tis—who is't? *Don Pedro* by all the Powers. What the Pox do's he here, or what the Pox do I here? I'm sure as matters stand, I ought to fly him like a Creditor; but he sees me, 'tis too late to slip him.

Enter Don Pedro.

Don Pedro. How now, *Lopez*, where are you going?

Lop. I'm going, Sir, I——I'm going——if you please I'm going about my Business.

Don Ped. From whence do you come?

Lop. Only, only Sir, from—taking the Air a little, I'm mightily muddled with a Whur——round about in my head for this day or two, I'm going home to be let blood, as fast as I can, Sir.

Don Ped. Hold Sir, I'll let you blood here.

This Rascal may have born some part in this late Adventure; He's a Coward, I'll try to frighten it out of him.

[*Seizing him by the Collar, and drawing his Poignard.*
You Traytor you, y' are dead.

Lop. Mercy *Don Pedro!*

Don Ped. Are you not a Villain? 　　　　　　　　　　[*Lop. kneeling.*

Lop. Yes if you please.

Don Ped. Is there so great a one upon Earth?

Lop. With respect to my Master; No.

Don Ped. Prepare then to die.

Lop. Give me but time, and I will. But Noble *Don Pedro*, Just *Don Pedro*, Generous *Don Pedro*, What is it I have done?

Don Ped. What if thou dar'st deny, I'll plunge this Dagger deep into thy Throat, and drive the falshood to thy heart again. Therefore take heed, and on thy Life declare; didſt thou not this laſt Night open my doors to let *Don Guzman* in?

Lop. Don Guzman?

Don Ped. Don Guzman? Yes *Don Guzman*, Traytor, him.

Lop. Now, may the Sky crush me, if I let in *Don Guzman*.

Don Ped. Who did you let in then? It wan't your Maſter sure? if it was him, you did your Duty, I have no more to say.

Lop. Why then if I let in any body else, I'm a Son of a Whore. [*Rising.*

Don Ped. Did he order you before-hand, or did you do't upon his Knocking?

Lop. Why he; I'll tell you Sir, he——pray put up that Brilliant, it sparkles so in my Eyes, it almoſt blinds me—thank you Sir.

[Don Ped. *puts it up.*

Why, Sir, I'll tell you juſt how the matter was, but I hope you won't consider me as a Party.

Don Ped. Go on, thou art safe.

Lop. Why then, Sir, when (for our Sins) you had left us, says my Maſter to me, *Lopez*, says he, Go and ſtay at old *Don Felix*'s House, till *Don Pedro* returns, they'll pass thee for his Servant, and think he has order'd thee to ſtay there. And then, says he, doſt hear, Open me the Door by *Leonora*'s Apartment to Night, for, I have a little Business, says he, to do there.

Don Ped. [*Aside.*] Perfidious Wretch!

Lop. Indeed, I was at firſt a little wreſty, and ſtood off; being Suspicious (for I knew the Man) that there might be some ill Intentions. But he knew me too, takes me upon the weak side; whips out a long Sword; and by the same Means makes me do the thing, as you have made me discover it. [*Aside.*] There's neither Liberty nor Property in this Land, since the Blood of the *Bourbon's* came amongſt us.

Don Ped. Then you let him in, as he bid you?

Lop. I did: If I had not, I had never liv'd to tell you the Story. Yes, I let him in.

Don Ped. And what follow'd?

Lop. Why he follow'd.

Don Ped. What?

Lop. His Inclinations.

Don Ped. Which Way?

Lop. The old Way; To a Woman.

Don Ped. Confound him.

Lop. In short, he got to Madam's Chamber, and before he had been there long, (tho' you know, Sir, a little time goes a great way in some matters) I heard such a clutter of small shot, Murder, Murder, Murder, Rape, Fire, Help, and so forth—But hold, here he comes himself, and can give you a more circumſtantial Account of the Skirmish.

Don Ped. I thank thee Heaven at laſt, for having pointed me to the Victim I am to sacrifice.   [*Ex.* Lop.

Enter Don John.

[*Drawing.*] Villain, defend thy self.
Don John. What do you mean?
Don Ped. To punish a Traytor.
Don John. Where is he?
Don Ped. In the Heart of a Sworn Friend.
Don John. [*Aside.*] I saw *Lopez* go from him; without doubt he has told him all.   [*To* Don Ped.
Of what am I suspected?
Don Ped. Of betraying the greateſt Truſt, that Man cou'd place in Man.
Don John. And by whom am I accus'd?
Don Ped. By me: Have at thy Traytor's Heart.
Don John. Hold! And be not quite a Madman!
Pedro, you know me well: You know I am not backward upon these Occasions; nor shall I refuse you any Satisfaction you'll Demand; but firſt, I will be heard, and tell you, That for a Man of Sense, you are pleas'd to make very odd Conclusions.
Don Ped. Why, what is't possible thou canſt invent to clear thy self?
Don John. To clear my self? Of what? I'm to be thank'd for what I have done, and not reproach'd. I find I have been an Ass, and pusht my Friendship to that Point, you find not Virtue in your self, enough to conceive it in another. But henceforward, I shall be a better husband on't.
Don Ped. I shou'd be loth to find Ingratitude cou'd e'er be juſtly charg'd upon me: But after what your Servant has confeſt——
Don John. My Servant! right, my Servant! The very thing I gueſt. Fie, fie, *Don Pedro*, Is't from a Servant's Mouth a Friend Condemns a Friend; or can Servants always Judge at what their Maſters outward Actions point? But some Allowances I shou'd make for the wild Agitation you muſt needs be in. I'm therefore Calm, and thus far pass all by.
Don Ped. If you are Innocent, Heaven be my Aid, that I may find you so; But ſtill——
Don John. But ſtill you wrong me, if you ſtill suspect. Hear then in short, my part of this Adventure. In order to Acquit myself of the Charge you laid upon me in your Absence, I went laſt Night, juſt as 'twas dark, to view the several Approaches to the House where you had left your Wife: And I observ'd not far from one of the Back Doors, Two Persons in close eager Conference: I was disguis'd, so ventur'd to pass near 'em, and by a word or two I heard, I found 'twas *Guzman* talking to *Jacinta*. My Concern for your Honour, made me at firſt resolve to call him to an

immediate Account. But then reflecting that I might possibly o'er-hear some part of their Discourse, and by that judge of *Leonora*'s Thoughts I rein'd my Passion in; and by the help of an advancing Buttress, which kept me from their sight, I learnt the black Conspiracy. *Don Guzman* said, he had great Complaint to make; and since his Honourable Love had been so ill return'd, he could with Ease forgive himself, if by some rougher Means he should procure, what Prayers and Tears, and Sighs, had urg'd in vain.

Don Ped. Go on.

Don John. His kind Assistant clos'd smoothly with him, and inform'd him with what Ease that very Night she'd introduce him to her Chamber. At last, they parted with this Agreement, That at some Overture in a Wall, he should expect her to inform him, when *Leonora* was in Bed, and all the Coast was clear.

Don Ped. Dispatch the rest—Is't possible after all he should be Innocent?

Don John. I must confess the Resolution taken, made me tremble for you; How to prevent it now and for ever, was my next care. I immediately order'd *Lopez* to go lye at *Don Felix*'s, and to open me the door when all the Family were in Bed. He did as I directed him. I enter'd, and in the dark found my way to *Leonora*'s Appartment; I found the Door open, at which I was surpriz'd. I thought I heard some stirring in her Chamber, and in an Instant heard her cry for Aid. At this I drew, and rusht into the Room, which *Guzman* Allarm'd at, cry'd out to her Assistance. His ready Impudence, I must confess, at first quite struck me speechless, but in a moment I regain'd my Tongue, and loud proclaim'd the Traytor.

Don Ped. Is't possible?

Don John. Yet more; Your Arrival hindring me at that time, from taking Vengeance for your wrong, I at this instant expect him here, to punish him (with Heavens Righteous Aid) for daring to attempt my ruin with the Man, whose Friendship I prefer, to all the Blessings Heaven and Earth dispense.——

And now *Don Pedro*, I have told you this, if still you have a Mind to take my Life? I shall defend it with the self same warmth, I intended to expose it in your service.   [*Draws.*

Don Ped. [*Aside.*] If I did not know he was in Love with *Leonora*, I could be easily surpriz'd with what he has told me. But—But yet 'tis certain he has destroyed the Proofs against him, and if I only hold him guilty as a Lover, why must *Don Guzman* pass for innocent; good Gods, I am again returning to my doubts.

Don John. [*Aside.*] I have at last reduc't him to a Ballance, but one lye more tost in, will turn the Scale.

To Don Ped.] One Obligation more my Friend you owe me; I thought to have let it pass, but it shall out. Know then, I lov'd, like you, the Beauteous *Leonora*; but from the moment, I observ'd how deep her dart had peirc't you, I tore my Passion from my bleeding heart, and sacrifis'd my happiness to yours. Now, I have no more to plead, If ſtill you think your Vengeance is my due, come pay it me.

Don Ped. Rather Ten Thousand Poiniards ſtrike me dead. O *Alvarada!* Can you forgive a Wild diſtraćted Friend? Gods! Whither was my jealous Frensie leading me? Can you forget this barbarous Injury?

Don John. I can: No more. But for the future, think me what I am, a faithful and a zealous Friend.—Retire, and leave me here. In a few moments I hope to bring you farther Proofs on't. *Guzman* I inſtantly expećt, leave me to do you Juſtice on him.

Don Ped. That muſt not be. My Revenge can ne'er be satisfy'd by any other hand but this.

Don John. Then let that do't. You'll in a Moment have an opportunity.

Don Ped. You miſtake; he won't be here.

Don John. How so?

Don Ped. He has not had your Challenge. His Siſter intercepted it, and desir'd I'd come to prevent the Quarrel.

Don John. What then is to be done?

Don Ped. I'll go and find him out immediately.

Don John. Very well: Or hold——[*Aside.*] I muſt hinder 'em from Talking. Gossiping may discover me.

Yes: Let's go and find him: Or, let me see——Ay——'twill do better.

Don Ped. What?

Don John. Why——That the Punishment should suit the Crime.

Don Ped. Explain.

Don John. Attack him by his own Laws of War—'Twas in the Night he would have had your Honour, and in the Night you ought to have his Life.

Don Ped. His Treason cannot take the guilt from mine.

Don John. There is no Guilt in fair Retalliation. When 'tis a point of Honour founds the Quarrel: The Laws of Sword-Men muſt be kept, 'tis true: But if a Thief glides in to seize my Treasure, methinks, I may return the Favour on my Daggers Point, as well as with my Sword of Ceremony six times as long.

Don Ped. Yet ſtill the nobler Method I wou'd chuse; it better satisfies the Vengeance of a Man of Honour.

Don John. I own it; were you sure you shou'd succeed: But the Events of Combats are uncertain. Your Enemy may 'scape you: You perhaps may only Wound him; You may be parted. Believe me *Pedro*, the Injury's too great for a Punćtillio Satisfaćtion.

Don Ped. Well, Guide me as you please, so you direct me quickly to my Vengeance. What do you propose?

Don John. That which is as easie, as 'tis just to execute. The Wall he past, to attempt your Wife, let us get over to prevent his doing so any more. 'Twill let us into a private Apartment by his Garden, where every Evening in his Amorous Solitudes, he spends some time alone, and where I guess his late fair Scheme was drawn. The Deed done, we can Retreat the way we Enter'd; let me be your Pilot, 'tis now e'en dark, and the most proper time.

Don Ped. Lead on; I'll follow you.

Don John. [*Aside.*] How many Villanies I'm forc'd to act, to keep one Secret. [*Exeunt.*

SCENE [II],

Don Guzman's *Apartments*.

Don Guzman, *sitting*, solus.

With what Rigour does this Unfaithful Woman treat me? Is't possible it can be she, who appear'd to Love me with so much Tenderness? How little stress is to be laid upon a Woman's Heart? Sure they're not worth those Anxious Cares they give. [*Rising.*] Then burst my Chains, and give me room to search, for nobler Pleasures. I feel my Heart begin to Mutiny for Liberty; there is a Spirit in it yet, will struggle hard for Freedom: but Solitudes the worst of Seconds. Ho, *Sancho, Galindo,* Who waits there? Bring some Lights. Where are you?

Enter Galindo, *rubbing his Eyes, and Drunk.*

Galin. I can't well tell. Do you want me, Sir?

Don Guz. Yes, Sir, I want you. Why am I left in the Dark, what were you doing?

Gal. Doing Sir! I was doing——what one does when one Sleeps, Sir.

Don Guz. Have you no Light without?

Galin. [*Yawning.*] Light!——No, Sir,——I have no Light. I'm us'd to hardship. I can sleep in the dark.

Don Guz. You have been Drinking, you Rascal, you are Drunk.

Gal. I have been Drinking, Sir, 'tis true, but I am not drunk. Every Man that is Drunk, has been drinking; Confess'd. But every Man that has been drinking, is not drunk. Confess that too.

Don Guz. Who is't has put you in this Condition, you Sot?

Galin. A very honeſt Fellow: Madam *Leonora's* Coachman, no body else. I have been making a little debauch with Madam *Leonora's* Coachman; yes.

Don Guz. How came you to drink with him, Beaſt?

Gal. Only *par* Complaisance, Sir. The Coachman was to be Drunk upon Madam's Wedding; and I being a Friend, was desir'd to take Part.

Don Guz. And so, you Villain, you can make your self Merry, with what renders me Miserable.

Galin. No, Sir, no; 'twas the Coachman was merry; I drank with Tears in my Eyes: The remembrance of your Misfortunes, made me so sad, so sad, that every Cup I swallow'd, was like a Cup of Poison to me.

Don Guz. Without doubt.

Galin. Yes; and to mortifie my self upon melancholly Matters, I believe I took down Fifty. Yes.

Don Guz. Go fetch some Lights you drunken Sot you.

Galin. I will, if I can find the Door, that's to ⎫ *Feeling for the Door and* say——The Devil's in the Door; I think 'tis ⎭ *running againſt it.* grown too little for me——Shrunk this wet Weather I presume.

[*Ex.* Galin.

Don Guzman *alone.*

Absence, the old Remedy for Love, muſt e'en be mine: To ſtay and brave the Danger, were Presumption: Farewel *Valencia*, then, and farewel *Leonora.* And if thou can'ſt, my Heart, redeem thy Liberty; secure it by a farewel Eternal to her Sex.

Re-enter Galindo *with a Candle, he falls and puts it out.*

Galin. Here's light, Sir——So.

Don Guz. Well done. You sottish Rascal ⎫ *Passing angrily into an-* come no more in my Sight. ⎭ *other Chamber.*

[*Ex.* Don Guz.

Galin. These Boards are so uneaven——
You shall see now I shall neither find the Candle ⎫ *Rising and feeling about* ——nor the Candleſtick; it shan't be for want ⎬ *for the Candle.* of searching however. ⎭

——O ho, have I got you? enough, I'll look for your Companion to Morrow.

Enter Don Pedro *and* Don John.

Don Ped. Where are we now?

Don John. We are in the Appartment I told you of——Softly,——I hear something ſtir,——Ten to one but 'tis he.

Galin. Don't I hear somewhat?——No——when One has Wine in One's head, one has such a bussle in One's ears.

Don Pedro. [*to* Don John.] Who is that is talking to himself?

Don John. 'Tis his Servant, I know his Voice, keep ftill.

Galin. Well; since my Mafter has banifh't me his sight, I'll redeem by my Obedience, what I have loft by my debauche. I'll go sleep twelve hours in some melancholy hole where the Devil shan't find me. Yes.

[*Exit* Galindo.

Don John. He's gone; but hush, I hear some body coming.

Don Guz. Ho there, will no body bring light? [*Behind the Scene.*

Don Ped. 'Tis *Guzman.*

Don John. 'Tis so, prepare.

Don Ped. Shall I own my weakness, I feel an inward Check; I wish this could be done some other way.

Don John. Diftraction all; is this a time to Ballance? think on the Injury he would have done you, 'twill fortifie your Arm and guide your Dagger to his heart.

Don Ped. Enough, I'll hesitate no more; be satisfy'd, hark, he's coming.

Don Guzman *passes the Stage.*

Don Guz. I think these Rogues are resolved to leave me in the dark all Night. [*Exit* Don Guz.

Don John. Now's your time, follow him and ftrike home.

Don Ped. To his heart if my Dagger will reach it.

[Don Pedro *follows him.*

Don John. [*Aside.*] If one be kill'd I'm satisfy'd; 'tis no great matter which.

Re-enter Don Guzman, Don Pedro *following him,*
with his Dagger ready to ftrike.

Don Guz. [*Aside.*] My Chamber door's lock't, and I think I hear some body tread.——Who's there?——No body Answers. But ftill I hear some thing ftir. Holo! there *Sancho,* are you all drunk, some Lights here quickly. [*Exit.*

Don Guzman *passes by the Corner where* Don John *ftands, and goes off the Stage;* Don Pedro *following him, ftabbs* Don John.

Don Ped. [*Aside.*] I think I'm near him now:——Traytor, take that, my Wife has sent it thee.

Don John. Ah, I'm dead.

Don Ped. Then thou haft thy due.

Don John. I have indeed, 'tis I that have betray'd thee.

Don Ped. And 'tis I that am reveng'd on thee for doing it.

Don John. I wou'd have forc'd thy Wife.

Don Ped. Die then with the Regret, to have fail'd in thy Attempt.

Don John. Farewell, if thou can'st forgive me—   [*dies.*
Don Ped. I have done the deed, there's nothing left, but to make our escape. *Don John* where are you; Let's begon, I hear the Servants coming.

Lopez *knocks hard at the Door.*

Lop. Open there quickly, open the door.
Don Ped. That's *Lopez,* we shall be discover'd. But 'tis no great matter, the Crime will justify the Execution; but where's *Don John, Don John* where are you?

Lopez *knocks again.*

Lop. Open the door there, quickly. Madam I saw 'em both pass the Wall, the Devil's in't if any good comes on't.
Leo. I am fright'ned out of my Sences, ho, *Isabella.*
Don Ped. 'Tis *Leonora.* She's welcome. With her own Eyes let her see her *Guzman* dead.

Enter Don Guzman, Leonora, Isabella, Jacinta *and* Lopez, *with Lights.*

Don Ped. Ha, what is't I see? *Guzman* Alive? Then who art thou?
                                                    [*Looking on* Don John.
Don Guz. Guzman alive? Yes *Pedro, Guzman* is alive.
Don Ped. Then Heaven is just, and there's a Traytor dead.
Isabella weeps.] Alas *Don John?*
Lop. [*Looking upon* Don John.] *Bonus Nocius.*
Don Guz. What has produc'd this Bloody Scene?
Don Ped. 'Tis I have been the Actor in't, my Poignard, *Guzman* I intended in your Heart; I thought your Crime deserv'd it, but I did you wrong, and my Hand in searching the Innocent, has by Heaven's Justice been directed to the Guilty. *Don John,* with his last breath, confesst himself the Offender. Thus my Revenge is satisfied, and you are clear'd.
Don Guz. Good Heaven, how equitable are thy Judgments!
Don Ped. [*To* Leo.] Come, Madam, my Honour now is satisfied, and if you please my Love may be so too.
Leo. If it is not

You to your self alone, shall owe your smart,
For where I've given my hand, I'll give my heart.

EPILOGUE

Spoken by *Mrs. Oldfield.*

WHAT say you, Sirs, d'ye think my Lady'll 'scape,
'Tis dev'lish hard to stand a Fav'rite's Rape?
Shou'd Guzman, like Don John, break in upon her,
For all her Vertue, Heaven! have Mercy on her;
Her strength, I doubt, 's in his Irresolution,
There's wond'rous Charms in Vig'rous Execution.
Indeed you Men are Fools, you won't believe,
What dreadful Things we Women can forgive;
I know but one, we never do pass by,
And that you plague us with Eternally;
When in your Courtly Fears to disoblige,
You won't attack the Town, which you besiege:
Your Guns are light, and planted out of reach,
D'ye think with Billetdoux to make a Breach;
'Tis small-shot all, and not a stone will fly,
Walls fall by Cannon, and by fireing nigh;
In sluggish dull Blockades you keep the Field,
And starve us e're we can with honour Yield.
In short!
We can't receive those terms you gently tender,
But Storm, and we can answer our Surrender.

THE

COUNTRY

HOUSE

A

FARCE

As Acted at both

THEATRES

With great Applause

Source

THIS play is a free translation of *La Maison de Campagne* of Florent-Carton Dancourt, first played at the Comédie Française on 27 January, 1688. It is the fourth of Dancourt's sixty odd stage productions, and it is just possible Vanbrugh may have seen it. In the original it only consists of one act; Vanbrugh made it into two acts without noting the scenes, though in later editions these are marked in conformity with the French method.

Vanbrugh's version follows the French, not too closely, but as a happy dog accompanies his master on a walk. He carefully avoids all allusions which would carry no weight in England. Both his omissions of these and his method of " breathing an English spirit " into French work can be illustrated from the few opening sentences as well as from any other passage.

SCÈNE PREMIÈRE:

ÉRASTE, LA FLÈCHE, LISETTE

Lisette. Encore une fois, Monsieur, si vous avez quelque considération pour elle, retournez à Paris, et qu'on ne vous voie point ici.

Éraste. Ma pauvre Lisette, que je lui parle un moment, que je la voie seulement, je t'en conjure!

Lisette. Mais vous êtes le maître: vous voilà dans le logis, il ne tient qu'à vous d'y demeurer. Je crois même que si Marianne vous y savait, elle aurait peut-être autant d'empressement de vous voir et de vous parler, que vous en témoignez vous-même.

Éraste. Et pourquoi donc ne veux-tu pas nous donner cette satisfaction à l'un et à l'autre?

Lisette. C'est que j'en sais les conséquences. Dès que vous serez ensemble, vous ne pourrez vous résoudre à vous quitter. Quelqu'un vous surprendra, et où en serons-nous, s'il vous plaît?

La Flèche. Eh bien! quand on nous surprendra, nous jettera-t-on par les fenêtres?

Lisette. Non: mais on me mettra à la porte, et on enverra Marianne dans un couvent.

Sometimes, but very rarely, he fails to be quite as racy as his original. When the Baron de Messy first appears, and Mrs. Bernard meets him, we have in Vanbrugh:

" Madam, the Baron de Messy is the best humour'd Man in the World; I've prevail'd with him to give us his company for a few days."

Dancourt wrote: " Ce baron n'est pas fat, au moins. Je le débauche, Madame, et je le fais rester ici." But the boot is nearly always on the other leg, and he adds little realistic touches. When Mawkin first comes in, Vanbrugh makes her say: " Ay, Cousin, here's Brother Janno and I are come from *Paris* to see you: Pray how does Cousin Mariane do? All the French has is: " Bonjour, mon cousin." Phrases such as " puffing and blowing like a cow in hard labour " are, of course, pure Vanburghian for the simple " tout essoufflé " of Dancourt.

Text

THE text is from the first edition of 1715. The copy in the " collection " of 1719 is the same, down to faults in setting. It is evident that unsold copies were bound up in this volume. The first edition, therefore, has been collated with later editions, the collected one of 1735 and the third of 1740, which varies considerably. The play does not occur in the collected editions of 1719 and 1730, but it does in those of 1735, 1759, 1765 and 1776.

Theatrical History

THAT excellent and lively farce *The Country House* was first acted at Drury Lane on 23 January, 1703, " At the Desire of Several Persons of Quality," being advertised in the *Daily Courant* of the 21st with " A Consort of Musick by the Best Masters, wherein the famous Signora . . . etc.: with several New Entertainments of Dancing by Monsieur Du-Ruell, lately arrived from the Opera in Paris. . . . None are to be admitted but printed Tickets, not above four hundred in number, at Five Shillings a Ticket." These were to be obtained beforehand at the fashionable chocolate-houses, namely, White's, Tom's and Will's. " And no persons to be admitted in Masks." Unfortunately we do not know who took the parts, except that it was the Drury Lane Company. Possibly Cibber played Barnard; Doggett his brother; and Mrs. Oldfield the young heroine. All we know for certain is that Mrs. Verbruggen played the part of Madam Barnard: for the next record we have of the play for the performance at the same theatre on 16 June, 1705, for Mill's benefit, states that " The Part of Madam Barnard in the Country House which was originally performed by Mrs. Verbruggen, to be performed by her daughter Mrs. Mountfort." It was acted with singing, etc., and *The Young Coquet,* and was repeated on the 28th with Mrs. Mountfort in her newly acquired part, with *The Young Coquet* and *The Quacks.*

Then it apparently slept until 14 January, 1715, for on being revived at Lincoln's Inn Fields on that date, it was advertised as " not acted 12 years." Then it appears to have been very popular, for it was acted nine times that spring. It was not, of course, long enough to fill more than a portion of the evening, and on this first occasion it was acted with *The Busy-Body,* with dances as well. Three days later it was acted after *The Confederacy* and singing, and on the next day it appeared with *The Cheats of Scapin* and dancing. It was often put on as part of *The Medley,* which was an entertainment of singing, dancing and farces, the others being sometimes *The Slip* and *The Beau Demolished,* sometimes *The Slip* and Doggett's play *The Country Wake.* In the autumn *The Medley* contained, besides *The Country House, The City Ramble* and *The Country Wake,* or *The City Ramble* and *Acis and Galatea.* It sometimes appeared, however, as the satyric play after more formidable stuff, as on 14 October, when it was acted at the conclusion of *A Duke and No Duke.*

It was acted only once in 1716, with *The Anatomist,* another farce, and then it rested until 22 November, 1721, when it was acted with *The Fatal Extravagance,* and at the beginning of December with *The Emperor of the Moon,* when probably Quin, Ryan, Mrs. Egleton and Mrs. Bullock took part. It was acted once in 1722, on 11 January, with *The Fatal Extravagance* and " an Entertainment of Dancing in Grotesque Characters, call'd The Jealous Doctor, or the Intriguing Dame "; and five times in 1723, with such plays as *A Woman's Revenge; or a Match in Newgate.* It kept on the stage in 1726, 1727 and 1728, with such old friends as *The Cheats of Scapin* and *The Emperor of the Moon,* and on 25 March, 1729, was joined with *The*

What D'ye Call It, which must have made an excellent evening's amusement. It was repeated the two following years, and on 9 February, 1732, was acted with *Rule a Wife and Have a Wife*, the cast of which included Quin, Ryan, Hippisley and Mrs. Younger, the entertainment concluding with dancing, during which Mrs. Bullock appeared in a Scottish dance. It was repeated on the 15th with *The Mistake*, and may have included Millward, Walker and Mrs. Egleton in its cast.

In the autumn of that year, when Quin and Mrs. Younger went over to Covent Garden, *The Country House* went with them, being acted there with *The Pilgrim* on 3 December. We may suppose that Quin played Barnard and Mrs. Younger Mrs. Barnard, for they had played Roderigo and Juletta in the former play. She was " a pleasing actress, especially in more sprightly parts, and rose high," but she left the stage early in her career to marry John Finch, son of the Earl of Nottingham. On the 10th it partnered *She Wou'd if She Cou'd*, on the 21st *The Merry Wives of Windsor*, and on the 29th Etherege's play once more.

It was acted four times at Covent Garden in 1733; and in 1734, on the 30 March, it appeared at Drury Lane, so long after its first performance there that the advertisement declared that it was " never acted there before." Cibber played Janno. It does not seem clear why he should have been mentioned, and one is tempted to guess that it was because it was his original part, and the public would like to see their old favourite in one of his creations. In the autumn it went back to Covent Garden, where it was acted with *The Way of the World* on 7 December. It was repeated three times in 1735, three times in 1737 and four times in 1739, with such plays as *The Merry Wives of Windsor* and *The Squire of Alsatia*. It appeared once more with *The Pilgrim* on 7 December, 1742, and with *The Provok'd Husband* on 3 December, 1746, " not acted for 5 years."

Then it does not appear again until 3 April, 1758, which seems to have been its last performance, and the first for which we have a cast. It was performed for the benefit of Shuter, who acted Janno; Dyer played the Marquis, Arthur was Luca, while Mrs. Green played Miss Mawkin. Dyer, who used also to play Moneytrap at this period, " was a very good copier of nature in some peculiarities of humour."

Dramatis Personæ

MEN.

Mr. Barnard.
Mr. Griffard, *Brother to Mr.* Barnard.
Erast, *in love with* Mariane.
Dorant, *Son to Mr.* Barnard.
The Marquis.
The Baron de Messy.
Janno, *Cousin to Mr.* Barnard.
Collin, *Servant to Mr.* Barnard.
Charly, *a Boy.*
A Soldier.
Servant to Erast.
A Cook.
Three Gentlemen Friends to Dorant.

WOMEN.

Madam Barnard.
Mariane, *her Daughter.*
Mawkin, *Sister to* Janno.
Lisett, *Servant to* Mariane.

The SCENE is laid in *Normandy in France.*

THE
COUNTRY HOUSE

ACT I. SCENE I.

Enter Eraſt. *and his Servant, with* Lisett.

Lisett.

ONCE more I'll tell ye, Sir, if you have any Consideration in the World for her, you muſt be gone this Minute.

Er. My dear *Lisett*, let me but speak to her, let me but see her only.

Lis. You may do what you will, here you are in our House, and I do believe she's as impatient to see you, as you can be to see her, but——

Er. But why won't you give us that Satisfaction then?

Lis. Because I know the Consequence, for when you once get together the Devil himself is not able to part ye; you will ſtay so long 'till you're surpriz'd, and what shall become of us then?

Serv. Why, then we shall be thrown out at the Window, I suppose.

Lis. No, but I shall be turn'd out of Doors.

Er. How unfortunate am I! these Doors are open to all the World, and only shut to me.

Lis. Because you come for a Wife, and at our House we don't care for People that come for Wives.

Serv. What wou'd you have us come for then?

Lis. Because such People generally want Portions.

Serv. Portions! No, no, never talk of Portions, my Maſter nor I neither don't want Portions; and if you'd follow my Advice, a Regiment of Fathers shou'd not guard her.

Lis. What's that?

Serv. Why, if you'll contrive that my Maſter may run away with your Miſtress, I don't much care faith if I run away with you.

Lis. Don't you so, Rogues Face, but I hope to be better provided for.

Er. Hold your Tongues. But where is her Brother? He is my Bosom Friend, and wou'd be willing to serve me.

Lis. I told you before, that he has been Abroad a hunting, and we ha'nt seen him these three Days; he seldom lies at home, to avoid his Father's ill Humour; so that it is not your Miſtress only that our old covetous Cuff

(213)

teizes——there's no body in the Family but feels the Effects of his ill Humour——by his good Will he wou'd not suffer a Creature to come within his Doors, or eat at his Table——and if there be but a Rabbit extraordinary for Dinner, he thinks himself ruin'd for ever.

Er. Then I find you pass your time comfortably in this Family.

Lis. Not so bad as you imagine neither perhaps, for thank Heaven, we have a Mistress that's as bountiful as he's stingy, one that will let him say what he will, and yet does what she will; but hark, here's somebody coming, it is certainly he.

Er. Can't you hide us somewhere?

Lis. Here, here, get you in here as fast as you can.

Serv. Thrust me in too.   [*Puts 'em into the Closet.*

Enter Mariane.

Lis. O, is it you?

Mar. So, *Lisett*, where have you been? I've been looking for ye all over the House: who are those People in the Garden with my Mother-in-Law? I believe my Father won't be very well pleased to see 'em there.

Lis. And here's somebody else not far off that I believe your Father won't be very well pleas'd with neither. Come, Sir, Sir.   [*Calls.*

Enter Erast *and Servant.*

Mar. O Heavens!   [*Cries out.*

Lis. Come, Lovers, I can allow you but a short bout on't this time, you must do your Work with a Jirk——one Whisper, two Sighs, and a Kiss, make haste, I say and I'll stand Centry for ye in the mean time.

[*Exit* Lisett.

Mar. Do you know what you expose me to, *Erast!* What do you mean?

Er. To die, Madam, since you receive me with so little Pleasure.

Mar. Consider what wou'd become of me, if my Father shou'd see you here.

Er. What wou'd you have me do?

Mar. Expect with Patience some happy turn of Affairs; my Mother-in-Law is kind and indulgent to a Miracle, and her Favour, if well managed, may turn to our Advantage; and cou'd I prevail upon my self to declare my Passion to her, I don't doubt but she'd join in our Interest.

Er. Well, since we've nothing to fear from her, and your Brother you know is my intimate Friend, therefore you may conceal me somewhere about the House for a few days, I'll hide any where.

Serv. Ay, but who must have the Care of bringing us Victuals? [*Aside.*

Er. Thrust us into the Cellar, up in the Garret: I don't care where it is, so that it be but under the same Roof with ye.

Serv. But I don't say so, for that Jade *Lisett* will have the feeding of us, and I know what kind of Diet she keeps——I believe we shan't be like the Fox in the Fable, our Bellies won't be so full but we shall be able to creep out at the same Hole we got in at.

Er. Must I then be gone? must I return to *Paris?*

Enter Lisett.

Lis. Yes, that you must, and immediately too, for here's my Master coming in upon ye.

Er. What shall I do?

Lis. Begone this Minute.

Mar. Stay in the Village till you hear from me, none of our Family know that you are here.

Er. Shall I see you sometimes?

Mar. I han't time to answer you now.

Lis. Make haste, I say; are you bewitch'd?

Er. Will you write to me?

Mar. I will if I can.

Lis. Begone, I say, is the Devil in you, [*Thrusting* Erast *and Servant out.*] come this way, your Father's just stepping in upon us.   [*Exeunt.*

Enter Mr. Barnard *beating* Collin.

Mr. Barn. Rogue! Rascal, did not I command you? Did not I give you my Orders, Sirrah?

Col. Why, you gave me Orders to let no body in; and Madam, her gives me Orders to let every body in——why the Devil himself can't please you both, I think.

Mr. Barn. But, Sirrah, you must obey my Orders, not hers.

Col. Why, the Gentlefolks ask'd for her, they did not ask for you—— what do you make such a Noise about?

Mr. Barn. For that Reason, Sirrah, you shou'd not let 'em in.

Col. Hold, Sir, I'd rather see you Angry than her too, for when you're Angry you have only the De'il in ye that's true enough; but when Madam's in Passion she has the De'il and his Dam both in her Belly.

Mr. Barn. You must mind what I say to you, Sirrah, and obey my Orders.

Col. Ay, ay, Measter——but let's not Quarrel with one another—— you're always in such a plaguy Humour.

Mr. Barn. What are these People that are just come?

Col. Nay, that know not I——but as fine Folk they are as ever Eye beheld, Heaven bless 'em.

Mr. Barn. Did you hear their Names?

Col. Noa, noa, but in a Coach they keam all besmear'd with Gould, with six breave Horses, the like on 'em ne're did I set Eyes on—— 'twou'd do a Man's Heart good to look on those fine Beast Measter.

Mr. Barn. How many Persons are there?

Col. Four——two as fine Men as ever Women boar, and two as dainty Deames as a Man wou'd desire to lay his Lips to.

Mr. Barn. And all this Crew sets up at my House.

Col. Noa, noa, Meaſter, the Coachman is gone into the Village to set up his Coach at some Inn, for I told him our Coach House was full of Faggots, but he'll bring back the six Horses, for I told him we had a rear good Steable.

Mr. Barn. [*Beating him.*] Did you so, Rascal? Did you so?

Col. Doant, doant, Sir, it wou'd do you good to see those Cattel, in faith they look as if they had ne're kept Lent.

Mr. Barn. Then they shall learn Religion at my House——Sirrah, do you take care they Sup without Oats to Night——What will become of me? Since I bought this damn'd Country House, I spend more in a Summer than wou'd maintain me seven Years.

Col. Why, if you spend Mony han't you good things for it? all the whole Country raund——come they not all to see you? Mind how you're belov'd, Meaſter.

Mr. Barn. Pox take such Love——how now, what do you want?

Enter Lisett.

Lis. Sir, there's some Company in the Garden with my Miſtress, who desire to see you.

Mr. Barn. Devil take 'em, what Business have they here? But who are they?

Lis. Why, Sir, there's the fat Abbot that always sets so long at Dinner, and drinks his two Bottles by way of Whet.

Mr. Barn. I wish his Church was in his Belly, that his Guts might be half full before he came—and who else?

Lis. Then there's the young Marquis that won all my Lady's Mony at Cards.

Mr. Barn. Pox take him too.

Lis. Then there's the merry Lady that's always in good Humour.

Mr. Barn. Very well.

Lis. Then there's she that threw down all my Lady's China t'other Day, and then laugh'd at it for a Jeſt.

Mr. Barn. Which I paid above 50*l.* for in earneſt——very well, and pray how did Madam receive all this fine Company?——With a hearty Welcome, and a Curtsie with her Bum down to the ground, ha.

Lis. No indeed, Sir, she was very Angry with 'em.

Mr. Barn. How! Angry with 'em, say you?

Lis. Yes indeed, Sir, for she expeƈted they wou'd have ſtaid here a

Fortnight, but it seems things happen so unluckily that they can't ſtay here above ten Days.

Mr. Barn. Ten days! How! what! four Persons with a Coach and six, and a Kennel of hungry Hounds in Liveries, to live upon me ten Days!
[*Exit* Lisett.

Enter a Soldier.

So, what do you want?

Sol. Sir, I come from your Nephew, Captain *Hungry.*

Mr. Barn. Well, what does he want?

Sol. He gives his Service to you, Sir, and sends you Word that he'll come and dine with you to Morrow.

Mr. Barn. Dine with me! no, no, Friend, tell him I don't dine at all to Morrow, it is my Faſt Day, my Wife died on't.

Sol. And he has sent you here a Pheasant and a couple of Partridges.

Mr. Barn. How's that, a Pheasant and Partridges, say you?——let's see——very fine Birds, truly——let me consider——to Morrow is not my Faſt Day, I miſtook, tell my Nephew he shall be welcome——And de'ye hear? [*to* Col.] do you take these Fowl and hang them up in a cool Place——and take this Soldier in, and make him drink——make him drink, do ye see——a Cup——ay, a Cup of small Beer—do ye hear?

Col. Yes, Sir——Come along; our small Beer is reare good.

Sol. But, Sir, he bad me tell ye that he'll bring two or three of his Brother Officers along with him.

Mr. Barn. How's that! Officers with him——here, come back—— take the Fowl again; I don't dine to Morrow, and so tell him. [*Gives him the Basket.*] Go, go. [*Thruſts him out.*

Sol. Sir, Sir, that won't hinder them from coming, for they retir'd off the Camp; and because your House is near 'em, Sir, they resolve to come.

Mr. Barn. Go, begone, Sirrah. [*Thruſts him out.*
There's a Rogue now, that sends me three lean Carrion Birds, and brings half a dozen Varlets to eat them.

Enter Brother.

Bro. Brother, what is the meaning of these Doings? If you don't order your Affairs better, you'll have your Fowl taken out of your very Yard, and carried away before your Face.

Mr. Barn. Can I help it, Brother? But what's the matter now?

Bro. There's a Parcel of Fellows have been hunting about your Grounds all this Morning, broke down your Hedges, and are now coming into your House——don't you hear them?

Mr. Barn. No, I don't hear them: but who are they?

Bro. Three or four Rake-helly Officers, with your Nephew at the Head of 'em.

Mr. Barn. O the Rogue! he might well send me Fowl——but is it not a vexatious thing, that I muſt ſtand ſtill and see myself plunder'd at this Rate, and have a Carrion of a Wife that thinks I ought to thank all these Rogues that come to devour me; but can't you advise me what's to be done in this Case?

Bro. I wish I cou'd, for it goes to my Heart to see you thus treated by a Crew of Vermin, who think they do you a great deal of Honour in ruining of you.

Mr. Barn. Can there be no way found to redress this?

Bro. If I were you, I'd leave this House quite, and go to Town.

Mr. Barn. What, leave my wife behind me? ay, that wou'd be mending the matter indeed.

Bro. Why don't you sell it then?

Mr. Barn. Because no Body will buy it; it has got as ill a Name as if it had the Plague; it has been sold over and over, and every Family that has liv'd in it has been ruined.

Bro. Then send away all your Beds and Furniture, except what is absolutely necessary for your Family, you'll save something by that, for then your Gueſts can't ſtay with you all Night however.

Mr. Barn. I've tried that already, and it signified nothing——For they all got drunk and lay in the Barn, and next Morning laugh'd it off for a Frolick.

Bro. Then there is but one Remedy left that I can think of.

Mr. Barn. What's that?

Bro. You muſt e'en do what's done when a Town's a fire, blow up your House that the Mischief may run no further——But who is this Gentleman?

Mr. Barn. I never saw him in my Life before, but for all that, I'll hold fifty Pound he comes to dine with me.

Enter the Marquis.

Marq. My dear Mr. *Barnard*, I'm your moſt humble Servant.

Mr. Barn. I don't doubt it, Sir.

Marq. What is the meaning of this, Mr. *Barnard?* You look as coldly upon me as if I were a Stranger.

Mr. Barn. Why truly, Sir, I'm very apt to do so by Persons I never saw in my Life before.

Marq. You muſt know, Mr. *Barnard*, I'm come on purpose to drink a Bottle of Wine with you.

Mr. Barn. That may be, Sir, but it happens that at this time I am not at all dry.

Marq. I left the Ladies at Cards waiting for Supper; for my Part, I never play; so I came to see my dear Mr. *Barnard*; and I'll assure you, I undertook this Journey only to have the Honour of your Acquaintance.

Mr. Barn. You might have spar'd your self that Trouble, Sir.

Marq. Don't you know, Mr. *Barnard*, that this House of yours is a little Paradise?

Mr. Barn. Then rot me if it be, Sir.

Marq. For my Part, I think, a pretty Retreat in the Country is one of the greatest Comforts in life; I suppose you never want good Company, Mr. *Barnard?*

Mr. Barn. No, Sir, I never want Company; for you must know I love very much to be alone.

Marq. Good Wine you must keep above all things, without good Wine and good Cheer I would not give a Fig for the Country.

Mr. Barn. Really, Sir, my Wine is the worst you ever drank in your Life, and you'll find my Cheer but very indifferent.

Marq. No matter, no matter, Mr. *Barnard*; I've heard much of your Hospitality, there's a plentiful Table in your Looks——and your Wife is certainly the best Woman in the world.

Mr. Barn. Rot me if she be, Sir.

Enter Collin.

Col. Sir, Sir, yonder's the Baron *de Messy* has lost his Hawk in our Garden; he says it is pearch'd upon one of the Trees; may we let him have'n again, Sir?

Mr. Barn. Go tell him, that——

Col. Nay, you may tell him your self, for here he comes.

Enter the Baron de Messy.

Sir, I'm your most humble Servant, and ask you a thousand Pardons that I should live so long in your Neighbourhood, and come upon such an Occasion as this to pay you my first Respects.

Mr. Barn. It is very well, Sir, but I think People may be very good Neighbours without visiting one another.

Baron. Pray how do you like our Country?

Mr. Barn. Not at all, I'm quite tir'd on't.

Marq. Is it not the Baron? it is certainly he.

Baron. How: my dear Marquis! let me embrace you.

Marq. My dear Baron, let me kiss you.   [*They run and embrace.*

Baron. We have not seen one another since we were School-fellows.

Marq. The happiest Rencounter!

Bro. These Gentlemen seem to be very well acquainted.

Mr. Barn. Yes, but I know neither one nor t'other of them.

Marq. Baron, let me present to you one of the beſt-natur'd Men in the World, Mr. *Barnard* here, the Flower of Hospitality——I congratulate you upon having so good a Neighbour.

Mr. Barn. Sir.

Baron. It is an Advantage I am proud of.

Mr. Barn. Sir.

Marq. Come, Gentlemen, you muſt be very intimate; let me have the Honour of bringing you better acquainted.

Mr. Barn. Sir.

Baron. Dear Marquis, I shall take it as a Favour, if you'll do me that Honour.

Mr. Barn. Sir.

Marq. With all my Heart——Come, Baron, now you are here we can make up the moſt agreeable Company in the World——Faith you shall ſtay and pass a few Days with us.

Mr. Barn. Now methinks this Son of a Whore does the Honour of my House to a Miracle.

Baron. I don't know what to say, but I shou'd be very glad you'd excuse me.

Marq. Faith, I can't.

Baron. Dear Marquis.

Marq. Egad I won't.

Baron. Well, since it muſt be so———But here comes the Lady of the Family.

Enter Madam Barnard.

Marq. Madam, let me present you to the Flower of *France*.

Baron. Madam, I shall think my self the happieſt person in the World in your Ladyship's Acquaintance, and the little Eſtate I have in this Country I eſteem more than all the reſt, because it lies so near your Ladyship.

Madam. Sir, your moſt humble Servant.

Marq. Madam, the Baron *de Messy* is the beſt humour'd Man in the World; I've prevail'd with him to give us his Company a few Days.

Madam. I'm sure you cou'd not oblige Mr. *Barnard* or me more.

Mr. Barn. That's a damn'd Lie I'm sure.   [*Aside.*

Baron. I'm sorry, Madam, I can't accept of the Honour———for it falls out so unlucky—for I've some Ladies at my House that I can't possibly leave.

Marq. No matter, no matter, Baron, you have Ladies at your House, we have Ladies at our House——let's join Companies——come, let's send for them immediately, the more the merrier.

Mr. Barn. An admirable Expedient truly.

Baron. Well, since it muſt be so, I'll go for them my self.

Marq. Make haſte, dear Baron, for we shall be impatient for your Return.

Baron. Madam, your moſt humble Servant——But I won't take my Leave of you———I shall be back again immediately——Monsieur *Barnard*, I'm your moſt humble Servant; since you will have it so, I'll return as soon as possible.

Mr. Barn. I have it so! 'sbud, Sir, you may ſtay as long as you please; I'm in no haſte for ye.   [*Exit Baron and Marquis.*

Mr. Barn. Madam, you are the Cause that I am not Maſter of my own House.

Madam. Will you never learn to be reasonable, Husband?

The Marquis returns.

Marq. The Baron is the beſt humour'd man in the World, only a little too ceremonious, that's all———I love to be free and generous; since I came to *Paris* I've reform'd half the Court.

Madam. You are of the moſt agreeable Humour in the World.

Marq. Always merry———But what have you done with the Ladies?

Madam. I left them at Cards.

Marq. Well, I'll wait upon 'em———but, Madam, let me desire you not to put your self to any extraordinary Expence upon our Accounts——— You muſt consider we have more than one Day to live together.

Madam. You are pleased to be merry, Marquis.

Marq. Treat us without Ceremony; good wine and Poultry you have of your own; Wild-Fowl and Fish are brought to your Door———You need not send abroad for any thing but a Piece of Butcher's Meat, or so——— Let us have no Extraordinaries.   [*Exit.*

Mr. Barn. If I had the feeding of you, a Thunder-bolt should be your Supper.

Madam. Husband, will you never change your Humour? if you go on at this Rate, it will be impossible to live with ye.

Mr. Barn. Very true; for in a little time I shall have nothing to live upon.

Madam. Do you know what a ridiculous Figure you make?

Mr. Barn. You'll make a great deal worse, when you han't Money enough to pay for the washing of your Smocks.

Madam. It seems you married me only to Dishonour me; how horrible this is!

Mr. Barn. I tell ye, you'll Ruin me. Do you know how much Money you spend in a Year?

Madam. Not I truly, I don't underſtand Arithmetick.

Mr. Barn. Arithmetic, O Lud! O Lud! Is it so hard to comprehend, that he who spends a Shilling and receives but Six-pence, must be ruin'd in the End?

Madam. I never troubled my Head with Accounts, nor never will; but if you did but know what ridiculous Things the World says of ye——

Mr. Barn. Rot the World——'Twill say worse of me when I'm in a Jail.

Madam. A very Christian-like Saying, truly.

Mr. Barn. Don't tell me of Christian——Adsbud, I'll turn Jew, and no Body shall eat at my Table that is not Circumcised.

Enter Lisett.

Lis. Madam, there's the Dutchess of *Twangdillo* just fell down near our Door, her Coach was overturn'd.

Madam. I hope her Grace has receiv'd no hurt.

Lis. No, Madam, but her Coach is broke.

Mr. Barn. Then there's a Smith in Town may mend it.

Lis. They say, 'twill require two or three Days to fit it up.

Madam. I'm glad on't with all my Heart, for then I shall enjoy the Pleasure of her Grace's good Company.———I'll wait upon her.

Mr. Barn. Very fine Doings. [*Exeunt severally.*

ACT II.

Enter Mr. *Barnard.*

NOW Heaven be my Comfort, for my House is Hell: [*Starts.*] How now, what do you want? who are you?

Enter a Servant with a Portmanteau.

Serv. Sir, here's your Cousin *Janno* and Cousin *Mawkin* come from *Paris.*

Mr. Barn. What a Plague do they want?

Enter Janno *leading in* Mawkin.

Jan. Come, Sister, come along———O here's Cousin *Barnard*——— Cousin *Barnard,* your Servant———Here's my Sister *Mawkin* and I are come to see you.

Mawk. Ay, Cousin, here's Brother *Janno* and I are come from *Paris* to see you: Pray how does Cousin *Mariane* do?

Jan. My Sister and I waunt well at *Paris;* so my Father sent us here for two or three Weeks to take a little Country Air.

(222)

Mr. Barn. You cou'd not come to a worse Place; for this is the worſt Air in the whole Country.

Mawk. Nay, I'm sure, my Father says it is the beſt.

Mr. Barn. Your Father's a Fool; I tell ye, 'tis the worſt.

Jan. Nay, Cousin, I fancy you're miſtaken now; for I begin to find my Stomach come to me already; in a Fortnight's time you'll see how I'll lay about me.

Mr. Barn. I don't at all doubt it.

Mawk. Father wou'd have sent Siſter *Flip* and little Brother *Humphry*, but the Calash would not hold us all, and so they don't come till to morrow with Mother.

Jan. Come, Siſter, let's put up our Things in our Chamber; and after you have wash'd my Face, and put me on a clean Neckcloth, we'll go and see how our Cousins do?

Mawk. Ay, come along, we'll go and see Cousin *Mariane*.

Jan. Cousin, we shan't give you much Trouble, one Bed will serve us; for Siſter *Mawkin* and I always lye together.

Mawk. But, Cousin; mother prays you that you'd order a little Cock-Broth for Brother *Janno* and I to be got ready as soon as may be.

Jan. Ay, *a propos*, Cousin *Barnard*, that's true; my Mother desires, that we may have some Cock-Broth to drink two or three times a-day between Meals, for my Siſter and I are sick Folks.

Mawk. And some young Chickens too, the Doctor said wou'd bring us to our Stomachs very soon.

Jan. You Fib now, Siſter, it waunt young Chickens, so it waunt, it was plump Partridges sure, the Doctor said so.

Mawk. Ay, so it was Brother——Come, let's go see our Cousins.

Jan. Ay, come along, Siſter——Cousin *Barnard*, don't forget the Cock-Broth.   [*Exeunt* Janno *and* Mawkin.

Mr. Barn. What the Devil does all this mean——Mother, and Siſter *Flip*, and little Brother *Humphrey*, and Chickens, and Partridges, and Cock-Broth, and Fire from Hell to dress 'em all.

Enter Collin.

Col. O Meaſter, O Meaſter——You'll not chide to Day, as you are usen to do, no marry will you not; see now what it is to be wiser than ones Meaſter.

Mr. Barn. What wou'd this Fool have?

Col. Why Thanks and Money to Boot, an Folk were greatful.

Mr. Barn. What's the Matter?

Col. Why the Matter is, if you have ſtore of Company in your House, you have ſtore of Meat to put in their Bellies.

Mr. Barn. How so? how so?

Col. Why a large and ſteatly Stag, with a pair of Horns of his Head, Heavens bless you, your Worship might have seen to wear 'em, comes towards our Geat a puffing and blowing like a Cew in hard Labour———— Now says I to my self, says I, if my Maſter refuse to let this fine Youth come in, why then he's a Fool de ye see—So I opens him the Geate, pulls off my Hat with both my Hands, and said you're welcome, kind Sir, to our House.

Mr. Barn. Well, well!

Col. Well, well, ay, and so it is well, as you shall ſtrait way find——So in a trotts, and makes directly towards our Barn, and goes Bounce, Bounce, againſt the Door, as boldly as if he had been Maſter on't——He turns 'en about and twacks'n down in the Stra, as who wou'd say, here will I lay me till to morrow Morning—But he had no Fool to deal with——For to the Kitchen goes I, and takes me down a Musquet, and with a Brace of Balls, I hits'n such a slap in the Face, that he ne'er spoke a Word more to me——Have I done well or no Meaſter?

Mr. Barn. Yes, you have done very well for once.

Col. But this was not all, for a Parcel of Dogs came Yelping after their Companion, as I suppose; so I goes to the back Yard Door, and as many as came by, Shu, says I, and drive 'em into the Gearden, so there they are as safe as in a Pownd——ha, ha——but I can but think what a power of Paſties we shall have at our House, ha, ha.   [*Exit* Collin.

Mr. Barn. I see Providence takes some Care of me, this cou'd never have happen'd in a better time.

Enter Cook.

Cook. Sir, Sir, in the Name of Wonder, what do you mean? is it by your Orders that all those Dogs were let into the Garden?

Mr. Barn. How.

Cook. I believe there's Forty or Fifty Dogs tearing up the Lettice and Cabbage by the Root, I believe before they've done they'll root up the whole Garden.

Mr. Barn. This is that Rogue's doings.

Cook. This was not all, Sir, for three or four of 'em came into the Kitchen, and tore half the Meat off the Spit that was for your Worship's Supper.

Mr. Barn. The very Dogs plague me.

Cook. And then there's a Crew of hungry Footmen devour'd what the Dogs left, so that there's not a bit left for your Worship's Supper, not a Scrap, not one Morsel, Sir.   [*Exit* Cook.

Mr. Barn. Sure I shall hit on some way to get rid of this Crew.

Enter Collin.

Col. Sir, Sir, here's the Devil to do without; yonder a parcel of Fellows swear they'll have our Venison, and s'blead I swear they shall have none on't, so ſtand to your Arms, Meaſter.

Mr. Barn. Ay, you've done finely, Rogue, Rascal, have you not?
[*Beating him.*

Col. 'Sblead, I say they shan't have our Venison, I'll die before I'll part with it. [*Exit.*

Enter Brother.

Bro. Brother, there's some Gentlemen within ask for you.

Mr. Barn. What Gentlemen? Who are they?

Bro. The Gentlemen that have been hunting all this Morning, they're now gone up to your Wife's Chamber.

Mr. Barn. The Devil go with 'em.

Bro. There's but one way to get rid of this Plague, and that is, as I told you before, to set your House on Fire.

Mr. Barn. That's doing my self an Injury, not them.

Bro. There's Dogs, Horses, Maſters and Servants, all intend to ſtay here till to Morrow Morning, that they may be near the Woods to hunt the earlier—besides I overheard 'em, they're in a kind of a Plot againſt you.

Mr. Barn. What did they say?

Bro. You'll be Angry if I shou'd tell ye.

Mr. Barn. Can I be more Angry than I am.

Bro. Then they said it was the greateſt Pleasure in the World to ruin an old Lawyer in the Country, who had got an Eſtate by ruining honeſt People in Town.

Mr. Barn. There's Rogues for ye.

Bro. I'm miſtaken if they don't play you some Trick or other.

Mr. Barn. Hold, let me consider.

Bro. What are you doing?

Mr. Barn. I'm conceiving, I shall bring forth presently——oh, I have it, it comes from hence, Wit was its Father, and Invention its Mother; if I had thought on't sooner, I shou'd have been happy.

Bro. What is it?

Mr. Barn. Come, come along, I say, you muſt help me to put it in Execution.

Enter Lisett.

Lis. Sir, my Miſtress desires you to walk up, she is not able all alone to pay the Civilities due to so much good Company.

Mr. Barn. O the Carrion! What, does she play her Jeſts upon me too. ———but mum, he laughs beſt that laughs laſt.

(225)

Lis. What shall I tell her, Sir, will you come?

Mr. Barn. Yes, yes, tell her I'll come with a Pox to her.

[*Exeunt* Mr. *Barnard* and *Brother.*

Lis. Nay, I don't wonder he shou'd be angry—they do try his Patience, that's the Truth on't.

Enter Mariane.

What, Madam, have you left your Mother and the Company?

Mar. So much Tittle Tattle makes my Head ake; I don't wonder my Father shou'd not love the Country, for besides the Expence he's at, he never enjoys a Minute's quiet.

Lis. But let's talk of your own Affairs—have you writ to your lover?

Mar. No, for I have not had time since I saw him.

Lis. Now you have time then, about it immediately, for he's a sort of desperate Spark, and a body does not know what he may do, if he shou'd not hear from you; besides you promised him, and you muſt behave your self like a Woman of Honour, and keep your Word.

Mar. I'll about it this Minute.

Enter Charly.

Char. Cousin, Cousin, Cousin, where are you going? Come back, I have something to say to you.

Lis. What does this troublesom Boy want?

Char. What's that to you what I want, perhaps I have something to say to her that will make her laugh——why sure! What need you care?

Mar. Don't snub my cousin *Charly*——well, what is't?

Char. Who do you think I met as I was coming here but that handsom Gentleman I've seen at Church ogle you, like any devil.

Mar. Hush, softly Cousin.

Lis. Not a Word of that for your Life.

Char. O, I know I shou'd not speak on't before Folks; you know I made Signs to you above, that I wanted to speak to you in private, did not I Cousin?

Mar. Yes, yes, I saw you.

Char. You see I can keep a Secret.——I am no Girl, mun——I believe I cou'd tell ye Fifty, and Fifty to that, of my Siſter *Sis*——O, she's the Devil of a Girl——but she gives me Mony and Sugar Plumbs——and those that are kind to me fare the better for it, you see Cousin.

Mar. I always said my Cousin *Charly* was a good-natur'd Boy.

Lis. Well, and did he know you?

Char. Yes, I think he did know me—for he took me in his Arms, and did so hug and kiss me——between you and I, Cousin, I believe he's one of the beſt Friends I have in the World.

Mar. Well, but what did he say to you?

Char. Why, he ask'd me where I was going; I told him I was coming to see you; you're a lying young Rogue, says he, I'm sure you dare not go see your Cousin—for you must know my Sister was with me, and it seems he took her for a Crack, and I being a forward Boy, he fancied I was going to make Love to her under a Hedge, ha, ha.

Mar. So.

Char. So he offer'd to lay me a *Lewis d'Or* that I was not coming to you; so, Done says I——Done, says he,——and so 'twas a Bett, you know.

Mar. Certainly.

Char. So my Sister's Honour being concerned, and having a mind to win his *Lewis d'Or*, de ye see——I bad him follow me, that he might see whether I came in or no—but he said he'd wait for me at the little Garden Door that opens into the Fields, and if I wou'd come thro' the House and meet him there, he'd know by that whether I had been in or no.

Mar. Very well.

Char. So I went there, open'd the Door, and let him in——

Mar. What then?

Char. Why, then he paid me the *Lewis d'Or*, that's all.

Mar. Why, that was honestly done.

Char. And then he talk'd to me of you, and said you had the charmingst Bubbies, and every time he named 'em, Ha! says he, as if he had been supping hot Milk Tea.

Mar. But was this all?

Char. No, for he had a mind, you must know, to win his *Lewis d'Or* back again; so he laid me another that I dare not come back, and tell you that he was there; so Cousin, I hope you won't let me lose, for if you don't go there, and tell him that I've won, he won't pay me.

Mar. What, wou'd you have me go and speak to a Man?

Char. Not for any harm, but to win your poor Cousin a *Lewis d'Or*. I'm sure you will—for you're a modest young Woman, and may go with-out Danger——Well, Cousin, I'll swear you look very handsom to Day, and have the prettiest Bubbies there; do let me touch 'em, I'll swear I must.

Mar. What does the young Rogue mean? I swear I'll have you whip'd.
[*Exit* Charly, Mariane.

Enter Collin.

Col. Ha, ha, od the old Gentleman's a Wag efaith, he'll be even with 'em for all this, ha——

Lis. What's the matter? What does the Fool laugh at?

Col. We an't in our House now, *Lisett*, we're in an Inn, ha, ha!

Lis. How in an Inn?

Col. Yes, in an Inn, my Meaſter has gotten an old ruſty Sword, and hung it up at our Geat, and writ underneath with a piece of Charcoal with his own fair Hand, *At the Sword Royal, Entertainment for Man and Horse;* ha, ha————

Lis. What Whim is this?

Col. Thou and I live at the Sword Royal, ha, ha————

Lis. I'll go tell my Miſtress of her Father's Extravagance.

[*Exit* Lisett.

Enter Mr. Barnard *and Brother.*

Mr. Barn. Ha, ha; yes I think this will do. Sirrah, now you may now let in all the World; the more the better.

Collin. Yes, Sir————Odsflesh! we shall break all the Inns in the Country ————For we have a brave handsome Landlady, and a curious young Lass to her Daughter————O, here comes my young Meaſter————We'll make him Chamberlain————ha, ha————

Enter Dorant.

Mr. Barn. What's the matter, Son? How comes it that you are all alone? You used to do me the Favour to bring some of your Friends along with ye.

Dor. Sir, there are some of 'em coming, I only rid before to beg you to give 'em a favourable Reception.

Mr. Barn. Ay, why not? It is both for your Honour and mine, you shall be Maſter.

Dor. Now, Sir, we have an Opportunity of making all the Gentlemen in the Country our Friends.

Mr. Barn. I'm glad on't with all my Heart, pray how so?

Dor. There's an old Quarrel to be made up between two Families, and all the Company are to meet at our House.

Mr. Barn. Ay, with all my Heart; but pray what is the Quarrel?

Dor. O Sir, a very Ancient Quarrel; It happened between their Great Grandfathers about a Duck.

Mr. Barn. A Quarrel of Consequence truly.

Dor. And 'twill be a great Honour to us if this shou'd be accommodated at our House.

Mr. Barn. Without doubt.

Dor. Dear Sir, you aſtonish me with this Goodness; how shall I express this Obligation? I was afraid Sir you wou'd not like it.

Mr. Barn. Why so?

Dor. I thought, Sir, you did not care for the Expence.

Mr. Barn. O Lord, I am the moſt altered Man in the World from what I was, I'm quite another thing mun; but how many are there of 'em?

Dor. Not above nine or ten of a side, Sir.

Mr. Barn. O, we shall dispose of them easily enough.

Dor. Some of 'em will be here presently, the rest I don't expect 'till to Morrow Morning.

Mr. Barn. I hope they're good Companions, jolly Fellows, that love to eat and drink well.

Dor. The merriest best-natur'd Creatures in the World, Sir.

Mr. Barn. I'm very glad on't, for 'tis such Men I want. But come, Brother, you and I will go and prepare for their Reception.

[*Exeunt Mr.* Barnard *and Brother.*

Dor. Bless me, what an Alteration is here! How my father's temper is chang'd within these two or three Days? Do you know the meaning of this?

Col. Why the meaning on't is, ha, ha――

Dor. Can you tell me the Cause of this sudden Change, I say?

Col. Why the cause on't is, ha, ha.――

Dor. What do you laugh at, Sirrah? do you know?

Col. Ha――Because the old Gentleman's a Drole, that's all.

Dor. Sirrah, if I take Cudgel――

Col. Nay, Sir, don't be angry for a little harmless Mirth――But here are your Friends.

Enter three Gentlemen.

Dor. Gentlemen you are welcome to *Pasty-Hall*; see that these Gentlemen's Horses are taken Care of.

1 *Gen.* A very fine Dwelling this.

Dor. Yes, the House is tolerable.

2 *Gen.* And a very fine Lordship belongs to it.

Dor. The Land is good.

3 *Gen.* This House ought to have been mine, for my Grandfather sold it to his Father, from whom your Father purchased it.

Dor. Yes, the House has gone thro' a great many Hands.

1 *Gen.* A Sign there has always been good House-keeping in it.

Dor. And I hope there ever will.

Enter Mr. Barnard, *and his Brother drest like Drawers.*

Mr. Barn. Gentlemen, do you call? will you please to see a Room, Gentlemen? here somebody take off the Gentlemen's Boots there?

Dor. Father! unkle! what is the meaning of this?

Mr. Barn. Here, shew a Room――Or will you please to walk into the Kitchin first and see what you like for Dinner.

1 *Gen.* Make no Preparations, Sir, your own Dinner will suffice.

Mr. Barn. Very well, I understand ye; let's see how many are there of ye, 1, 2, 3, 4; well, Gentlemen, it is but half a Crown a-piece for your selves, and six Pence a-head for your Servants; your Dinner shall be ready in half an Hour; here shew the Gentlemen into the *Apollo*.

2 Gen. What, Sir, does your Father keep an Inn?

Mr. Barn. The Sword Royal, at your Service, Sir.

Dor. But, Father, let me speak to ye; would you shame me?

Mr. Barn. My Wine is very good, Gentlemen, but to be very plain with ye, it is dear.

Dor. O, I shall run distracted.

Mr. Barn. You seem not to like my House, Gentlemen, you may try all the Inns in the County and not be better entertained; but I own my Bills run high.

Dor. Gentlemen, let me beg the Favour of ye.

1 Gent. Ay, my young 'Squire of the Sword Royal, you shall receive some favours from us.

Dor. Dear Monsieur *la Guarantiere*.

1 Gen. Here, my Horse there.

Dor. Monsieur *la Rose*.

2 Gent. Damn ye, you Prig.

Dor. Monsieur *Trofignac*.

3 Gent. Go to the Devil.   [*Exeunt three Gentlemen.*

Dor. O, I'm disgrac'd for ever.

Mr. Barn. Now, Son, this will teach you how to live.

Dor. Your Son! I deny the Kindred; I'm the son of a Whore, and I'll burn your House about your Ears, you old Rogue you.   [*Exit.*

Mr. Barn. Ha, ha——

Bro. The young Gentleman's in a Passion.

Mr. Barn. They're all gone for all that, and the Sword Royal's the best General in Christendom.

Enter Erast's *Servant talking with* Lisett.

Lis. What, that tall Gentleman I saw in the Garden with ye?

Serv. The same, he's my Master's Unkle, and Ranger of the King's Forests——He intends to leave my Master all he has.

Mr. Barn. Don't I know this Scoundrel? What, is his Master here? What do you do here, Rascal?

Serv. I was asking which must be my Master's Chamber.

Mr. Barn. Where is your Master?

Serv. Above Stairs with your Wife and Daughter; and I want to know where he's to lie, that I may put up his things.

Mr. Barn. Do you so, Rascal?

Serv. A very handsome Inn this—Here, Drawer, fetch me a Pint of Wine.

Mr. Barn. Take that, Rascal, do you Banter us?   [*Kicks him out.*

Enter Madam Barnard.

Madam. What is the meaning of this, Husband? Are not you ashamed to turn your House into an Inn——and is this a Dress for my Spouse, and a man of your Character?

Mr. Barn. I'd rather wear this Dress than be ruin'd.

Madam. You're nearer being so than you imagine; for there are some Persons within that have it in their Power to punish you for your ridiculous Folly.

Enter Erast *leading in* Mariane.

Mr. Barn. How, Sir; what means this? who sent you here?

Er. It was the luckiest Star in your Firmament that sent me here.

Mr. Barn. Then I doubt, that at my Birth, the Planets were but in a scurvy Disposition.

Er. The killing one of the King's Stags that run hither for Refuge is enough to overturn a Fortune much better establish'd than yours——However, Sir, if you will consent to give me your Daughter, for her Sake I will secure you harmless.

Mr. Barn. No, Sir, no Man shall have my Daughter that won't take my House too.

Er. Sir, I will take your House, pay you the full Value on't, and you shall remain as much its Master as ever.

Mr. Barn. No, Sir, that won't do neither; you must be Master on't your self, and from this Minute begin to do the Honours on't in your own Person.

Er. Sir, I do consent.

Mr. Barn. Upon that Condition, and in order to get rid of my House, here take my Daughter——And now, Sir, if you think you've a hard Bargain, I don't care if I toss you in my Wife to make you amends.

> *Since all Things now are sped,*
> *My Son in Anger, and my Daughter wed;*
> *My House dispos'd of, which was the Cause of Strife,* ⎫
> *I now may hope to lead a happy Life,*   ⎬
> *If I can part with my ingaging Wife.*   ⎭

Æsop : part I

Prol. l. 12. *Patentees.* Q1 and Q2 " Pattentees," but " Patentees " later.

l. 13. *Zeal,* Qs and 1711. 1725 " Zeal "

l. 20. *lye* Qs ly 1711 etc. " lie "

l. 24. *borne* Qs only, " born." This correction has been made consistently throughout the play.

Dram. Pers. *Pinkethman.* Qs, in each case, " Pinkerman." In *The Pilgrim* he appears as " Pinkeman." It may be worth while to note that his nickname was Pinky, to account for these errors. Cf. *The Epistle to Augustus:*

> And idle Cibber, how he breaks the laws
> To make poor Pinkey eat with vast applause.

a Herald. Qs " a Herauld," but " Herald " in the play.

Fruitful. He is so called in the play, but in the Q1 and Q2 Dramatis Personæ both he and his wife are called Breedwell.

p. 14, l. 11. *pity* 1711. Q1 and Q2 " pitty," but " pity " later.

p. 15, l. 13. *blind.* Q2 etc. Q1 only, " bind." The meaning is the same.

p. 15, l. 15. *Magistrates:* Qs, 1711, 1725, " Magistrates." 1719 " Magistrates," turn

p. 15, l. 16. *Tyrants:* Q1 and Q2 " Tyrants." 1711, 1725, " Tyrants; " 1719 " Tyrants, breaks. ."

p. 15, l. 42. *from whence I sprung.* This passage is another instance of how much better blank verse Vanbrugh wrote when he was writing prose than when he was consciously writing verse.

p. 16, l. 2. *your future* 1711 etc. Q1 and Q2 " Your future "

p. 16, l. 34. *easy.* It may be as well to note once, to palliate any false judgments of which the editor may be guilty, that the earlier text does not necessarily have the older spelling. In this instance, 1711 spells " easie." Such anomalies are frequent.

p. 16, l. 37. *Damsel* 1711 etc. Qs " Damsell " here, but " Damsel " later.

p. 18, l. 12. *by the outside alone.* In *Ésope* here follows the fable of *Le Renard et la Teste Peinte.*

p. 18, l. 13. *Periwig* Q " Periwigg " here and lower, but more often " Periwig."

p. 18, l. 18. *my Rival.* This suggestion is not in Boursault. The passage " Have her dream of nothing . . ." is the purest Vanbrugh.

p. 19, l. 7. *swoon* Q2, 1711 etc. " swoon; " Q1 " swoond," here and later.

p. 19, l. 12. *Heroes* Qs only, " Heros."

p. 20, l. 17. *Conversation.* 1711 etc. Q1 and Q2 " Conversation,"

p. 21, l. 5. *Exit Æsop running.* In the French he utters a homily of some seven lines before doing so: the Fable ends differently in conformity.

p. 21, l. 8. *sense* 1711 etc. Qs " sence," but " sense " four lines lower.

p. 22, l. 27.   *Struggled*   Qs only "strugled"

p. 23, l. 33.   *Beak*   Qs only "Beake"

p. 23, l. 42.   *Avaunt* 1719, 1725.   Q1, Q2 and 1711 "*Avant*"

p. 25, l. 7.   *let*   Qs "Let"

p. 25, l. 15.   *what Title must we give him.*   This discussion is Vanbrugh's.   There is just one modest remark of Æsop's in the French.

p. 26, l. 2.   *cram'd* Qs.   1711, 1719, 1725 "cramb'd"

p. 27, l. 23.   *his* 1711 etc.   Qs "his,"

p. 28, l. 1.   *Country* 1711 etc.   Qs here, and elsewhere, "*Countrey*," but as often as not "Country."

p. 28, l. 15.   *I'se*   Q1 "I's."   "I'se" above.

p. 28, l. 30.   *Joan*   Qs misprint "Jone" here, but "Joan" later.

p. 29, l. 23.   *wholesome* 1711 etc.   Qs "wholsome"

p. 30, l. —.   *Æsop.*   At this point, for some reason, Q1 begins to spell "Æsope" at the head of each page, and often in the text.   Q2 "Æsop" throughout.

p. 32, l. 8.   *loser by his gain.*   Qs and 1711 have:

And makes the wise Man lose, by what he gains.

1719 is a distinct improvement, and is adopted here as being, if not Vanbrugh's, likely approved by him.

p. 32, l. 28.   *genealogist* 1711 etc.   Qs "geneologist" every time.   Once at the Herald's College Vanbrugh would no doubt have corrected the error.   Q1 "A Geneologist?"   Q2 "A Geneologist!"

p. 33, l. 42.   *Symmetry* Q2 etc.   Q1 "Simmetry."

p. 34, l. 22.   *high,*   Qs high?

p. 34, l. 40.   *bubbled*   Qs print "bubled"

p. 35, l. 5.   *there?* Q2 etc.   Q1 "who waits there."   Vanbrugh here omits the fable of *Le Corbeau et le Renard* with its moral anent flatterers.   Boursault's *Ésope* only threatens vaguely.   He does not call in a cudgeller.

p. 36, l. 9.   *Dickins.*—Qs   1711 etc. "Dickens," as in *The Provok'd Husband.*

p. 36, l. 21.   *awkward*   Qs "aukward," but "awkward" earlier.   A similar correction is made later.

p. 36, l. 25.   *Ladyship.*   Q1 "Ladiship," but "Ladyship" elsewhere.

p. 37, l. 29.   *Enter Learchus* etc.   Qs misprints "Learcus" here and elsewhere.   This scene comes first in the act in *Ésope.*   The last scene in the French is between two children, a scene Vanbrugh omits, since he has considerably swollen this one.   The turn at the end of the act is entirely Vanbrugh's.

p. 38, l. 13.   *bear*   Qs only *bare;* a similar correction is made in the fables of the puffed-up toad and the crab, and in the Æsop-Oronces scene in Act IV.

p. 38, l. 34.   *pulls too*   so all early texts.   I have usually altered this, but here the weight of texts is too strong against me.

p. 38, l. 39.   *Larum* 1711 etc.   Qs "Laram"

p. 40, l. 26.   *Cuckow* 1711 etc. but Qs "Cookow" twice.

p. 42, l. 34.	*Pigmy* Q2, 1711 etc. Q1 " Pigmie " here, but " Pigmy " otherwise· 1711 etc. " a Pigmy."
p 43, l. 28.	*the Deux* 1711 etc. " the Deuce," but Vanbrugh has " Deux " in another place, and in other plays, e.g. *The Mistake.*
p. 47, l. 41.	*then you had* Q1. " than you had " Q2, 1711 etc.
p. 49, l. 22.	*Enter Oronces.* This scene in *Ésope* precedes that of Fruitful. There is no Mrs. Fruitful in the French, and the scene ends with the fable of *Les Colombes et le Vautour.*
p. 50, l. 33.	*ſtroke.* Q2, 1711 etc. Q1 only " spoak, stroak; " by then rather archaic.
p. 51, l. 10.	*wed* Q2, 1719, 1725. Q1 " wedd " 1711 " weded "
p. 51, l. 24.	*muſt be* Q1 only " must be,"
p. 51, l. 25.	*Chuse that,* Qs only. 1711 etc. " Chuse that "
p. 51, l. 41.	*whilſt . . . fixt* Q2, 1711 etc. Q1 " whils't . . . fix't " " fix't " is clearly wrong. You can have " fix'd," but you could not have " fixet."
p. 52, l. 3.	*Verge* Q2, 1711 etc. Q1 " Virge "
p. 52, l. 32.	*Act V.* Vanbrugh says he added " Act V ": he has re-written it. It resembles Boursault's in some respects, but to follow the differences in detail would weary the reader as much as the editor. Ward has a note to the effect that Vanbrugh may have based his last act on an event which happened early in the life of Beau Nash: but this is doubtful, as Vanbrugh's story is no nearer Nash's than it to the French.
p. 53, l. 11.	*a great many* 1711, 1725. Qs and 1719 " great many "
p. 53, l. 15.	*Curtsy* 1711, 1719. Qs, in text and as catch-word in Q1, and 1725, " Cursy "
p. 53, l. 22.	*an Ace* Qs only " Ams Ace," which does not seem to make sense. For " ames ace " see the note on Hazard in the notes on *A Journey to London.*
p. 53, l. 42.	*wheedle* Q1 only " wheadle "
p. 54, l. 23.	*lik'd* Q1 only " lik't "—but this is impossible. " Lik'd " or " likt " (?) but not " liket."
p. 54, l. 33.	*linnen* Qs " linen," but Q1 consistently elsewhere " linnen "
p. 55, l. 23.	*Politician* Q1 only, " Polititian "
p. 56, l. 21.	*defer* Qs only, " deferr " but " defer " later.
p. 59, l. 2.	*Fidlers* so all early editions, and Q1 " fidling " later, while 1719 has " fiddling." Q1 has " fiddles " later. This seems to be a case for inactivity in an editor.
p. 60, l. —.	Q1 here begins to print *Es:* instead of *Æs:* Q2 corrects. 1719 prints " Esop " throughout the whole play. There is no warrant for this except the French *Ésope.*
p. 63, l. 32.	*does,* Q1 " does."
p. 63, l. 33.	*Council* 1719 only, " Counsel." 1725 restores " Council "
p. 64, l. 38.	*o're* in conformity with usage. Qs " ore." 1711 " o'er "
p. 65, l. 2.	*o'rewhelm'd* similarly. In both cases the older spelling, corrected, is adopted.
p. 65, l. 18.	*Sparrows are* Q2 1711 etc. Q1 " Sparows are,"

p. 65, l. 19.   *already* Q2, 1711 etc.   Q "already,"
Q1, at the bottom of the last page, notes two errata, which have
been silently corrected.

Æsop : part II

Q1 has Æsop on the title page, Esope at the head of the play, and *Æsope* at the
head of the pages. It varies between *Æs, Es,* and Æ. in the text. Q2 has Æ. throughout.

p. 67, l. 23.   '*pray*' Q1, Q2 and 1711. The inverted commas are dropped in 1719
and 1725. They presumably stand for I——you. Cf. Part I. V, i.

p. 67, l. 31.   *Frigat* Q1 and Q2.   1711 etc. "Frigot"

p. 67, l. 32.   *guilded* Qs only; but this spelling was still common.

p. 68, l. 1.   *mercy*   Q1 and Q2 "merry"

p. 68, l. 19.   *Wrack*   Qs only "Rack"

p. 69, l. 2.   *you?* Qs "You?"

p. 69, l. 32.   *Pay*   Q1 and Q2 misprint "Pair"   1711 corrects.

p. 69, l. 38.   *Patience.* Qs only, the remainder "Patience?" but it might just as
well be an exclamation as a query.

p. 70, l. 6.   *coolly*   Q1 and Q2 "cooly"

p. 70, l. 10.   *to the purpose.*   In 1711 etc. all this above passage is, very sensibly,
printed as prose.

p. 70, l. 14.   *separation*   Qs "seperation."

p. 70, l. 38.   *o'er* Q2.   Q1 "ore"

p. 71, l. 32.   *talk'd* Q2.   Q1 misprints "taulk'd"

p. 71, l. 33.   *Fowler* Q1 and 2 "Fouler," but "Fowler" earlier.

p. 72, l. 11.   *Guarantee* Q1 and 2 "Garantee"

p. 72, l. 16.   *Exeunt.* Qs and 1719 have not got this stage direction, but only
"*Enter a Country Gentleman, who* . . ." 1711 and 1725 followed
here. Qs "*too and fro*"

p. 72, l. 17.   *Country.* Part II spells preferably "Countrey"; but here the spelling
is kept uniform throughout. See note ante.

p. 74, l. 16.   *Council* See note ante.

p. 74, l. 34.   *Uncle* Q2.   Q1 "Unkle," but "Uncle" later.

p. 75, l. 13.   *Head peice* Qs and 1711 consistently.   1719 modernises.

p. 76, l. 7.   *Mankind* 1711.   Qs "mankind"

p. 76, l. 28.   *Rack* 1711, 1725.   Qs and 1719 "Wrack"

p. 76, l. 32.   *Rewards* Q1.   Q2 "the Rewards"

p. 76, l. 42.   *And so Sir you* Q1.   Q2 "And so, Sir, you"

p. 76, l. 42.   *lay* 1719, 1725.   Q1 and 1711 "play"   Q2 "play,"

p. 77, l. 6.   200 *miles* Q1.   Q2 "200. Miles"

p. 77, l. 8.   *Well:* Q1.   Q2 "Well!"

p. 77, l. 18.   *A Fool* Q1.   Q2 "Fool"

p. 79, l. 3.   *Putt* Q1.   Q2 "Put"

p. 80, l. 6.   *favour.* Qs "favour,"

p. 80, l. 7.   *went,* Qs "went."

p. 81, l. 1.   *Wig* Q2.   Q1 "Wigg"

The Pilgrim

A pamphlet issued by Messrs. Dobell states that two copies of the 1701 Dryden in the possession of G. Thorn-Drury, Esq., K.C., contain the Prologue with certain variations, some of which are adopted here, and marked 1701.

Prol. l. 12. *muzzled* Q " muzled " Oxford text correction adopted.

l. 16. *Maurus* 1701. Q misprints " *Marus.*" (See Explanatory Notes.)

l. 26. *lower* 1701. Q " longer "

l. 29. *flounders* 1701. Q " founders."

l. 40. *Cat-Calls* Q " Cat-Call's." *again* 1701 " for gain "

Dram. Pers. *Pinkethman.* Q Pinkeman.

p. 96, l. 29. Enter Alinda and Juletta. Vanbrugh shortens this scene very considerably.

p. 98, l. 11. *Rascals?* F and 1753. Q " Rascalls? "

p. 98, l. 13. *undo me?* F. Q " undoe me! "

p. 98, l. 24. *beg* F and 1753. Q " begg "

p. 99, l. 6. *point at? Still* F " look for? Still " Q " point at, Still "

p. 100, l. 22. *Kneel to* Q " Kneel too "

p. 100, l. 35. *Penance* Q " Pennance " F " penance "

p. 103, l. 1. *Coalpit* F " Coal-pit " Q " Colepit "

p. 103, l. 5. *Enter Servant drunk.* This and the stammering servant are Vanbrugh's invention. Fletcher has simply " *Enter Porter and Servants,*" these having previously been sent off the scene.

p. 104, l. 14. [SCENE II.] This direction is restored from F.

p. 104, l. 27. *flay* F " fley " Q " flea " 1753 " flay." Since F is more modern than Q the spelling has been completely modernised, though the archaic spelling was used by Vanbrugh earlier in Æsop.

p. 105, l. 8. *Mony* Q " Money," but " Mony " otherwise in the play.

p. 105, l. 17. *yielded* F. Q " yeilded "

p. 106, l. 29. *Thief-like* F. Q " Theif-like," but " thief " lower down.

p. 106, l. 33. *for't* Q " fort "

p. 107, l. 2. *alas* Q " alass "

p. 108, l. 39. *Prithee* Q " Prethee," here and later, but as often " Prithee."

p. 110, l. 15. *whither* Q " whether "

p. 110, l. 21. *he'll* Q " he'l " As " ll " occurs most frequently in such cases, it has been silently substituted wherever the more archaic " l " is printed.

p. 111, l. 19. *call'd* Q " cal'd "

p. 115, l. 5. *me?* 1753. Q " me! "

p. 116, l. 28. [SCENE III.] A change of scene is clearly necessary here and is marked in F, where it is Scene VI.

p. 117, l. 26. *Coal-house* Q " Cole-house " F " coal house "

p. 118, l. 32. *lie* F. Q " lye "

p. 120, l. 29. *weary of me?* F.   Q " weary of me! "

p. 122, l. 27. *boil* Q " boyl," but " boild " lower.

p. 126, l. 32. [SCENE II.]   The scene must change here.   This is marked Scene III in F, Scene II being at the entry of Roderigo, but the place need not be changed for that.

p. 127, l. 12. *Trenchmores* Q " Frenchmores "   F " trenchmores "

p. 127, l. 33. *Triton* F.   Q " Tryton "

p. 128, l. 2. *Enter mad Taylor.*   The tailor is of Vanbrugh's invention.

p. 129, l. 34. *best now* Q. " best know "

p. 134, l. 1. [SCENE II.]   This necessitates a change of scene, as is the case at [SCENE III] and [SCENE IV.]   Scene II here is Scene III in F, Scene II being at the entry of Alinda and Juletta.

p. 134, l. 19. *Bonfires* F " bonfires "   Q " Bonefires "

p. 137, l. 4. *Name.   The seeming Boy too, we* Q " Name, the seeming Boy too.   We "

p. 142, l. 1. *Song.*   The idea of the character is from the story told by the Curate in Part II, Chapter I of *Don Quixote.*

Sec. Masque:

l. 1   *Chronos.* Q and 1753 " Chronus."

l. 28   *been.* Q " been," 1753 corrects.

l. 30   *Musick,* following the spelling in the play. Q " Musique."

l. 32   *Day,* Oxford. Q " Day." 1753 " Day; "

l. 38   *sky,* Q " Skie "—but the same line above " Sky "

Epilogue:

l. 18   *its Head* Q " it's Head "

l. 20   *Scandal* Q " Scandall "—but in Prologue " Scandal "

l. 40   *married* Q " maried "

The False Friend

p. 159, l. 22. *gracious Sir.* Q " gracious, Sir."

p. 162, l. 19. *Astre* So Q and 1719.   Later editions misprint "*Astrea*" which makes nonsense.   The French has " astre."

p. 165, l. 40. *Difficulties are* Q misprints " ate "

p. 165, l. 40. *Rocombolle* the French has " rocambolle " but Vanbrugh's spelling is more correct.

p. 166, l. 27. *Mine's not* Q misprints " nor "

p. 167, l. 1. *Conge* so Q, 1719 and 1730.   1776 has " *Congé* "

p. 167, l. 14. *Heaven's* 1719. Q " Heavens "

p. 168, l. 23. *Love.   Widower.* Q " Love?   Widower? "

p. 169, l. 2. *Apprehensions* Q "Appresions' 1719 " apprehensions "

p. 171, l. 14. *Deuce* First two editions " Deux "

p. 171, l. 18. *e'en* Q " e'n "

p. 173, l. 28. *Lady's* Q " Ladies "

p. 176, l. 4. *hates* Q " hate's "

p. 176, l. 15.   *Jacinta.*   Q " Jacinte."
p. 176, l. 23.   *I am in.*   Q " I am."
p. 177, l. 16.   *what wrong*   Q " Were it even so? What wrong "
p. 179, l. 22.   *Enter Lopez.*   Leigh Hunt and Ward gratuitously change the scene
        here; there seems no necessity for it.
p. 180, l. 18.   *o'th'*   Q " ot'h "
p. 180, l. 26.   *has.*   Q " has? "
p. 181, l. 26.   *Ladies* 1719.   Q " Lady's "
p. 182, l. 32.   *Regulator* 1719.   Q " Regulater "
p. 183, l. 32.   *Scene changes.*   There is none in the French: Leonora comes in
        holding on to Don John. (Don André.)
p. 186, l. 26.   *wrackt*   Q and 1719 " wreckt "
p. 188, l. 14.   *'twas you.*   Q " 'twas you? "
p. 189, l. 3.   *Night! . . . again!* 1730.   *Night? . . . again.* 1719   *Night? . . .*
        again? Q.
p. 189, l. 4.   *Wrack* 1719 and 1730.   Q " Wreck "
p. 189, l. 33.   *Yes;* 1719 and subsequently.   Q " Yes? "
p. 191, l. 32.   *am I!* 1719 and subsequently.   Q " am I? "
p. 195, l. 31.   *Mercy, Don Pedro!*   Q omits " *Lopez* " before this remark.
p. 195, l. 39.   *plunge*   Q " plung "   1719 corrects.
p. 196, l. 28.   *Bourbon's*   Q " Boubon's "
p. 197, l. 39.   *Two Persons*   Q " the Two Persons "   1719 " two Persons "
p. 198, l. 21.   *Appartment;* 1719.   Q "Appartment,"
p. 198, l. 23.   *for Aid.* 1719.   Q " to Aid."
p. 198, l. 24.   *Assistance.*   Q "Assistance,"   1719 " assistance."
p. 198, l. 38.   *told* 1719.   Q " tol'd "
p. 201, l. 39.   *told you of.* 1719.   Q " told you off."
p. 202, l. 23.   *I'm satisfy'd; 'tis* 1719.   Q " I'm satisfy'd 'tis "
p. 203, l. 22.   *Bonus Nocius.*   This " buenas noches " of the valet is not in the
        French version, nor, it need hardly be said, in the Spanish. It
        would seem to indicate that Vanbrugh's Spanish was a little wanting.
p. 203, l. 29.   *Judgments!*   It is to be regretted that in Q Don Guzman makes
        this a question; " Judgments? "

The Country House

Title.   The edition of 1740 calls it La Maison Rustique, or The Country House.
Dramatis Personæ. This varies slightly from the first edition in 1735 and 1740.
        Erast becomes *Erastus* and Mariane *Mariamne.* Charly is " a
        little boy."
p. 213, l. 6.   In 1715 Erast's first speech runs: " Let me but see her, let me but
        speak to her only." This is clearly loose in sense, as well as contrary
        to the French. The text of 1735 and 1740 has been adopted here.

p. 213, l. 20. *want Portions.* 1735 and 1740 read: "Any thing but Wives; because they can't be put off without Portions."

p. 213, l. 21. *Portions!* 1715 "Portion!"

p. 213, l. 21. *Portions,* 1735 and 1740 "Portions;"

p. 215, l. 39. *keam* 1735 and 1740. 1715 "ceam"

p. 216, l. 18. *belov'd, Meaſter.* 1735 and 1740 read, perhaps more logically: ". . . good Things for it? Come they not to see you the whole Country raund? Mind . . ." This is also nearer the French: "Morguoi! vous vous divartissez bien aussi: toujours grand chère et biau feu; la maison ne désemplit point, et n'an vous viant voir de par tout, jarnigué! c'est qu'an vous aime."

p. 217, l. 8. *Captain Hungry.* So 1735, 1740, 1759, 1765 and 1776. 1715 reads "*Hungary.*"

p. 217, l. 27. *retir'd off.* 1735 etc. "retir'd a little distance off." There is no corresponding phrase in the French.

p. 217, l. 29. *begone, Sirrah.* 1715 "begone, Rogue." But this seems to have strayed in here from the next line.

p. 217, l. 32. *Enter Brother.* 1735 and 1740 "*Enter Mr.* Barnard's *Brother*" 1776 "*Enter Mr.* Griffard."

p. 217, l. 40. *I don't hear them:* 1735 etc. 1715 "I did not hear them:"

p. 218, l. 11. *What, leave* 1735 etc. "What, and leave"

p. 218, l. 15. *as if it had the Plague;* 1735 etc. "as if the Plague were in't;"

p. 218, l. 28. *I'll hold* 1735 etc. 1715 "I hold"

p. 219, l. 1. *so I came* 1715 "so I come"

p. 219, l. 18. *the beſt Woman* 1735 etc. "one of the best Women."

p. 220, l. 10. *Dear Marquis* 1715 "Dear, Marquis"

p. 220, l. 37. *unlucky* 1735 etc. "unluckily"

p. 220, l. 39. *no matter, Baron,* 1715 misprints "Marquis"

p. 221, l. 14. *in the World.* 1735 etc. "in the World, Marquis."

p. 221, l. 38. *horrible this is!* 1715 "horrible this is?"

p. 222, l. 6. *Jail.* 1740. 1715 "Gail." 1735 "Jayl." 1776 "jail."

p. 222, l. 11. *fell down* 1735, 1740. 1715 "set down"

p. 222, l. 16. *fit it up.* 1735 etc. "fit it up again."

p. 222, l. 18. *I'll wait* 1715 "I wait"

p. 223, l. 20. *a propos* 1740. 1715 "*a propo*" 1735 "*a propôs*"

p. 223, l. 31. *partridges* 1715 misprints "pigeons"

p. 223, l. 40. *ſtore . . . ſtore* 1735 "good store . . . good store"

p. 224, l. 40. *hit on* 1715 "hit of"

p. 225, l. 36. *able all alone* 1715. Subsequent editions "able, by herself,"

p. 226, l. 10. *your own* 1715 and 1735. 1740 et seq. "our own"

p. 226, l. 17. *Enter Charly.* Vanbrugh splits up Le Cousin in Dancourt to make Janno and Charly. There is no cause for it.

p. 226, l. 20. *troublesom* 1715 only. Subsequently "troublesome."

p. 226, l. 24. *handsom.* 1715 only. Subsequently "handsome."

p. 226, l. 33. *Sis* 1715. Subsequent editions "*Cicely*"

p. 227, l. 7. *Lewis d'Or* so all editions except 1715 which prints "*Lewis d'Ore*" throughout.

p. 227, l. 12.   *bad* 1715.   Subsequent editions " bid."

p. 227, l. 14.   *Garden Door* 1715.   Subsequent editions " Garden Gate," here and later.

p. 227, l. 18.   *What then?* 1715 " What then."

p. 227, l. 23.   *supping* 1715.   Subsequent editions " sipping "

p. 227, l. 28.   *go there* 1715.   Subsequent editions " go to him "

p. 227, l. 33.   *bubbies there;* 1715 " bubbies there "

p. 227, l. 33.   *touch 'em* 1715.   Subsequent editions " feel 'em "

p. 227, l. 34.   *I must* 1715.   Subsequent editions " you must "

p. 228, l. 24.   *Now, Sir, we have* 1735 etc. " Sir, we have now "

p. 229, l. 12.   *chang'd* 1735 etc.   1715 " alter'd "   In view of " alteration " just above, the later editions seem preferable.

p. 229, l. 19.   *take Cudgel* 1715.   Subsequent editions " take the Cudgel "

p. 229, l. 26.   *tolerable* 1715 " tollerable "   1735 " Tolerable "

p. 230, l.   2.   *six Pence a-head* 1735 etc.   1715 " six Pence a Piece "

p. 230, l.   6.   *shame me* 1715.   1735, 1740, 1776 " disgrace me "

p. 230, l. 30.   *Enter Erasts's Servant* 1715, 1735, 1740 misprint " *Enter* Dorant's *Servant* "   The French has La Flèche, who is Éraste's servant, as the context proves.   1776 corrects.

p. 230, l. 32.   *Ranger of the King's* 1735 etc.   1715 " Ranger of all the King's." The omission seems justified, to avoid the jingle of the later " all he has."

p. 231, l.   4.   *my Spouse* 1735 etc.   1715 " my Husband "

p. 231, l. 11.   *How, Sir;* 1715, 1735, 1740 " How, Sirs."

p. 231, l. 18.   *secure you harmless* 1715.   Subsequent editions " bear you harmless "

p. 231, l. 30.   *Since all Things now are sped* 1715.   Later editions " *Well then, since all Things thus are fairly sped* "

p. 231, l. 32.   *My House dispos'd of, which was the Cause of Strife*   The later editions have " *My* House *dispos'd of, the sole Cause of Strife,*"   A few minor divergences of text between the 1715 and subsequent editions have not been noted where 1715 has been followed.

Æsop : part I

Preface. *Conduct of the War.* See notes to *The Relapse.*

Feathers, i.e. fops, who still wore feathers in their hats. Cf. Part II, Scene iii.

Prologue. This is a preliminary flurt at the morality-mongers, and bears no relation to Boursault's Prologue.

p. 13. *Pike-man:* as we should say, " Straight as a guardsman."

p. 13. *Barb,* a Barbary horse, an Arab, famous for their beauty; cf. " The best stallion is a well-chosen Barb, or beautiful Spanish horse." Newcastle, *System of Horsemanship,* I, v (1658). They were probably first imported into Europe by the Moors in Spain. Though as early as 1121 two Eastern horses are said to have been imported into England, the first authentic record is that of the " Markham Arabian " brought in by James I. This horse was not a great success, and was poorly thought of by the famous horse-lover, the Duke of Newcastle. Both Charles II and James II encouraged Barb blood, but it was the reign of William III that saw the introduction of the three famous Arabs from which all our thoroughbreds are descended, though the third, the " Darley Arabian," was not imported until after the date of this play.

For barb, or Barbary, used as a term of beauty, cf. Congreve, *Love for Love,* I (1695): " a *Barbary* shape."

p. 13. *Heaven as he is;* clumsy English for

Plust aux Dieux, tel qu'il est, qu'Euphrosine luy plût!

p. 15. *false Musters.* Officers were responsible for paying their soldiers, and impressed for the money on the basis of their rolls. These were often unchecked, so much so that men long dead were often found on the rolls.

p. 15. *Pulvilio.* A scented powder, frequently mentioned in the comedies of the period, and by the more sober Addison. Cf. *The Way of the World* (1700), IV, i: " Have you pulvill'd the Coach-man and Postillion, that they may not stink of the Stable . . .? "

p. 19. *Deess.* So all early texts. *Déesse,* of course.

p. 22. *Talk of the Devil.* The earliest mention of this saying in the N.E.D. is of 1672: " Talk of the Devil and see his Horns." *Cataplus.* The next mention is Prior, in 1721:

Forthwith the Devil did appear,
For name him, and he's always near.
Hans Carvel.

Vanbrugh almost seems to have invented the familiar use.

p. 22. *mumping.* To mump is to over-reach. Cf. Wycherley, *The Gentleman Dancing Master,* IV (1676): " He is . . . some debauch'd person who will mump you of your daughter." And Buckingham's *Rehearsal*, II, ii. (1672): "I am resolv'd hereafter, to bend all my thoughts for the service of the *Nursery*, and mump you proud Players, I gad."

p. 22.   *crump*; a hunch: also crump-back. N.E.D. quotes this passage.

p. 23.   *cornet*; a kind of head-dress, with lappets of lace hanging over the ears. Cf. Countess d'Annoy's *Travels* (1697): "I immediately threw off my Bonnets and my Cornets." (N.E.D.)

p. 25.   *Ten Thousand pounds to be made a Lord*. People nowadays talk as though the buying of titles were a new corruption. After all, baronetcies were invented to raise money: and wealth has always been a good claim to a title.

p. 31.   *scowre*. Scour. See notes to *The Relapse*.

p. 33.   *Welch Woman*, whence a genealogist. The Welsh have always been noted for their love of genealogical lore, a point Peacock did not fail to make use of.

p. 34.   *that made 'em*. The whole of this speech, it will be observed, is in excellent Vanburghian blank verse.

p. 34.   *bubbled*; cheated. See notes to *The Relapse*.

p. 36.   *The Dickins*. See notes to *The Provok'd Husband*.

p. 43.   *goloshoes*; galoshes. Cf. Etherege's *The Man of Mode*, I (1676):

'Tis but despising a coach, humbling yourself
To a pair of Goloshoes.

p. 44.   *Botcher*; a repairing tailor. Cf. "A sorry Taylor may make a Botcher, or a bad Shoomaker may make a Cobler." Baxter, *Div. Life* (1663). (N.E.D.)

p. 45.   *runners*; race-horses. N.E.D. quotes this passage.

p. 45.   *blind stallions*. Stallions are still often blindfolded when being taken along roads.

p. 45.   *Pad*. A pad is a riding horse, and the word is still in use. It is a horse for a path.

p. 45.   *Routs*. N.E.D. says "some kind of horse," and quotes merely this passage to support the statement. Probably a hack, a route-horse.

p. 52.   *channel*; gutter. See notes to *A Journey to London*.

p. 54.   *opposition*. Heavenly bodies are said to be in opposition when they are opposite one another as seen from the earth, i.e. differing in longitude by 180°. Astrologically "This aspect is of enimity most perfect." Scot's *Discovery of Witchcraft* (1665). See also notes to *The Provok'd Wife*.

p. 54.   *Snap-sack*—obviously knapsack. Common, the N.E.D. says *c.* 1650–1700. From, of course, knap-sack, i.e. sack for luncheon.

p. 54.   *with a witness*. Vengeance. See notes to *The Confederacy*.

p. 57.   *shift yourself*; change your clothes. See notes to *The Confederacy*.

p. 58.   *Lilly Burleighre*, usually spelt Lilli-burlero. It is clear Learchus was a Whig. This song, with a tune by Purcell (Uncle Toby Shandy's favourite tune), was supposed to have been composed by the Earl (later Marquis) of Wharton, and was a great revolutionary song, so much so that Wharton claimed that he had sung a king out of three kingdoms. The words may readily be found in Percy's *Reliques,* and the tune most easily in Novello's cheap edition of Purcell tunes, under the title of *A New Irish Melody.*

Æsop : part II

p. 67. *Play upon the Patentees.* The whole of this scene is a burlesque view of the quarrel which led to the secession of the L.I.F. group from the patentees of Drury Lane in 1695.

p. 67. *the Patent,* viz. for the companies united in 1682, agreed to by Charles Killigrew, Betterton, Charles Davenant and Smith.

p. 67. *White-Staff,* i.e. the Lord Chamberlain, under whose authority the theatre was.

p. 68. *under a Petticoat.* "When it became necessary . . . to lessen the charge, a resolution was taken to begin with the salaries of the actors; . . . To make this project more feasible, they propos'd to begin at the head of them. . . . To bring this about with a better grace, they under pretence of bringing younger actors forwards, order'd several of Betterton's and Mrs. Barry's parts to be given to young Powel and Mrs. Bracegirdle. . . . But . . . tho' the giddy head of Powel accepted the parts of Betterton, Mrs. Bracegirdle had a different way of thinking . . . she knew the stage was wide enough for her success without entering into any such rash and invidious competition with Mrs. Barry, and therefore wholly refused acting any part that properly belong'd to her. But this proceeding, however, was warning enough to make Betterton be upon his guard . . ." etc., which led to the secession. Cibber, *Apology,* VI.

p. 68. *little Ben.* "Little Ben is, of course, Betterton, the leader of the seceding actors." Ward. But Betterton was not "amongst" the rest, he led them, and among them Doggett, who created the part of Benjamin in Congreve's *Love for Love,* the first play acted in L.I.F. in April, 1695. Doggett had no right to leave Drury Lane, and was arrested in 1697. He was found at Norwich, and as the State had to pay the expenses of his journey, he did himself proud on the way to London. I am inclined to think that Ben means Doggett.

p. 68. *took orders to be Chaplain.* After the secession the patentees found themselves forced to raise the salaries of the remaining actors so as to attract talent. "*Powell* and *Verbruggen,* who had then but forty shillings a week, were raised each of them to four pounds, and others in proportion." Cibber. "Chaplain" may be an oblique reference to Cibber, who had made his name as the Chaplain in Otway's *The Orphan* (1680). Now that Cibber was taking leading parts, as in this play, no doubt some inferior actor was promoted to his parts.

p. 68. *Curst;* disagreeable. See notes to *The Confederacy.*

p. 69. *At Amboyna.* The outrages of the Dutch upon the English at Amboyna occurred in 1623, and the affair was not settled until 1654, when Cromwell forced monetary compensation to the families from the Dutch. The theme was still popular, thanks to Dryden's tragedy, *Amboyna, or the Cruelties of the Dutch to the English in Amboyna* (1673), reprinted 1691.

p. 72.   *none of your Turin play;* meaning again, no separate peace. The Duke of Savoy, Victor Amadeus II, one of the allies against France, " was beguiled into a separate peace, signed privately at Loretto, and publicly at Turin, on August the 29th, 1696." Ward.

The companies, of course, were not reunited until the failure of the Queen's Opera House as a theatre marked it out for opera alone; thus in 1708 the actors went back to Drury Lane.

p. 73.   *Crocus Me^m.* Crocus metallorum. " Crocus was a name given to various oxides and peroxides, e.g. crocus of copper, cuprous oxide. This particular one was a crude oxide of antimony, liver of antimony, which, mixed with wine, was used as an emetic." Chambers' *Dictionary*, 1738.

p. 77.   *contemptibly;* presumably contemptuously.

p. 79.   *You old Putt you.* See notes to *The Pilgrim.*

p. 79.   *a Feather*—in his hat.

p. 80.   *Plod-Shooes.* Cf. Preface to *The Relapse.*

p. 81.   *A Band:* i.e. a parson; literally the bands a parson wore. See any contemporary portrait of a divine. Cf. Holme's *Armoury*, 1688: " A short Bobb, a Head of Hair, is a Wig that hath short locks and a hairy crown." (N.E.D.) Here meaning a merchant, a solid citizen.

p. 81.   *a Feather:* a fop. Cf. Preface, and note ante. The N.E.D. gives no instances of these uses, but their meaning is obvious enough.

The Pilgrim

Prologue

l. 3.   *Tom Dove,* a bear famous in the annals of bear-baiting. Dryden refers to him also in the Epilogue " At the opening of their Theatre upon the union of the two Companies in 1682."

They roar so loud, you'd think behind the Stairs
Tom Dove and all the Brotherhood of Bears:

l. 6.   *tho' they never Pay.* Authors who had had a play accepted were allowed the privilege of free entry into the theatre.

l. 8.   *He who writes Letters to himself;* i.e. the foplings. The reference is to *The Way of the World* which had been acted earlier in the month. (See Act I, viii, Ed. 1710.) Witwoud is describing Petulant: Where he wou'd send in for himself, that I mean, call for himself, wait for himself, nay and what's more, not finding himself, sometimes leave a Letter for himself.

l. 16. *Maurus.* Maurus in Latin, a moor, blackamoor, whence Sir Richard Blackmore (*d.* 1729). As the rest of the Prologue is about him, all the references may be explained here. He had, indeed, acquired the degree of B.A. at Oxford (1674), and subsequently proceeded to M.A. But his medical degree was a somewhat doubtful one granted him at Padua. At one time he tried to get his living as a schoolmaster; he wrote moral tracts, inveighing against the " obscene and profane pollutions " of the stage before Collier appeared on the scene; and practised without an English degree, hence " Pedant, Canting Preacher, and a Quack." His first monstrous epic was *King Arthur,* in ten books, 1695, in the Preface of which he attacked Dryden, who was here getting some of his own back. Others of his works are mentioned with due scorn in the Prologue. The reference ending " But rides triumphant between Stool and Stool " is to his own statement that he would write wherever he could, in coffee-houses, or in his coach as he went from patient to patient. " One made the Doctor, and one dubb'd the Knight " is a reference to the fact that he was admitted to the College of Physicians under James and knighted by William for adherence to the principles of the Revolution. Dryden had already had a cut at him in the Preface to the *Fables* (1700).

We may here note the extraordinary vigour of this Prologue. Dryden was now seventy years old, and ailing, so that the play was being produced for his benefit. Yet these couplets are well worthy of the author of the character of Zimri, and the idea is largely that of the Epilogue Dryden wrote to Etherege's *Man Of Mode* (1676).

l. 35. *Vandal Hopkins.* This reference appears to be to John Hopkins (*d.* 1570), who with Sternhold produced rhymed versions of the Psalms which were popular for three centuries. But he had tampered with eighteen only, while Blackmore spread his hand over all. For Hopkins, though accounted a good poet by some, the epithet Vandal is explicable if we accept the opinion of others that he spoiled the graces of the Psalms rather than added to them. Campbell opined that " they turned into bathos what they found sublime," an opinion Dryden may well have shared. The reference may be a double one, and partly to Charles Hopkins, who by his tragedy of *Boadicea,* 1697, might seem to challenge Blackmore's possession of the field of early English history.

p. 97. *louse yourselves,* viz. free yourselves of lice. The phrase occurs often in Stevens's translation of Quevedo's *Il Gran Buscón* (1707).

p. 98. *motion—a Puppit Pilgrim.* Puppet shows were known as the motions, too commonly to need illustration from the period. Cf., however, *Two Gentlemen of Verona,* II, i: " Oh! excellent motion; oh exceeding puppet." The word is contemptuous.

p. 99. *entitul'd;* " entitled." It should be either this or " intituled." The N.E.D. gives no example of the mixed form.

p. 102. *the flea-chamber.* In Spain rooms were sometimes set apart for fleaing or lousing. See Quevedo's work referred to ante, Book II, Chapter I (Duff's edition, 1926): " He went into an appartment reserved for lousing, and before closing the door reversed a little notice-board, similar to those that hang in vestries, on one side of which was written EN-GAGED FOR LOUSING."

p. 104.   *Lirry Poop*, usually spelt "liripipe" in books on costume, was the long pendent hood. It is here used metaphorically, as we might say "flap-doodle." The Fletcher passage is quoted by the N.E.D. as meaning a silly person. It also gives as authority Miller's M.S. Devon Glossary, which defines it as "A silly empty creature, an old dotard."

p. 105.   *Kissing*, to meet closely. Cf. *Romeo and Juliet*, II, vi: "Like fire and powder, Which as they kiss consume."

p. 106.   *t'invade*. This is one of those instances where an adapter trying to make a phrase clear confuses it worse. Fletcher has: "The more unhallowed soul hast thou to offer it."

p. 109.   *more joyful to a Wedding*. Cf.:

> I will encounter darkness as a bride
> And hug it in my arms.   (*Measure for Measure.*)

> I will be
> A bridegroom in my death, and run into't
> As to a lover's bed.   (*Antony and Cleopatra.*)

p. 109.   *prepar'd to die*. This is a common Jacobean theme; cf. Hamlet refraining from killing his uncle at his prayers. But it sounds a little strangely at this period.

p. 113.   *a Royal*; a gold coin, as we might say, a sovereign. The N.E.D. quotes Fabyan, *Chron.* VII (1513): "This yere, was a new coine ordeyned by the Kynge, the whiche was namyd the royall, and was and yet is in value of x shillynges." Later in the century it was worth an Angel and a half, viz. 11/3.

p. 114.   *flurt*, also spelt "flirt": a sharp tap or flick, N.E.D., which quotes the Fletcher passage; and for another illustration, which shows Vanbrugh not to have been using an archaism, *Bagford Ball* (c. 1691): "I'll give you a good flurt on the ear."

p. 115.   *kekkle*; spelt "keckle" in 1753 and by the N.E.D. To "keckle" means to gulp with difficulty. "The hypocrite . . . can swallow a Cammell with the same throat, which did euen keckle at a gnat." Whately, *God's Husb.* 1619.

p. 116.   *I'll ferk him*, viz. beat him. Cf. Congreve's *The Double Dealer* (1693): "You firk him, I'll firk him myself." And *Hudibras* II, ii, 447 (1664), when Hudibras in trying to persuade Ralph to beat himself:

> Then strip thee of thy Carnal *Jerkin*
> And give thy *outward-fellow* a Ferking.

And *Henry V*, IV, iv: "I'll fer him, and ferk him, and ferret him."

p. 116.   *such Diversion*. Madmen were a theme for laughter in Elizabethan times, of which we get a hint in *Twelfth Night*, but the actual display in several pieces. Cf. *The Duchess of Malfi*, IV, ii:

> A great physician, when the Pope was sick
> Of a deep melancholy, presented him
> With several sorts of madmen, which wild object
> Being full of change and sport, forced him to laugh,
> And so the imposthume broke:

The popularity of such an amusement seems to have been waning at this time, and Evelyn found the sight distressing on the 21st April, 1675. But Bedlam was still visited. Cf. Swift's *Tale of a Tub*, IX.

p. 117. *the Malt-Tax*. This naturally unpopular excise was granted to Charles II in 1660 at 2/6 per barrel of ale. At the date of this play it had lately been augmented by two additions of 9d. a barrel granted William and Mary. But the point of the allusion is not the excise, but a war-tax of a little over 6d. per bushel imposed in 1697 on malt made in England and Wales. Stephen Dowell, *Taxation and Taxes in England.*

p. 117. *Tanzey*, a bitter purgative herb, *tanacetum vulgare*, but the name is also locally given to other herbs. The word was also applied, as here, to an omelet flavoured with tansy. The N.E.D. quotes the Fletcher passage as illustration.

p. 119. *hit the Nick*, hit the exact mark; similar to "in the nick of time." The N.E.D. quotes the Fletcher passage.

p. 121. *errant*, "arrant." See notes to *A Journey to London*.

p. 122. *Enter Roderigo* in the gown he had put on in the previous act.

p. 127. *Trenchmore*, "a boisterous country dance." N.E.D. Cf. Fletcher's *The Island Princess*: "All the windows of the town dance a new trenchmore." E. W. Naylor in *Shakespeare and Music* says it was also known as French-more, but gives no nearer instance than "a French brawl." *L.L.L.*, III, i. Selden in his *Table-Talk* has: "But in King Charles [I]'s time, there has been nothing but trenchmore and cushion dance, *omnium gatherum; tolly polly, hoite cum toite*," as opposed to the graver corantoes and galliards "kept up with ceremony" of the earlier reigns.

p. 127. *curran-sawce*. Fletcher, "green sawce." I have been unable to find out the exact meaning of this. Perhaps some form of currant sauce was used as a condiment with roast pork, as we use apple sauce, which is, to be sure, green.

p. 128. *Warm Ware*: presumably "warm wear"; but the other meaning is possible.

p. 128. *dizen'd*, i.e. "bedizened," dressed him out; contemptuous. The N.E.D. quotes the Fletcher passage.

p. 129. *The Organs at Wrexham*. "Heere is Wrexham to be seene, . . . much spoken of for a passing faire towre steeple that the Church hath, and the Musical Organs that be therein." *Holland Camden's Brit.* 677 (1610).
"The Church of Wrexham is commended for a fair and spacious building, and it is questionable, whether it claimeth more praise for the artificial Tower thereof, or for the Organs. These were formerly most famous (the more because placed in a Parochial, not Cathedral Church) for beauty, bigness and tunableness. . . . What is become of Wrexham Organs I know not, and could heartily wish, they had been removed into

some Gentlemans house, seeing such as accuse them for superstitious in Churches must allow them lawful in private places." 1661 Fuller's *Worthies*, Denbigh (1662) 33.

Fletcher was apparently having a fling at the fanatics of his day.

p. 129. *Basilus Manus.* This is somewhat obscure, and perhaps obscene. It might mean a hand-gun of sorts. There was a gun called a Basilisk, of which Basilus might be a corruption. The 1750 Beaumont and Fletcher emends this to *Besar los Manos*, and is followed by 1778. This makes a clear meaning, viz. that all that is left to old impotence is to kiss hands.

p. 129. *White-pot.* To make an excellent "whitepot." "Take two quarts of cream, boil in it, in a short time, half an ounce of mace, a piece of cinnamon, and half a nutmeg; then cut a white penny-loaf exceeding thin, then lay the slices at the bottom of a dish, and cover them with marrow; add likewise a dozen yolks of eggs to the cream, well beaten in rose-water, and sweeten it with a sufficient quantity of sugar; then take out the spices, beat up the cream well, and fill a broad bason in which the bread, raisins, and marrow was laid, and bake it; when it is enough, scrape white sugar on it, and serve it up." *Closet of Rarities* (1706), Nares.

Cf. *Hudibras*, I, i, 296 (1663): with regard to his paunch, the knight

> had a special Care
> To keep well-cramm'd with thrifty Fare
> As White-pot, Butter-milk, and Curds,
> Such as a Country-house affords.

And Dr. King's *Art of Cooking* (1708):

> Cornwall Squab-pie, and Devon White-pot brings
> And Leic'ster Beans and Bacon fit for Kings.

p. 130. *ye old put you.* "Put" is a duffer, a country clod-pole. *Dictionary of the Canting Crew* (1700) gives, "A silly, shallow-pated fellow." Mr. Masefield's "closhy putt" has made the word familiar to-day. Cf. *Æsop*, II.

p. 131. *Witness; vengeance.* See notes to *The Confederacy*.

p. 132. *Champion-country.* Champaign country, viz. flat, open country. Cf. Milton:

> From his side two rivers flow'd
> Th' one winding, the other strait and left between
> Fair Champain with less rivers interveind.
>
> *Paradise Regain'd*, III, 255.

The stage directions of *Camilla* (1706), have "A Champian Country . . ."

p. 134. *temper*, in Elizabethan English, can often be translated by our word temperament, but it here means calmness.

p. 139. *Bilboa Master.* A "bilboa" or "bilbo" was a sword. (Fletcher has Bilbo Master.) So called from its place of origin, as in the case of Toledo. The use of the word is common during and after the Shakespearean period. Cf. the speech of Bluff in *The Old Batchelour*, III, vii,

Ed. 1710: " Bilbo's the Word, and Slaughter will ensue." The meaning here is fire-eater, swashbuckler.

p. 141. *Gillian*, a wench. (Fletcher has " waiting-woman.") It is from the Latin Julian or Juliana, and variants are gill, or jill. Fletcher uses the word in *The Night Walker*, II, iii: " De'e bring your Gillians hither? nay, she's punished, your conceal'd love's cas'd up." (1625.) Ben Jonson's *Gypsies* has: " Each Jack with his Gill." See also Wycherley, *Love in a Wood* (acted 1671). "Dramatis Personæ: Mrs. Crossbite, an old cheating jill." Cf. *The Oxford Bowlers*, by Mr. Vanbrughe, with its obvious pun:

> Some Nantz then of Bowling Since we have had our Fill
> Let's lay aside our *Jack* Boys and each Man take his Gill.

p. 141. *the late great Poet*. This play was acted in April, but was evidently not printed until after Dryden's death, which took place on May 1.

p. 141. *to Celebrate this Day*. The day was New Year's Day, 1700. The new century did not, of course, really begin until March 25, 1701, as pedants have not failed to point out. Even Scott is satiric, saying it is a mistake a post-boy would not have made, for if told to ride twenty miles he would not think his journey done after riding nineteen. But all sensible men begin their century with the double zero: it may be contrary to reason, but it is in conformity with feeling, for who considers anything which happened in 1900 as happening in the last century rather than this?

Song. *St Hermo*. " The meteoric appearances, called by sailors in the Mediterranean the lights of St. Elmo, and by the ancients Castor and Pollux. Their appearance is supposed to presage the safety of the vessel and the termination of the storm." Scott, Edition of Dryden. Cf. Horace, *Lib.* III, *Car.* XXIX:

> " tunc me biremis praesidio scaphae
> tutum per Ægaeos tumultus
> aura feret geminusque Pollux ";

and Lucian, Πλοῖον ἤ εὐχαί, 9.

Masque. This singularly beautiful masque, worthy of Dryden at his best, is allegorical of the closing century. Diana represents the reign of James I, with whom hunting was a passion, and happy vinous evenings a relaxation. Mars stands for the Civil Wars and Venus for the courtly debaucheries of the early Restoration. Malone believes the music to have been by Daniel Purcell; the Latreille MS. records a 1704 Bill stating the masque to be " set to musick by the famous Mr. Henry Purcell," which must be an error, as Henry Purcell died in 1695. It was re-set by Dr. Boyce, and revived with success at Drury Lane in 1749.

l. 144. *wexing*, " waxing." The corruption was first introduced by Spenser, for the sake of a rhyme, according to Johnson, and Dryden used it frequently.

l. 144. *Tyrian Dye*, viz. purple, the colour of blood.

l. 145. *The Queen of Pleasure*. Probably the lovely and much-loved Mary of Modena, the wife of James II, in exile with her husband. Dryden would readily introduce her in this masque. Cf. his beautiful Jacobite lament, printed as *The Lady's Song* in the 1704 *Miscellany*, the second stanza of which begins:

> While Pan and fair Syrinx, are fled from our shore.

Epilogue. Just as the Prologue was a reply to Blackmore, so this is a reply to Collier, and full of sturdy common sense. It is usually said that this is Dryden's recantation, but taken with his Preface to the *Fables* (1700) it cannot be considered such: he gives away a point or two to make his general position more tenable. In this Epilogue he argues that the stage is the chronicle and brief abstract of the time, and puts the blame on to the town, as corrupted by the Court. Lansdowne, in the Prologue to *The Jew of Venice* (1701), follows the lead in putting the blame entirely on the audience:

> . . . for without mincing, to be plain
> The guilt's your own, of every odious scene;
> The present time still gives the stage its mode:
> The vices that you practise, we explode.

Defoe in his *Review* (II, No. 26, 1705) has: " But, Gentlemen and Ladies, if you would have a Reformation in the Play house, you must Reform your Taste of Wit, and let the Poet see you can Relish a Play, tho' there be neither Bawdy nor Blasphemy in it." But Dryden was evidently very sceptical as to whether human nature would change.

l. 1.   the Parson. Collier.

Last line. Oats. Titus " Oates," whose morals were not unimpeachable, and who as a Tory would be hated by Dryden. But Dryden was also making a pun upon " wild oats." " Wild Oats " was sometimes used as a kind of nickname.

Hains. The actor, but perhaps by way of a pun, and also to stress Dryden's Tory proclivities, Bryan Haines, the Tory evidence against Shaftesbury and College, thus making the whole line a Popish Plot reference. But the obvious meaning is Haines the actor, who was a gay, somewhat irresponsible person, who in 1677 had been fined for " reciteinge . . . a Scurrilous & obscoene Epilogue." In the reign of James II he became a convert to Catholicism, declaring that the Virgin had appeared to him. When questioned on the point by Lord Sunderland, Haines professed that " As I was lying in my bed, the Virgin appeared to me and said— '*Arise, Joe.*' " " You lie, you rogue," the Earl replied, " if it had really been the Virgin herself she would have said *Joseph*, if it had only been out of respect to her husband." Quin tells the story. See Genest, II, 237. Haines was afterwards reconverted. The " facetious Tom Brown " attacked Dryden for his conversion, and in *The Reasons of Mr. Haines the Player's Conversion and Reconversion* (1691) has a dialogue between Haines and Bayes (Dryden) on the subject. Haines died in 1701, in which year was published an amusing book, *The Life of the late famous Comedian, Jo Hayns*, full of his escapades.

The False Friend

Prologue. *When Portugal declares.* After much havering, Portugal joined the confederacy against France in 1703.

p. 165. *Rocombolle*, metaphorically cream, zest, or seasoning. It is actually Allium scorodoprasum, a sort of wild garlic. Cf. King, *Art of Cookery* (1708):

> Where rocombole, shallot, and the rank garlic grow.

p. 167. *Groyn*; at that time a common name for Corunna.

p. 168. *I'll expect you.* I'll await you.

p. 174. *Portocarero.* Luis Manuel Fernandez de Portocarrero (1635–1709), Cardinal-Archbishop of Toledo, of noble birth, took an active, even predominant part in the politics of his time. His evident conviction that government should reside in the hands of the strong made him support first the French, then the Austrian faction, and after that again the party of Philip V when he succeeded in 1700. Thus he earned a reputation for dishonesty, especially in England, where he was regarded much as Macchiavelli was at the time of James I. His " scandalous " history was published in England in 1704, and society was mildly excited when in 1712 his nephew was attached to the Spanish embassy. Lady Stafford described him as " a grandee of the first class." The name is of Vanbrugh's insertion. It would obviously not do in Spain, nor would Le Sage's phrase do in England: " C'est une chose plus difficile que de prendre au Roi de France, Rouën ou la Rochelle."

p. 175. The attentive reader will observe a deal of blank verse in this act.

p. 183. *Capitolade*; a hash of twice-cooked meat.

p. 191. *bate*; abate.

p. 196. *Bourbon's.* This remark, naturally, occurs neither in the Spanish nor the French.

p. 198. *Overture*; opening, from the French ouverture.

The Country House

p. 215. *the Fox in the Fable.* This is the forty-second fable in John Ogilby's *The Fables of Æsop Paraphras'd in Verse*, first printed in 1651, and popular throughout the century, to judge by the number of editions, though probably not so popular as *Reynard the Fox*. It is not unlike the Vanbrugh-Boursault fable of the goat (see I *Æsop*, I); though in Boursault a fox tells the goat what to do. In Ogilby a " jeering Weesell from the Wall " draws the moral for the distended fox, who, instead of disgorging, resigns himself, saying:

> —I can
> But be uncas'd, and bravely die by man.